GCSE
CHEMISTRY

Bob McDuell
Deputy Headmaster
Berry Hill High School, Stoke-on-Trent

EDUCATIONAL

First published 1979
Revised 1981, 1983, 1986, 1987, 1989, 1994
Reprinted 1991, 1993, 1995

Letts Educational
Aldine House
Aldine Place
London W12 8AW

British Library Cataloguing in Publication Data

A CIP record for this book is available from the British Library.

ISBN 1 85758 302 7

Printed in Great Britain by
WM Print Limited, Walsall, West Midlands WS2 9NE

Letts Educational is the trading name of BPP (Letts Educational) Ltd

Preface

This book is intended as a complete guide for a student preparing for GCSE examinations. It is important to prepare thoroughly for the examination and to plan the revision period. This publication helps you to identify the requirements of your particular syllabus, gives you the required core content, and helps you with examination technique with both self tests and examination-type questions.

This book has been ensuring success for examination students at 16+ since 1979 and certainly longer than any other revision aid. Many students have written to thank me for the help that this guide has provided. It has been well received by teachers over the years because it is not a 'crammer' to replace the teacher but an organized revision course, the like of which was not available before its publication. However, Chemistry syllabuses and examination papers continue to change. To meet changes in syllabus and style of question, this book has undergone repeated revisions and differs in many ways from earlier editions.

This edition has been completely revised for the new GCSE syllabuses based on the Science National Curriculum. There are fewer syllabuses nationally and so the analysis is more detailed. The content has been reorganized into 35 chapters and the order has been arranged to match the strands of the National Curriculum. The question sections have been rewritten to incorporate new-type questions. In previous editions reviewers have praised the commonsense advice on Coursework Assessment. All syllabuses contain a new Coursework Assessment. A new section has therefore been written for this book which will provide students with the help they need.

I would like to thank the staff at Letts Educational for all their help in the production of this new edition. Especially, I would like to thank Wayne Davies, my editor, for his splendid and thoroughly professional job in turning my manuscript into a first-rate product.

I have received willing cooperation and advice from staff in different Examination Boards and am grateful to the Midland Examining Group, the Northern Examinations and Assessment Board, the Northern Ireland Council for the Curriculum Examinations and Assessment, the Scottish Examination Board, the Southern Examining Group, the University of London Examinations and Assessment Council, and the Welsh Joint Education Committee for permission to reproduce examination questions. Where examination questions have been used the answers are my interpretation and are entirely my responsibility.

Finally, I wish to thank my wife, Judy, and Robin and Timothy for their patience and encouragement, and my own students and former users of this book for their helpful suggestions.

Bob McDuell 1994

Contents

Questions and answers

Coursework

Introduction

Knowing how best to prepare for an examination is most important. This book will help you by providing a complete revision course. It contains all of the necessary factual material, self test units, hints on taking examinations and on coursework, sample questions of all types and sample answers. To get the best from this book you should start the following procedure.

How to use this book

The first thing to do is to find out which syllabus you are studying. Your teacher will tell you this. Remember that some Examination Boards have more than one syllabus. Look up your syllabus in the Syllabus Analysis section of this book (pages 9–17). Here you will find out information which will help you. **Remember, whichever syllabus you are doing you will need to study the Core, i.e. Chapters 1–28.**

The syllabus analysis will tell you:

1. details about the three tiers of entry which are available for the syllabus.
2. the lengths of papers for each tier.
3. the types of questions which the papers will contain.
4. the additional chapters which are required for your syllabus (from Chapters 29–34).
5. the address of the Examining Board. You may wish to contact them for past examination papers as the examination approaches. Also, if you are a private candidate not attached to a school or college, you may wish to find a Centre where you can take the examination.

You are advised to work through as many of the chapters as possible. Read the chapter several times. Make some brief notes on a postcard as you go along and learn these. These postcards can be useful for revision as the examination approaches. Read the Summary at the end of the chapter. When you are confident, have a go at the Self Test Questions for the chapter and compare your answers with the answers given. If you get less than half right go back and look at the chapter again. Keep a record of your progress through the chapters using the chart on page 18.

When you have worked through the chapters, and not more than six months before the final examination, look at the sections on types of examination questions and sample examination questions. If your syllabus does not have a multiple choice paper, you may still find the sample multiple choice paper useful for identifying weaknesses which you can then overcome by looking again at the relevant chapters.

The National Curriculum, GCSE and the separate sciences

The National Curriculum provides a course which all students in State schools in England and Wales must follow. A similar curriculum arrangement applies in Northern

Ireland. Scottish arrangements are explained on page 12. The National Curriculum is divided into four Key Stages:

Key Stage 1 – pupils up to the age of 7.
Key Stage 2 – pupils between 7 and 11.
Key Stage 3 – pupils between 11 and 14.
Key Stage 4 – pupils between 14 and 16.

At the end of Key Stage 3 you will have taken tests. These tests, together with assessments made by your teacher, were checked by an outside agency. These results will have been reported to your parents.

At Key Stage 4 there is now some flexibility. At the end of the Key Stage you will be assessed by GCSE examinations and coursework completed in your school or college. There are various possible routes. These include:

1. Entry for a Double Science GCSE which counts as two GCSE subjects.
2. Entry for a Single Science GCSE which counts as one GCSE subject.
3. Entry for Separate Sciences – Chemistry, Physics and Biology. These should be taken with the same examination board and will count as three GCSE subjects.

This book covers the essential content of GCSE Chemistry courses.

Attainment Targets (ATs)

The Science National Curriculum is divided into four broad areas of study called Attainment Targets:

AT1 Scientific Investigation (also known as Sc1)

This AT assesses your scientific skills in carrying out experimental and investigative work. It will be assessed by your teacher (see pages 254–257).

AT2 Life and Living Processes (Sc2)
AT3 Materials and their Properties (Sc3)
AT4 Physical Processes (Sc4)

GCSE Chemistry is based on AT1 and AT3. AT2 is covered in Biology and AT4 in Physics. To make up the equivalent of one GCSE subject, additional material has been added to the core of Chemistry.

Strands, Programmes of Study and Statements of Attainment

Each AT is split up into three, four or five sections or **strands** of related knowledge, understanding, concepts and skills.

AT 1 is divided into three strands:

(i) Asking questions, predicting, making hypotheses.
(ii) Observing, measuring and manipulating variables.
(iii) Interpreting your results and evaluating the scientific evidence.

AT 3 is divided into four strands:

(i) The properties, classification and structure of materials.
(ii) Explanations of the properties of materials.
(iii) Chemical changes.
(iv) The Earth and its atmosphere.

Some parts of strand (iv) have been transferred to the Physics syllabuses. This involves aspects of the study of weather and means you will not now study these in Chemistry.

To complete their GCSE syllabuses, the Examination Boards have added new strands (see page 8).

For each strand there is a description in terms of a **Programme of Study** which details the range of knowledge which could be examined. Additionally there are a set of **Statements of Attainment**. These describe what you are expected to achieve at each of the ten levels of the National Curriculum. How the contents of this book relate to the Statements of Attainment is described in the margins of the main text. Examination papers for GCSE test both the Programme of Study and the Statements of Attainment.

Tiers of Entry

Unlike previous GCSE examinations, all syllabuses provide three alternative tiers of entry. Whatever they are called by your Examination Board, there is a Basic Tier (intended for candidates aiming at grades around E–G), a Central Tier (intended for candidates around B–E) and a Higher Tier (intended for candidates aiming at A★–B). Most candidates will enter for the Central Tier. The Higher Tier will consist of difficult questions and unless you are confident that you can cope with the Statements of Attainment at levels 9–10 you would be unwise to enter this Tier.

There will probably be common questions between tiers, e.g. parts of the same question may appear on Basic, Central and Higher Tier papers.

You can change your tier of entry right up to the examination and so leave the choice as late as possible. The Syllabus Analysis gives further details of tiers of entry for each syllabus.

The following table shows how National Curriculum levels will be converted to GCSE grades for your final result. You will notice especially that there is no direct correlation between grades C, D and E and levels 7 and 6.

Grade	Level
A★	10
A	9
B	8
C	7
D	
E	6
F	5
G	4

Spelling, punctuation and grammar

On all written papers, apart from multiple choice papers, and on coursework a mark has to be added for the quality of your spelling, punctuation and grammar. The mark for the written paper will be added by the examiner who marks your paper. Your teacher will add the mark for coursework and this mark will be checked externally by somebody outside your school.

Up to 5% of the total mark can be added for spelling, punctuation and grammar. This means 4 marks on a paper out of 80, 5 marks on a paper out of 100 and 6 marks on a paper out of 120. These marks are important and they could make the difference between whether you get the grade you want or not. The following advice may help you.

Correct spelling, especially of scientific words, is important. As you carry out your revision it is wise to make a list of scientific words and learn the spellings. Words like separate, apparatus, fluorine, potassium, neutral, environment, tectonics and soluble are very frequently misspelt. A high mark assumes correct spelling of words including technical terms. Make sure you can spell all of the words in the Glossary (pages 258–262).

Many examination papers do not require you to write in complete sentences. Unless it specifically asks you to write in complete sentences, there should be no penalty for the good candidate who writes the answer in note form. Most papers have opportunities for extended writing within the paper. Ensure, if you write in sentences, that the sentences start with a capital letter and finish with a full stop. Keep your sentences simple.

When you have written a sentence or series of sentences read the sentence(s) slowly to yourself. Does it sound right to you? Be careful with the following pairs of words:

its	it's
their	there
has	as

With some preparation you can improve your performance in spelling, punctuation and grammar.

Assessment objectives

It is very easy to concentrate your revision on learning facts. Factual recall and understanding are very important aspects of GCSE Chemistry examinations and are probably the best starting place for all students. But you should be aware that factual recall and understanding only account for about 50% of the marks. There are other skills to be tested and you should prepare yourself to answer questions testing these other skills.

There follows a list of **Assessment Objectives**. These are the intellectual and practical skills which you are asked to demonstrate. They are the same in all syllabuses, although they may be numbered differently.

You should be able to

★① ask questions, predict and hypothesize.

★② observe, measure and manipulate variables.

★③ interpret your results and evaluate scientific evidence.

④ demonstrate the knowledge, skills and understanding specified by your syllabus.

⑤ communicate scientific observations, ideas and arguments effectively.

⑥ select and use reference materials and translate data from one form to another.

⑦ interpret, evaluate and make informed judgements from relevant facts, observations and phenomena.

⑧ solve qualitative and quantitative problems.

Of these assessment objectives the starred ones (1–3) are assessed in your Coursework (refer to pages 254–257). Number 4 refers to recall and understanding, which is the area most teachers and students concentrate on when organizing revision.

You will find examples of questions testing the other assessment objectives in the question section of this book, but perhaps one or two points should be made at this stage.

Assessment objective 5 requires you to communicate scientific information effectively. It usually requires some extended writing. You could be asked, for instance, about the effects of increasing carbon dioxide in the atmosphere or the economics of a particular industrial process. Often some information will be given to you. It is essential to make a rough plan to your answer before you write it. Try to make different points and not the same ones over and over again, and try to get these points into some logical sequence.

Assessment objective 6 may be linked to mathematical skills. You could be given information in a table and asked to display it in a graph or be given information in a pie diagram and be required to use it in some other form. These skills will be practised during Coursework and so you should be able to carry them out correctly on written papers.

Assessment objective 7 will require you to use information given in the question to make some kind of interpretation, evaluation or conclusion. You will probably not have carried out identical processes before, but you are expected to use your experience in similar situations. Make sure that the information is in a logical order and check at the end that your comments are reasonable and do fit the information you were given.

Assessment objective 8 will include all of the chemical calculations which have always been part of GCSE Chemistry. Make sure you use the information given to you and remember if you have a Periodic Table that this is another source of information. Show your working to enable the examiner to give credit if you get the wrong answer but have made some progress correctly through the question. Always check your answer to see that it is reasonable and give units where necessary. This section will also include problems for you to solve which do not need calculations.

Syllabus analysis

All syllabuses require you to study the Common Core – Chapters 1–28.

Chemistry core

The core is based on the Programmes of Study and Statements of Attainment for National Curriculum Science Sc3. It is divided into four strands (i–iv).

(i) The properties, classification and structure of materials

Programme of Study

Pupils should:

- carry out a more detailed study of selected elements and their compounds, covering metals and nonmetals, in order to understand the limitations and different ways which elements can be classified and ordered in the Periodic Table.
- recognize patterns in the properties in groups and periods and relate these to electronic structures.
- be able to make predictions from the reactivity series of metals.
- investigate the process of neutralization.
- study the properties, structure and uses of materials, including metals, ceramics, glass, plastics and fibres.
- have the opportunity to separate and purify the components of mixtures and make different types of mixtures which have everyday applications, such as emulsions, foams, gels and solutions.
- be introduced to the idea of composite materials illustrated by some common examples including reinforced concrete, glass-reinforced plastic, bone and synthetic fibres.

Statements of Attainment

Pupils should:

4(a) be able to classify materials as solids, liquids and gases on the basis of simple properties which relate to their everyday use.

5(a) know how to separate and purify the components of mixtures using physical processes.

5(b) be able to classify aqueous solutions as acidic, alkaline or neutral using indicators.

6(a) be able to distinguish between metallic and nonmetallic elements, mixtures and compounds using simple chemical and physical properties.

7(a) be able to relate the properties of a variety of classes of materials to their everyday uses.

7(b) know that the Periodic Table groups families of elements with similar properties which depend upon their electronic structure.

8(a) know the major characteristics of metals and nonmetals as reflected in the properties of a range of their compounds.

8(b) understand the structure of the atom in terms of protons, neutrons and electrons and how this can explain the existence of isotopes.

9(a) understand how the properties of elements are related to their electronic structure and their position in the Periodic Table.

10(a) be able to use data on properties of different materials in order to make evaluative judgements about their uses.

(ii) Explanations of the properties of materials

Programme of Study

Pupils should:

- investigate the quantitative relationships between the volume, temperature and pressure of a gas, and use the kinetic theory to explain changes of state and other phenomena.
- develop models to explain the difference between elements and compounds in terms of atoms, molecules, ions and covalent and ionic bonds.
- use their knowledge of the structure of the atom to explain the existence of isotopes and radioactivity.
- become aware of the characteristics of radioactive emissions and determine the half-life of a nuclide.
- study the different methods of detecting ionizing radiation and its effects on matter and living organisms, developing an understanding of the beneficial and harmful effects.

Statements of Attainment

Pupils should:

6(b) understand the physical differences between solids, liquids and gases in simple particle terms.

7(c) understand the changes of state, including the associated energy changes, mixing and diffusion in terms of the proximity and motion of particles.

7(d) understand the relationships between the volume, pressure and temperature of a gas.

7(e) understand the difference between elements, compounds and mixtures in terms of atoms, ions and molecules.

8(c) understand radioactivity and nuclear fission and harmful and beneficial effects of ionizing radiations.

8(d) be able to relate the properties of molecular and giant structures to the arrangement of atoms and ions.

9(b) understand the nature of radioactive decay, relating half-life to the use of radioactive materials.

10(b) understand chemical reactions in terms of the energy transfers associated with making and breaking chemical bonds.

10(c) be able to relate the bulk properties of metals, ceramics, glass, plastics and fibres to simple models of their structure.

(iii) Chemical changes

Programme of Study

Pupils should:

- investigate a range of types of reaction, including thermal and electrolytic decomposition, ionic reactions in solution, salt formation, oxidation and reduction, fermentation and polymerization and, where possible, relate these to models and to everyday processes such as corrosion and the manufacture of new materials.
- investigate the different factors affecting the rate of chemical reactions and relate these to the practical problems associated with the manufacture of new materials and to everyday biochemical change. Chemical and electrolytic reactions should be represented first in word and later symbolic equations and these should be used as a way of describing and understanding reactions.
- begin to explore through experiment and the use of data the quantitative aspects of chemical equations including masses of solids and volumes of gases. The work should involve determination of formulae, and subsequently, quantitative electrolysis.

- study chemical reactions in which there is energy transfer to and from the surroundings. At a later stage they should become aware that the energy transfer is associated with the making and reforming of chemical bonds and can be determined qualitatively by experiment and the use of data.
- study the energy requirements and the social, economic, environmental and health and safety factors associated with the manufacture of materials. This should involve studying the processes involved in metal extraction, cracking oil, chlor-alkali industry and the production of plastics and fertilizers.
- relate this research to experimental methods used in the laboratory. During the work they should be made aware that some reactions are significantly reversible and may reach an equilibrium, and that this may be a major consideration in some manufacturing processes.

Statements of Attainment

Pupils should:

4(b) know that materials from a variety of sources can be converted into new and useful products by chemical reactions.

4(c) know that the combustion of fuel releases energy and produces waste gases.

5(c) understand that rusting and burning involve a reaction with oxygen.

6(c) understand oxidation processes, including combustion, as reactions with oxygen to form oxides.

6(d) be able to recognize variations in the properties of metals and make predictions based on the reactivity series.

6(e) know that some chemical reactions are exothermic, while others are endothermic.

6(f) know about the readily observable effects of electrolysis.

7(f) understand the factors which influence the rate of a chemical reaction.

7(g) be able to relate knowledge and understanding of chemical principles to manufacturing processes and everyday effects.

8(e) be able to explain the physical and chemical processes by which different chemicals are made from oil.

8(f) be able to use symbolic equations to describe and explain a range of reactions including ionic interactions and those occurring in electrolytic cells.

9(c) be able to interpret chemical equations quantitatively.

9(d) be able to use scientific information from a range of sources to evaluate the social, economic, health and safety and environmental factors associated with a major manufacturing process.

10(d) be able to interpret electrolytic processes quantitatively.

(iv) The Earth and its atmosphere

All syllabuses here have transferred the study of the weather from Sc3 to Physics. This section therefore only contains a study of the Earth and rocks.

Programme of Study

Pupils should:

- study, through laboratory work and fieldwork, the evidence which reveals the mode of formation and later deformation of rocks and the sources of energy that drive such processes.
- study the scientific processes involved in the weathering of rocks, transport of sediments and soil formation.
- understand how geological time scales are measured.
- examine data which suggest that the Earth has a layered structure, including contrasting densities between surface rocks and the whole Earth, transmission of earthquake waves and magnetic evidence.
- investigate the evidence which favours the theory of plate tectonics including the nature of the rock record.
- consider how plate movements are involved in the recycling of rocks and the global distribution of the Earth's physical resources.

- consider theories from earlier times concerning movements of the Earth's crust, and how these were changed through advances in several fields of science and technology.

Statements of Attainment

Pupils should:

4(d)   know that weathering, erosion and transport lead to the formation of sediments and different types of soil.

6(g)   understand the scientific processes involved in the formation of igneous, sedimentary and metamorphic rocks, including the time-scales over which these processes operate.

8(f)   be able to interpret evidence of modes of formation and deformation of rocks.

9(d)   be able to describe and explain the supporting evidence, in simple terms, for the layered structure of the inner Earth.

10(e)   understand the theory of plate tectonics and the contribution this process makes to the recycling of rocks.

New Statements of Attainment and Extension Topics

The following Statements of Attainment are typical of the ones added to the Chemistry content (Sc3) of National Curriculum Science to make up a full GCSE in Chemistry as a single subject. They form the basis of the extension topics that each syllabus provides in addition to the Chemistry Core.

You will notice they extend the experience in Chemistry in a number of particular areas:

1️⃣   Quantitative Chemistry, especially calculations involving the mole and calculations from titrations.

2️⃣   Qualitative Chemistry, testing for common ions.

3️⃣   Industrial Chemistry, the Chemistry behind some important chemical processes.

4️⃣   Organic (or carbon) Chemistry.

In preparation for your GCSE Chemistry examination it is important to ensure you understand these topics. The particular extension topics that you will have to study are detailed in the following pages under the name of your Examination Board and syllabus.

Strand on Quantitative Chemistry

3.5k   recognize the factors affecting solution, i.e. heat, surface area, stirring, volume of solvent.

3.7p   understand the effect of temperature on the solubility of solids and gases in water.

3.7q   recognize that atoms have mass centred largely in the nucleus.

3.7r   understand that atomic masses are measured relative to carbon-12.

3.7s   understand the term relative atomic mass and use this to determine relative formula masses (relative molecular masses).

3.9i   recognize the quantitative effect of temperature on the solubility of solids in water and use solubility curves.

3.9j   understand that one mole of different substances contain equal numbers of specified particles.

3.9k   use relative formula mass to determine the number of moles present in a given mass of material.

3.9l   use experimental results to calculate the formula of a simple compound.

3.10j   understand the term concentration of a solution expressed in moles per litre (mol/dm^3).

3.10k   calculate solution concentrations in mol/l and g/dm^3 from the results of acid/base titrations (back titrations not included).

Strand on Making New Materials

3.7t use appropriate methods to prepare soluble and insoluble salts.

3.8m describe the important chemistry of the Contact Process.

3.8n describe the important chemistry of the Haber–Bosch Process.

3.9m describe the important chemistry of the industrial manufacture of nitric acid from ammonia.

3.9n relate the position of metals in the reactivity series to the method of extraction from their ores.

Strand on Analytical Chemistry

3.5l use anhydrous copper(II) sulphate or cobalt chloride to test for the presence of water.

3.8o describe the chemical tests for the anions:

    carbonate using dilute acid;

    chloride using silver nitrate solution;

    sulphate using barium chloride solution.

3.8p use flame tests to identify compounds of the following metals: Ca, Cu, K, Na.

3.8q describe tests to identify the gases: ammonia, carbon dioxide, hydrogen chloride, oxygen.

3.8r use sodium hydroxide solution to identify salts of Cu, Mg and Al.

3.8s use aqueous ammonia to identify salts of Zn and Mg.

3.9o use sodium hydroxide solution to identify salts of Ca, Fe(II), Fe(III), Zn.

3.9p use aqueous ammonia to identify salts of Cu, Fe(II), Fe(III), Al.

Strand on Carbon Compounds

3.4j relate that fossil fuels and biological substances are carbon-based compounds.

3.7u recall that oil is the major source of organic chemicals and that chemicals obtained from oil are hydrocarbons.

3.8t describe the important physical properties and uses of a variety of organic compounds from different homologous series.

3.9q explain the important chemical properties of a variety of organic compounds from different homologous series.

Midland Examining Group (MEG)

Address: 1 Hills Road, Cambridge CB1 2EU

Chemistry 1781

All candidates complete a Coursework Assessment on Sc1   25%

Basic Tier   One paper   targeted at levels 4–6 $1\frac{1}{2}$ hours   75%
Short answer (multiple choice, sentence completion, matching pairs, etc.) and structured questions.

Central Tier   One paper   targeted at levels 5–8   2 hours   75%
Short answer, structured questions with some extended response.

Further Tier   One paper   targeted at levels 7–10 $2\frac{1}{4}$ hours   75%
Structured questions, some requiring extended answers.

The syllabus is divided into seven strands:

    C1 Raw materials (Chapters 1, 11, 14, 15, 20, 21, 22, 23, 24)

    C2 Reactions (Chapters 6, 11, 12, 13, 16, 17, 18, 25)

    C3 Structures and properties (Chapters 1, 6, 7, 8)

C4   Patterns and trends (Chapters 2, 3, 4, 5, 9, 10, 19)
C5   Rocks (Chapters 26, 27, 28)

Additional strands:

C6   Utilizing the Earth's resources (Chapters 3, 8, 11, 13, 15, 20, 31, 32, 33, 35)
C7   Obtaining and using chemical data (Chapters 8, 13, 18, 19, 25, 29, 30, 31, 32)

Nuffield Chemistry 1786

All candidates complete a Coursework Assessment on Sc1   25%

Basic Tier   One paper   targeted at levels 4–6 $1\frac{1}{2}$ hours   75%
Short answer (multiple choice, sentence completion, matching pairs, etc.) and structured questions, with some questions requiring extended responses.

Central Tier   One paper   targeted at levels 5–8   2 hours   75%
Structured questions with some extended response.

Further Tier   One paper   targeted at levels 7–10 $2\frac{1}{4}$ hours   75%
Structured questions, some requiring extended answers.

The syllabus is divided into topics strands:

C1   The Elements of Chemistry (Chapters 1, 2, 12, 13, 16, 17, 18, 25)
C2   Petrochemicals (Chapter 20)
C3   Chemicals from Plants (Chapter 34)
C4   Chemicals and Rocks (Chapter 28)
C5   Materials and Structures (Chapters 6, 7)
C6   Glasses and Ceramics (Chapter 7)
C7   Metals and Alloys (Chapter 3)
C8   Polymers (Chapter 21)
C9   Foams, Emulsions, Sols and Gels
C10   Keeping Water Clean (Chapter 30)
C11   Dyes and Dyeing
C12   Chemicals in the Medicine Cupboard
C13   Fuels and Fires (Chapter 11)
C14   Batteries (Chapter 19)
C15   Soil (Chapter 26)
C16   Fertilizers (Chapter 22)
C17   The Periodic Table (Chapter 5)
C18   Atoms and Bonding (Chapters 4, 8)
C19   Geology (Chapters 26–8)

There are three Extension strands:

(v)   Chemistry in the Environment (Chapters 11, 29, 30, 35)
(vi)   The Chemistry of Food and Drink (Chapters 11, 25, 32, 34)
(vii)   Colloids and Detergents (Chapters 1, 30, 34)

Salters' Chemistry 1791

All candidates complete a Coursework Assessment on Sc1   25%

Basic Tier   One paper   targeted at levels 4–6 $1\frac{1}{2}$ hours   75%
Approximately 80 marks covering all strands. Two sections:
A   25–35% of total marks – short answer (multiple choice, sentence completion, matching pairs, etc.).
B   65–75% of total marks – structured questions.

Central Tier   One paper   targeted at levels 5–8   2 hours   75%
Approximately 108 marks covering all strands. Two sections:
A   45–55% of total marks – short answer, structured questions.
B   45–55% of total marks – structured questions with some extended response.

Further Tier   One paper   targeted at levels 7–10 $2\frac{1}{4}$ hours   75%
Approximately 120 marks covering all strands. Two sections:
A   45–55% of total marks – short answer, structured questions.
B   45–55% of total marks – questions requiring extended answers.

The syllabus is divided into six strands:

C(i)   the properties, classification and structure of materials (Chapters 1–5)
C(ii)   explanation of the properties of materials (Chapters 6, 7, 8, 10)
C(iii) chemical changes (Chapters 11–25)
C(iv)   the Earth (Chapters 26–28)
C(v)   energy transfer and chemical change (included in Chapters 9, 11, 17, 19, 35)
C(vi)   chemistry of food, water and health (included in Chapters 22, 30, 31, 34)

Northern Examinations and Assessment Board (NEAB)
Welsh Joint Education Committee (WJEC)

Addresses: NEAB 12 Harter Street, Manchester M1 6HL
WJEC 245 Western Avenue, Cardiff CF5 2YX

Science: Chemistry

All candidates complete a Coursework Assessment on Sc1   25%

Option P   (levels 4–6) $1\frac{1}{2}$ hours   75%

Option Q   (levels 6–8)   2 hours   75%

Option R   (levels 8–10) $2\frac{1}{2}$ hours   75%

The syllabus is divided into the following themes (Extension topics underlined):

Chemical Patterns and Classification	Properties and uses of material (Chapter 8)
	Mixtures (Chapter 7)
	Particle model of matter (Chapter 6)
	Gas laws (Chapter 10)
	Metals, nonmetals and the Periodic Table (Chapters 3, 4, 5)
	Reactivity series of metals (Chapter 12)
	Acids (Chapter 2)
	Aqueous chemistry (Chapters 25, 30, 32)
	Different sorts of particles (Chapters 7, 8)
	Structure of the atom (Chapter 4)
Formulae and Equations	Chemical equations (Chapters 13, 16, 25)
Energy and Reactions	Energy transfer in chemical reactions (Chapter 19)
	Rates of reaction (Chapter 17)
Making New Materials and their Properties	Types of chemical reaction (Chapters 11, 14, 16)
	The chemical industry (Chapter 20)
	Industrial processes (Chapters 3, 15, 24)
	Organic chemistry (Chapters 20, 34, 35)
	Properties and uses of materials (Chapter 8)
Atmosphere	Origins and maintenance of the atmosphere and the oceans (Chapters 30, 35)
Rock Cycle and Earth	Rocks: weathering, formation, age (Chapter 26)

N.B. All of the Core chapters (1–28) are needed, either directly or indirectly.

Northern Ireland Council for the Curriculum Examinations and Assessment (NICCEA)

Address: Beechill House, 42 Beechill Road, Belfast BT8 4RS

All candidates complete a Coursework Assessment on Sc1   24%

This assessment is slightly different from coursework schemes in England and Wales. The following pattern will apply:

Assessment Category	Weighting
A Planning (strand i)	7%
B Carrying out investigations (strand ii)	7%
C Interpreting (strand iii)	7%
D Using Information Technology	3%

For details of Information Technology strand see your syllabus or ask your teacher.

Basic Tier (P)	Two papers	targeted at levels 4–6
Paper 1	1 hour	38%
Paper 2	1½ hours	38%
Central Tier (Q)	Two papers	targeted at levels 6–8
Paper 1	2 hours	38%
Paper 2	2 hours	38%
Further Tier (R)	Two papers	targeted at levels 8–10
Paper 1	2 hours	38%
Paper 2	2 hours	38%

Except for Paper 1 in tier P, all papers will consist of 20 objective questions and a number of structured questions of varying length. All questions are compulsory.

The content of the syllabus is set out in four sections.

I   Atomic structure and bonding (Chapters 4, 8)
II   Patterns and classification
        Solids, liquids and gases (Chapter 6)
        Materials and their properties (Chapters 1, 2, 3, 7)
        Acids, bases and salts (Chapters 2, 32)
III   Chemical reactions and reactivity
        Chemical change (Chapters 11–12, 14–24)
        Equations (Chapter 13)
        Quantitative chemistry (Chapter 25)
        Rates of reaction (Chapter 17)
IV   Chemistry of the elements and their compounds
        The Periodic Table (Chapter 5)
        Water (Chapter 30)
        Organic chemistry (Chapter 20–21)

The following additional chapters should be studied – 29, 30, 31, 32, 34, 35.

Scottish Examination Board

Address: Ironmills Road, Dalkeith, Midlothian EH22 1LE

For students at S3 and S4, there are three levels of entry:

Foundation	Grades 5 & 6
General	Grades 3 & 4
Credit	Grades 1 & 2

Candidates studying Science as a subject can enter at Foundation, General or Credit levels. Candidates entering for Chemistry as a separate subject can enter only at General or Credit levels.

Candidates can take papers at both General and Credit levels or at just one. If both levels are taken, the candidate will be awarded the better of the two grades.

The grade will be awarded on a scale of 5–1, with grade 1 denoting the highest performance. Grade 5 will be awarded when General level has just been missed. Grade 7 indicates that none of the components has been completed.

There will be one paper of $1\frac{1}{2}$ hours for each level. The paper will consist of multiple choice questions, grid questions, short answer questions and extended answer (essay-type) questions. Grid questions are a type of multiple choice question.

The syllabus is divided into three equal elements:
Knowledge and Understanding
Problem Solving
Practical Abilities – These are assessed within the school or college.

Knowledge and Understanding

The contents of this element is divided into 15 topics. These are shown below with the chapters which should be studied in this book.

1 Chemical Reactions (Chapter 7)
2 Speed of Reactions (Chapter 17)
3 Atoms and the Periodic Table (Chapters 4, 5, 6)
4 How Atoms Combine (Chapter 8)
5 Fuels (Chapters 19, 20, 35)
6 Structures and Reactions of Hydrocarbons (Chapters 20, 21)
7 Properties of Substances (Chapters 8, 16)
8 Acids and Alkalis (Chapters 2, 25, 32)
9 Reactions of Acids (Chapters 2, 13)
10 Making Electricity (Chapters 11, 12, 19)
11 Metals (Chapters 3, 12, 15)
12 Corrosion (Chapter 14)
13 Plastics and Synthetic Polymers (Chapter 21)
14 Fertilizers (Chapters 18, 22)
15 Carbohydrates and Related Substances (Chapter 34)

Problem Solving

This element is divided into 12 sections:

1 Selecting relevant information from different sources, including data books, picture keys, flowcharts, tables, bar and line graphs, pie charts, or diagrams.
2 Constructing tables of data and suggesting appropriate headings.
3 Constructing bar and line graphs.
4 Selecting a suitable format for the presentation of data.
5 Choosing an appropriate procedure from a given selection.
6 Suggesting, using words or labelled diagrams, an appropriate experimental procedure.
7 Choosing, from a given selection, a factor which might affect the fairness of a test.
8 Identifying the factors which might affect the fairness of a test.
9 Drawing a conclusion from chemical information including experimental results.
10 Deducing valid explanations of results and conclusions.
11 Using a conclusion to predict what might happen in a related situation.
12 Deducing an appropriate generalization.

Practical Abilities

There are two categories of Practical Abilities in Standard Grade Chemistry: (a) Techniques and (b) Investigations.

There are ten techniques listed in the syllabus, put into five groups A–E:

Group A	Group B	Group C	Group D	Group E
1 Bubbling gases into solutions and observing changes	1 Filtration	1 Mixing substances and observing changes	1 Titrations	1 Preparing compounds by neutralization and evaporation
2 Electrolysis of solutions	2 Collecting a sample of a gas over water, when the gas has been produced by chemical reaction	2 Carrying out solubility tests		2 Distillation
3 Heating solids and observing changes				

You need to be tested carrying out one technique from each group. For the techniques in Groups A, B and C, you will be assessed out of 6 marks for each. For the techniques in Groups D and E, which are more involved, you will be assessed out of 9 marks for each. This gives a total of 36 marks for Techniques.

For Investigations, you will be assessed doing one whole investigation (see Coursework section pages 254–257). This will require you to show planning skills, experimental skills, evaluation skills and recording and reporting skills. Your investigation will be marked out of 28.

You will therefore get a total mark out of 64 for Practical Abilities which is converted to a grade using the following table:

Marks range	Grade
57–64	1
49–56	2
42–48	3
35–41	4
28–34	5

Southern Examining Group (SEG)

Address: Stag Hill House, Guildford GU2 5XJ

Science: Chemistry 2424

All candidates complete a Coursework Assessment on Sc1   25%

Foundation Tier   (levels 4–6)

Paper 2	$1\frac{1}{4}$ hours, most of the questions from SEG Double Science Sc3 questions	40%
Paper 5	$1\frac{1}{4}$ hours, testing additional materials	35%

Intermediate Tier   (levels 6–8)

Paper 3	$1\frac{1}{4}$ hours, most of the questions from SEG Double Science Sc3 questions	40%
Paper 6	$1\frac{1}{4}$ hours, testing additional materials	35%

Higher Tier   (levels 8–10)

Paper 4	$1\frac{1}{4}$ hours, most of the questions from SEG Double Science Sc3 questions	40%
Paper 7	$1\frac{1}{4}$ hours, testing additional materials	35%

The syllabus is divided into the following topics:

A The properties, classification and structure of materials
  1 Purpose and properties (Chapter 8)
  2 Mixtures and composites (Chapter 7)
  3 Acids and bases (Chapter 2)
  4 Periodicity (Chapter 5)

B Explanation of properties of materials
  5 Kinetic theory (Chapters 6, 10)
  6 Elements and compounds (Chapter 7)
  7 Atomic structure and radioactivity (Chapters 4, 9)

C Chemical changes
  8 Chemical reactions (Chapters 11, 16, 21)
  9 Rate of reaction (Chapter 17)
  10 Chemical equations (Chapters 13, 16, 25)
  11 Energy in chemistry (Chapter 19)
  12 Chemical technology (Chapter 20)

D The Earth and its atmosphere
  13 Practical geology (Chapter 26)
  14 Plate tectonics (Chapter 28)
  15 Atmosphere (Chapter 11)

  EXTENSION
  16 Nitrogen and its compounds (Chapters 11, 22)
  17 Chemistry and the environment (Chapters 30, 35)

E Mineral Chemistry
  18 Limestone, chalk and marble (Chapter 31)
  19 Transition elements and their compounds (Chapters 11, 33)
  20 Sulphur and its compounds (Chapters 24, 32)

F Organic Chemistry
  21 Hydrocarbons (Chapters 20, 25)
  22 Compounds from natural products (Chapter 34)

N.B. All of the Core chapters (1–28) are needed, either directly or indirectly.

University of London Examinations and Assessment Council (ULEAC)

Address: Stewart House, 32 Russell Square, London WC1B 5DN

Syllabus A 1036

All candidates complete a Coursework Assessment on Sc1		25%

Foundation Tier (levels 4–6)

Paper 2F	$1\frac{1}{2}$ hours, assessment of core (40%) + extension (5%)	45%
Paper 3F	$1\frac{1}{2}$ hours, assessment of extension	30%

Intermediate Tier (levels 6–8)

Paper 2I	$1\frac{1}{2}$ hours, assessment of core (40%) + extension (5%)	45%
Paper 3I	$1\frac{1}{2}$ hours, assessment of extension	30%

Higher Tier (levels 8–10)

Paper 2H	$1\frac{1}{2}$ hours, assessment of core (40%) + extension (5%)	45%
Paper 3H	$1\frac{1}{2}$ hours, assessment of extension	30%

All questions on all written papers will be compulsory. There will be a variety of questions on each paper, including structured questions involving both short answer and extended prose responses.

The syllabus is divided into the following topics:

Materials and their properties (Chapters 1–5)
Elements, compounds, mixtures (Chapters 6–7)
Periodicity, atomic structure and bonding (Chapters 5–8)
Chemical changes (Chapters 11–25)
Chemicals from oil (Chapters 20–21)
Energy changes (Chapter 19)
Electrochemistry (Chapter 19)
Rates of reaction and equilibrium (Chapter 18)
Quantitative Chemistry (Chapter 25)
Atmosphere (Chapter 3)
Lithosphere (Chapters 26–28)

These topics include two new strands:

Strand (v)   Making useful materials
Strand (vi)   Analysing materials and the environment

Additional chapters of the book you should study:

29, 30, 31, 32, 34

Syllabus B 1038

All candidates complete a Coursework Assessment on Sc1   25%

Foundation Tier   (levels 4–6)

    Paper 2F $1\frac{1}{2}$ hours, multiple choice and structured questions   40%
    Paper 3F $1\frac{1}{2}$ hours, structured and free response questions   35%

Intermediate Tier   (levels 6–8)

    Paper 2I $1\frac{1}{2}$ hours, multiple choice and structured questions   40%
    Paper 3I $1\frac{1}{2}$ hours, structured and free response questions   35%

Higher Tier   (levels 8–10)

    Paper 2H $1\frac{1}{2}$ hours, multiple choice and structured questions   40%
    Paper 3H $1\frac{1}{2}$ hours, structured and free response questions   35%

All written papers will assess both core and extension material.

The syllabus is divided into the following topics:

Particles and kinetic theory (Chapter 6)
Periodicity, atomic structure and bonding (Chapters 4, 7, 8)
Rates of reaction and equilibrium (Chapter 18)
Energy changes (Chapter 19)
Quantitative Chemistry (Chapter 25)
Elements, compounds and mixtures (Chapter 7)
Chemicals from oil (Chapters 20–21)
Metals and nonmetals (Chapter 3)
Atmosphere and lithosphere (Chapters 26–28, 35)

These topics include two new strands:

Strand (v)   Making useful materials
Strand (vi)   Analysing materials and the environment

Additional chapters of the book you should study:

29, 30, 31, 32, 34

International General Certificate of Secondary Education (IGCSE)

Address: University of Cambridge Local Examination Syndicate, 1 Hills Road, Cambridge, England CB1 2EU

This is a syllabus based upon GCSE used in various parts of the world with examinations in June and November each year.

Two papers are to be taken. For candidates aiming for grades C–G there is a $\frac{3}{4}$ hour multiple choice paper and a 1 hour structured paper. For candidates aiming at grades A–C there are two structured papers, each of 1 hour.

The written papers test the following chapters in this book: 1, 2, 3, 4, 5, 6, 7, 9 (only part), 11, 12, 13, 14, 15, 16, 17, 18, 19, 20, 21, 22, 23, 24, 25, 29, 30, 31, 32, 33, 34, 35.

The written papers account for 80% of the total mark with 20% allocated to coursework. This coursework covers the practical skills of following instructions, making observations and measurements, drawing conclusions and planning.

Study checklist

Syllabus studied

....

Dates of examination

....

Chapter	Date completed	Problems encountered/things to act on later
1		
2		
3		
4		
5		
6		
7		
8		
9		
10		
11		
12		
13		
14		
15		
16		
17		
18		
19		
20		
21		
22		
23		
24		
25		
26		
27		
28		

Additional chapters	Date completed	Problems encountered/things to act on later

Revision and examinations

Learning and remembering

Revision for examinations is most important and effective revision should start as early as possible. Certainly regular revision should start early in Year 11.

Plan your revision in advance and try to keep to your plans.

Revision is more than just sitting down and reading through a book. It is important to produce a plan. List all of the topics in the syllabus and make an assessment of the topics that you think you know well and the ones you know less well. Concentrate on mastering the topics that you do not fully understand. Do not leave out big sections of the syllabus because examinations are designed to cover as much of the syllabus as possible.

Learning is best done in fairly small chunks. Half an hour of intensive study followed by a short break and a change of subject is probably best, but everybody is different and you have to learn what is best for you. Set yourself definite revision targets – to complete certain sections by a certain date – and make sure you achieve them!

As you work through the sections write down the important points. This is helpful for triggering your memory and, if you keep these notes, for last minute revision.

Learn basic definitions, as many questions revolve around knowing these.

Hints on taking examinations

In this section there is information that you should find useful for both revising and taking your examinations. As a chief examiner responsible for setting and marking GCSE papers and as an assessor of coursework, I continually see candidates not achieving what they should because of basic flaws in their preparation or examination technique. This section is intended to be very practical and to ensure that you do your best both in preparation and in taking the examinations.

Understanding the syllabus

Syllabuses are very clear about what should be studied. However, you should understand some of the language of the syllabus. The following terms frequently appear on syllabuses.

- *'The characteristics of'* – You are required to describe the main properties/reactions of the substance concerned.
- *'The identification of'* – Recognizing the substance by means of simple test tube reactions is required.
- *'The formation of'* – Knowledge of the reaction or reactions leading to the making of the substance is required, without details of apparatus and/or collection methods.
- *'The manufacture of'* – A knowledge of the essential reactions involved in the commercial production of the material is required. Details of the industrial plant are not required.
- *'The preparation of'* – Knowledge of the reaction(s) and apparatus necessary for obtaining, purifying and collecting the material is required.

- *'The use of'* – A brief statement of both commercial and domestic applications of the material is required, with emphasis being placed on the property of the material that makes it suitable.

Often syllabuses provide useful notes that tell you, and your teachers, the detail which is required.

Underline important points in the questions as you read them.

The importance of reading the questions thoroughly

It is frequently stated in reports by examiners that candidates misread questions or fail to use the information given in the question. If the question concerns the industrial preparation of nitric acid, there would be no marks for a candidate whose answer refers to the laboratory preparation of nitric acid. If information (e.g. a table comparing two allotropes, an equation, relative atomic masses, a graph, etc.) is given in a question, it must be required to answer the question fully.

The question 'Explain what you would *see* if excess iron filings are added to copper(II) sulphate solution' requires more than a correct equation. You would be expected to mention that copper(II) sulphate solution is blue and when excess iron filings are added the blue solution goes colourless and a brown solid (copper) is deposited. It is obvious that most of the marks are awarded for these observations.

Where there is a choice of questions to be made, read all the questions through carefully before making any choice.

There are a number of instructions that appear on examination papers and candidates are often not clear what they mean. Here are some of the common instructions:

- *'Define'* – Just a statement or definition is required.
- *'State'* – Just a short answer is required, with little or no supporting argument.
- *'State and explain'* – Again a short answer is required, but with a little more reasoning.
- *'Describe'* – This is often used with reference to a particular experiment. The answer should include reference to what is seen during the experiment.
- *'Outline'* – The answer must be brief and the main points must be picked out.
- *'Predict'* – You are not expected to recall the answer but to link other pieces of information together logically to work out an answer. No supporting material is required in your answer.
- *'Suggest'* – Either there is no unique answer or you are applying your knowledge to a situation outside the syllabus.
- *'Find'* – This is a general term which may mean calculate, measure, determine, etc.
- *'Calculate'* – A numerical answer is required. You should show your working as well as your answer. Do not forget to put in the correct units.

Spending too much time on one question

A candidate who completes only half of the questions required can only achieve a maximum of 50 per cent and can have little chance of being successful. It is important to divide your time equally between the questions. It is a good idea to prepare a timetable for the examination before entering the examination room and then to stick to it.

Take time to choose questions – poor choice could cost you a grade.

For example, if you are preparing to take a $2\frac{1}{2}$ hour examination paper consisting of 40 fixed response questions and four longer questions to be chosen from eight, your plan might be:

13.30. Start the fixed response questions. There is no point in reading all the fixed response questions before you start as they are compulsory.
13.55. You should have reached item 20.
14.30. Complete fixed response questions. Note that more time is allowed for later items in the fixed response section. Read the eight longer questions and select the four to be attempted.
14.40. Attempt the question you feel you can do best. This is important as it will increase your confidence and will benefit you if, for any reason, you cannot complete the paper. If you have not finished at 15.00, stop writing and move on to the next question.
15.00. Start the second long question of your choice.
15.20. Start the third long question of your choice.
15.40. Start the fourth long question of your choice.
16.00. Examination finishes.

If you have any time left go back and complete any unfinished questions.

It is unwise to abandon a question when you have spent some time on it, in order to do another question instead. You will be wasting time with no certainty that you can do better with the other question.

Doing the wrong number of questions

Despite clearly stating the number of questions to be attempted, examiners see many papers where candidates have attempted the wrong number of questions.

It is believed by some candidates that if too many questions are attempted the examiner will mark all the questions and credit the candidate with marks from the best answered questions. This is not so and the examiner will award marks for the first questions attempted. It can never benefit the candidate to do more questions than required. If you find you have time to spare that enables you to attempt other questions, your answers may not be sufficiently detailed.

If you have done too many questions, make sure you have thoroughly crossed out any questions that you do not want to be marked.

Lack of planning and poor presentation

It is important to plan your answers carefully. This becomes more important as the questions get longer and more involved. A plan takes only a few minutes and it will help to ensure that you have covered the full extent of the answer required.

Some candidates believe that there is some credit given for long answers. When marking a longer question an examiner is looking for the inclusion of certain facts or statements. Marks are awarded when these are included. Unless these long answers contain the required facts or statements, no marks can be awarded.

You can lose marks for bad presentation and untidy work. Examiners cannot award marks for answers they cannot read.

Chemical equations

Your answers to questions in chemistry should include equations whenever relevant. If you are in doubt about the relevance of an equation, include it in your answer.

An equation is a useful summary of a chemical reaction. If three marks are awarded for an equation, one mark will be awarded for the correct word equation, one mark for the correct formulae throughout the equation and one mark for correctly balancing the equation. You are advised to include, therefore, both word and symbol equations.

If the question asks for a test for carbon dioxide, an equation (see Unit 31.3) should be included for the reaction between limewater and carbon dioxide.

Check that the symbol equation is balanced before you move on. If it is impossible to balance the equation completely, it suggests that you may have missed one or more of the reactants or products or that you may have written one or more of the formulae incorrectly.

State symbols, e.g. (s), (l), (g) or (aq), are used in this book. They are a useful addition to your equations.

Chemical calculations

All chemistry papers contain chemical calculations. They are usually not very well attempted by candidates. The figures are chosen to minimize arithmetic and it should not be necessary to resort to a calculator.

On many candidates' papers only answers are given and the working is not shown. If the answer is incorrect, the examiner cannot award any marks if no working is shown. If the working is given, it may still be possible, despite the wrong answer, to award a good mark. Remember most of the marks will be awarded for the essential *chemistry* rather than the arithmetic.

Remember to give units, where appropriate, to your answer. Before moving on to the next question, check that your answer is reasonable. I have seen a candidate, after making an arithmetical mistake, write 'because the ratio 41977:28493 is a simple ratio, the law of multiple proportions is verified'. If he had realized that this ratio is not simple he might have looked back and found the mistake.

The amount of space given for the answer and the mark allocation are good guides to how much detail is required.

Attention to detail

One of the distinguishing features between a good candidate and an average candidate is the ability to incorporate details into the answer. As a guide, in any answer, you should include:

❶ Names of chemicals used and produced. Include states, colours and concentrations of the chemicals.

❷ Give the conditions of any reaction, i.e. temperature, catalysts, etc.

❸ Explain why the reaction takes place. Relate your answer, if possible, to the Periodic Table or the reactivity series.

❹ Write the equations in words and symbols.

Drawing diagrams

Diagrams should be included whenever they improve your answer. They should help you avoid having to write a long descriptive account of your experiment.

Do not spend a long time doing an artistic diagram. The important feature of your diagram must be clarity. Draw the diagrams about half as big again as the diagrams in this book. Draw your diagrams freehand with a pencil and have an eraser available in case you make any mistakes. You may use stencils but they restrict your diagrams in size. When the diagram is finished, look carefully to make sure you have not made any obvious mistakes, e.g. in a gas preparation, a thistle funnel must enter the solution in the flask or the gas will escape. Finally, label every piece of apparatus and all chemicals in ink.

The following points are worth remembering:

❶ Do not waste time drawing stands and clamps. The examiner assumes you will support the apparatus correctly. They also detract from the important features of the diagram.

❷ Do not waste time drawing Bunsen burners for heating part of your apparatus. Just draw an arrow and label it HEAT.

❸ Try to draw each piece of apparatus to the correct size in relation to the other pieces of apparatus.

❹ Draw a round-bottomed flask if heating is required and a flat-bottomed or conical flask if it is not. If a round-bottomed flask is used, it must be drawn above the level of other apparatus to enable heat to be applied.

❺ A common mistake in diagrams is to omit corks and bungs.

❻ If a gas is to be bubbled through a liquid, ensure that the tube goes below the level of the liquid in the wash bottle, and the outlet for the gas is above the level of the liquid (see figure below).

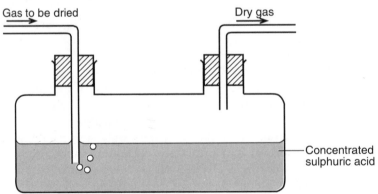

❼ When collecting a gas in a gas jar using a beehive shelf, ensure that the level of the water in the trough is above the top of the beehive shelf, that there is water inside the beehive shelf and that there is a hole in the top of the beehive shelf through which the gas can pass.

❽ When collecting a gas by upward or downward delivery (e.g. Fig. 22.1 or Fig. 31.3), ensure that the delivery tube reaches to the end of the gas jar.

❾ Having drawn an arrangement to dry a gas, do not collect it over water.

Chapter 1
Separation techniques in chemistry

3.5a know how to separate and purify the components of mixtures using physical processes.

A chemist is frequently involved in separating mixtures or purifying substances. There are a number of methods available as outlined below.

1.1 Separating insoluble impurities from a soluble substance

E.g. removing sand and other impurities from salt solution

When crushed rock salt is added to water, the salt **dissolves** and forms a salt **solution**. The sand and other impurities remain undissolved, and this material can be removed by **filtration** (Fig. 1.1).

The salt solution passing through the filter paper contains no solid impurities. In order to obtain a sample of pure salt, the salt solution is **evaporated** (Fig. 1.2).

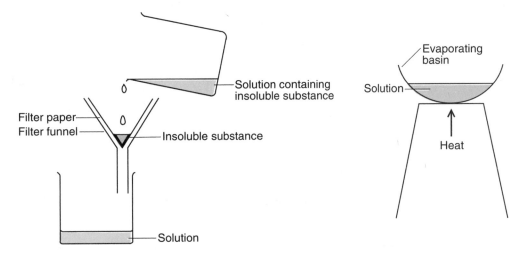

Fig. 1.1 Filtration

Fig. 1.2 Evaporation

Undissolved material can also be removed by **centrifuging**. This is used when small quantities of material are used, e.g. blood samples.

1.2 Separating a liquid from a solution of a solid in a liquid

E.g. producing pure water (distilled water) from sea water

This process is called **distillation**. When the flask is heated the solution boils and steam passes into the condenser. In the condenser, the steam is cooled by cold water passing through the outer condenser tube. The steam **condenses** and the **distillate** (distilled water) collects in the receiver. The impurities are left in the flask (Fig. 1.3).

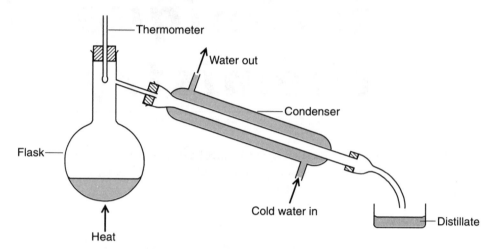

Fig. 1.3 Distillation

1.3 Separating a liquid from a mixture of miscible liquids

E.g. removing ethanol from a mixture of ethanol and water

(Miscible liquids are liquids that mix together completely to form a single layer.)

This process is called **fractional distillation** (Fig. 1.4). It relies on the difference in boiling points of the two liquids (e.g. water 100 °C, ethanol 78 °C).

When the flask is heated the ethanol boils more readily than the water. The water (with the higher boiling point) condenses in the fractionating column and drips back into the flask. The ethanol distils over first. When all the ethanol has distilled over, the temperature (recorded on the thermometer) rises, and water distils over and is collected in a different receiver.

1.4 Separating a mixture of immiscible liquids

E.g. separating a mixture of water and hexane

Water and hexane are **immiscible** and form two separate layers. The hexane layer forms above the water (or aqueous) layer because water is denser than hexane. These two liquids could be separated using a tap funnel.

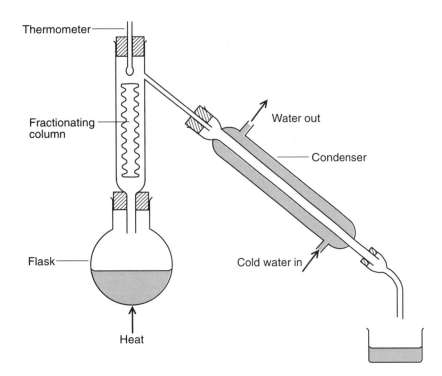

Fig. 1.4 Fractional distillation

1.5 Separating a mixture of similar compounds in solution

E.g. separating the dyes present in a sample of ink

This process is called **chromatography**. It is a very sensitive method that can be used to separate similar compounds in solution.

If a spot of dye solution is put on to a filter paper and the spot enlarged by slowly dropping solvent on to the centre of the spot, the different components of the dye spread out at different rates. Each component forms a definite ring on the filter paper.

Chromatography experiments are often carried out using square sheets of filter paper. Spots of dye solutions are put along the baseline of a sheet of filter paper. The filter paper is coiled into a cylinder and the cylinder is put into a tank containing a small volume of solvent. The lid is put on the tank and the solvent slowly rises up the filter paper. When the solvent has nearly reached the top of the filter paper, the cylinder is removed and the position that the solvent has reached is marked.

In Fig. 1.5, dyes A and B are either pure substances or a mixture of dyes not separated with the solvent used. Dye C is composed of a mixture of A and B, because the original spot has separated into two spots corresponding to A and B. Chromatography was originally devised to separate coloured substances in solution. It can, however, be used to separate colourless substances in solution, which can then be seen by spraying or dipping the filter paper into a suitable chemical (called a locating agent), which colours the spots produced.

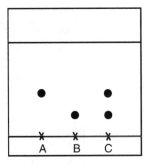

x Original position of each substance

● Final position of each substance

Fig. 1.5 A chromatogram

1.6 Separating a solid which sublimes from a solid which does not sublime

E.g. separating ammonium chloride (which sublimes) from sodium chloride (which does not sublime)

A substance is said to **sublime** if, on cooling, its vapour changes directly from gas to solid without going through an intermediate liquid state. Usually a substance which sublimes also changes from solid to vapour without melting to a liquid.

If a mixture of ammonium chloride and sodium chloride is heated, the ammonium chloride turns directly to a vapour but the sodium chloride remains unchanged. When the vapour is cooled, solid ammonium chloride collects free from sodium chloride.

1.7 Recognizing a pure substance

A **pure substance** has a **definite melting point**. The presence of an impurity **lowers the melting point** but also causes the substance to melt over a **range of temperature**. Calcium chloride is used to lower the melting point of sodium chloride in the extraction of sodium.

The boiling point of a substance depends on pressure. At atmospheric pressure, the boiling of a pure substance takes place at a particular temperature called the **boiling point**. The presence of dissolved impurities **increases the boiling point** slightly.

1.8 Emulsions, gels and foams

A solution consists of a solute distributed throughout the solvent. In a solution of sodium chloride in water, for example, the sodium chloride cannot be seen. The sodium and chloride ions fill gaps between the water molecules. The sodium chloride is still there, hence the salty taste.

There are other mixtures which can exist. These are often very important in industry and everyday life.

An **emulsion** is a mixture of two liquids. Unlike a true solution it is possible to see the distributed substance under a microscope and the emulsion is not transparent. Fig. 1.6 shows an oil-in-water emulsion. Droplets of oil are distributed through the aqueous layer. Milk is an example of an oil-in-water emulsion. Having the fat distributed through the liquid makes the fat more digestible.

An oil-in-water emulsion is formed by shaking oil and water together. On standing, however, the oil and water will start to separate. An emulsifying agent added to the mixture will help to keep the emulsion stable. Other common emulsions include salad cream, butter and cream cake mixes.

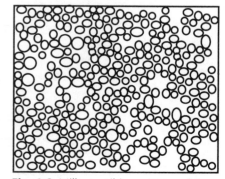

Fig. 1.6 Milk: an oil-in-water emulsion. Droplets of oil distributed in a watery liquid

When a mixture of starch and water is heated, the starch granules absorb water and swell. A thick white paste is formed which is jelly-like in appearance. This is called a **gel**. Cornflour is used to thicken gravy and sauces. Other common gels include wallpaper paste, toothpaste and fruit jellies, where the gel formed by gelatin and water contains 99% water.

A **foam** consists of a liquid or solid filled with bubbles of gas. When egg whites are briskly whisked, a stiff foam is formed. The mixture consists of tiny bubbles of air distributed through the stretched protein structure. When the mixture is heated at a low temperature, the protein sets and a meringue is formed.

Summary

A pure substance contains no impurities and melts at a definite melting point. An impure substance melts at a lower temperature and over a range of temperature.

An insoluble substance, e.g. sand, can be removed from a solution by filtering. Centrifuging is an alternative method when working on a small scale.

Evaporation can be used to recover dissolved salt from a salt solution. The salt solution would pass through a filter paper without change.

Distillation can be used to recover a solvent from a solution, e.g. getting water from a salt solution. Distillation involves boiling followed by condensation. Distilled water is produced when a solution is distilled where water is the solvent.

Fractional distillation can be used to separate mixtures of liquids with different boiling points. Fractional distillation is used when the liquids mix completely, i.e. they are miscible. If the liquids are immiscible, they can be separated using a tap funnel.

Chromatography is used to separate a mixture of compounds dissolved in a solvent. It is often used to separate mixtures of coloured compounds.

Sublimation is used to separate a mixture where one of the substances sublimes. Ammonium chloride, which sublimes, is often one of the substances in the mixture.

Chapter 2
Acids and bases

2.1 Acids

3.5b be able to classify aqueous solutions as acidic, alkaline or neutral, using indicators.

Acids form an important group of chemicals. They are generally thought of as being corrosive and having a sour taste.

Acids can be detected by using an **indicator** such as **litmus**. Indicators are dyes, or mixtures of dyes, which change colour when acids or alkalis are added. A wide range of indicators is available, each having its own characteristic colour in acid and alkali.

E.g. litmus   re**d** in aci**d**
                         b**l**ue in a**l**kali

A very useful indicator is called **Universal Indicator**. This is a mixture of dyes and so gives a greater range of colour changes. The colours of Universal Indicator are shown in Fig. 2.1.

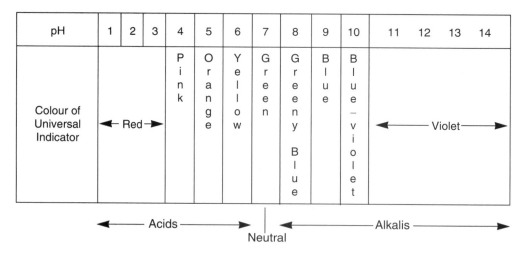

Fig. 2.1 Colours of Universal Indicator

Universal Indicator can not only show whether a substance is acid, alkaline or neutral but can also show how strong the acid or alkali is. Table 2.1 gives a list of some common acids.

Table 2.1 Common acids

Acid	Formula	
Hydrochloric acid	HCl	⎫
Nitric acid	HNO_3	⎬ Mineral acids
Sulphuric acid	H_2SO_4	⎭
Ethanoic acid (acetic acid)	CH_3COOH	Contained in vinegar
Citric acid	$C_6H_8O_7$	Contained in lemon juice

2.2 General reactions of acids

Although there are a large number of different acids, there are a number of general chemical reactions common to all acids.

1 Acids turn indicators to their characteristic colour, e.g. litmus turns red.

2 Acids react with a fairly reactive metal to form a salt and evolve hydrogen.

E.g. $$Mg(s) + H_2SO_4(aq) \rightarrow MgSO_4(aq) + H_2(g)$$
magnesium + sulphuric acid $\rightarrow$ magnesium sulphate + hydrogen

An exception is nitric acid. This acid tends to release oxides of nitrogen when reacted with metals, although very dilute nitric acid does liberate hydrogen with magnesium.

3 Acids react with metal oxides to form a salt and water. In most cases the acid needs warming.

E.g. $$CuO(s) + 2HNO_3(aq) \rightarrow Cu(NO_3)_2(aq) + H_2O(l)$$
copper(II) oxide + nitric acid $\rightarrow$ copper(II) nitrate + water

4 Acids react with metal carbonates to form a salt, carbon dioxide and water.

E.g. $$CaCO_3(s) + 2HCl(aq) \rightarrow CaCl_2(aq) + CO_2(g) + H_2O(l)$$
calcium carbonate + hydrochloric acid $\rightarrow$ calcium chloride + carbon dioxide + water

5 Acids react with alkalis to form a salt and water.

E.g. $$NaOH(aq) + HCl(aq) \rightarrow NaCl(aq) + H_2O(l)$$
sodium hydroxide + hydrochloric acid $\rightarrow$ sodium chloride + water

2.3 Importance of water

Hydrogen chloride gas will dissolve in both water and methylbenzene (toluene) but the solutions have different properties. Table 2.2 compares results of some tests for each solution.

Table 2.2 Testing hydrogen chloride solutions

Test	Solution of hydrogen chloride in water	Solution of dry hydrogen chloride in dry methylbenzene (toluene)
1 Dry Universal Indicator paper	Turns red showing strong acid	Turns green – neutral
2 Add magnesium ribbon	Hydrogen evolved	No reaction
3 Add calcium carbonate	Carbon dioxide evolved	No reaction
4 Electrical conductivity	Good conductor	Nonconductor
5 Temperature change on forming solution	Rise in temperature	Little change

These results show that the solution in water behaves as an acid but the solution in methylbenzene shows no acidic properties.

The electrical conductivity of the solution in water indicates the presence of ions.

When hydrogen chloride gas dissolves in water it changes from molecules to ions:

$$HCl(g) \xrightarrow{\text{water}} H^+(aq) + Cl^-(aq)$$

This ionization is accompanied by a rise in temperature. **It is the hydrogen ions that cause acidic properties and these are formed in the presence of water**.

You will come across different names and symbols for the hydrogen ion in solution which attempt to show how the hydrogen ion becomes associated with water molecules:

$$H^+(aq) \quad \textbf{hydrated proton} \text{ or } \textbf{hydrated hydrogen ion}$$
$$H_3O^+(aq) \quad \textbf{oxonium} \text{ or } \textbf{hydronium ion}$$

Remember that the hydrogen ion is simply a proton. (This is because a hydrogen atom consists of a single proton and a single electron; when H^+ is formed the electron is removed.)

2.4 Definitions of an acid

An acid can be defined in various ways. These include:

1 An acid is a substance that contains hydrogen which can be wholly or partially replaced by a metal. This hydrogen is called replaceable hydrogen.

2 An acid is a substance which forms hydrogen ions when it is dissolved in water.

3 An acid is a proton donor. It provides protons or H^+ ions.

The general reactions of an acid (see Unit 2.2) can now be seen as reactions of hydrogen ions in solution.

E.g.
$$Mg(s) + 2H^+(aq) \rightarrow Mg^{2+}(aq) + H_2(g)$$
$$O^{2-}(s) + 2H^+(aq) \rightarrow H_2O(l)$$
$$CO_3^{2-}(s) + 2H^+(aq) \rightarrow CO_2(g) + H_2O(l)$$
$$OH^-(aq) + H^+(aq) \rightarrow H_2O(l)$$

2.5 pH scale

As the reactions of an acid are those of the hydrogen ions in solution, clearly the more hydrogen ions are present, the stronger the acid will be. The strength of an acid is measured on the **pH scale**. Figure 2.1 relates the colour of Universal Indicator to the pH number. The pH number is a measure of the hydrogen ion concentration.

pH 1	strong acid
pH 2–pH 6	weak acids
pH 7	neutral
pH 8–pH 13	weak alkalis
pH 14	strong alkali

The smaller the pH the larger is the concentration of hydrogen ions, and so the stronger the acid is. The pH can be measured with Universal Indicator or by using a pH meter.

2.6 Strong and weak acids

Some acids completely ionize when they dissolve in water. These are called **strong acids**, i.e. the solution will contain a high concentration of hydrogen ions.

E.g. sulphuric acid

$$H_2SO_4(l) \xrightarrow{\text{water}} 2H^+(aq) + SO_4^{2-}(aq)$$

Other acids do not completely ionize on dissolving in water, i.e. some of the molecules remain un-ionized in the solution. These are called **weak acids**.

E.g. ethanoic acid (acetic acid)

$$CH_3COOH(l) \underset{water}{\rightleftharpoons} H^+(aq) + CH_3COO^-(aq)$$

In a molar solution of ethanoic acid only about four molecules in every thousand change into ions.

Table 2.3 lists some common strong and weak acids.

Table 2.3 Strong and weak acids

Strong acids	Weak acids
Hydrochloric acid	Ethanoic acid
Sulphuric acid	Carbonic acid
Nitric acid	Sulphurous acid

2.7 Bases

A **base** is a substance that can accept hydrogen ions, i.e. a proton acceptor. A base will react with an acid to form a salt and water only.

E.g.
$$CuO(s) + H_2SO_4(aq) \rightarrow CuSO_4(aq) + H_2O(l)$$
copper(II) oxide + sulphuric acid → copper(II) sulphate + water
$$O^{2-}(s) + 2H^+(aq) \rightarrow H_2O(l)$$

If a base is soluble in water, the solution is called an **alkali**. Examples of alkalis include sodium hydroxide NaOH, potassium hydroxide KOH and calcium hydroxide $Ca(OH)_2$. An alkali contains a high concentration of hydroxide ions (OH^-) in solution.

When an acid reacts with an alkali, the reaction is between hydrogen ions and hydroxide ions.

$$H^+(aq) + OH^-(aq) \rightarrow H_2O(l)$$

This reaction is called a **neutralization** reaction.

2.8 Strong and weak alkalis

If an alkali completely ionizes on dissolving in water, a **strong alkali** is produced.

E.g. sodium hydroxide
$$NaOH(s) \xrightarrow{water} Na^+(aq) + OH^-(aq)$$

If an alkali does not completely ionize in water, a **weak alkali** is formed.

E.g. ammonium hydroxide (solution of ammonia gas in water)
$$NH_4OH(aq) \rightleftharpoons NH_4^+(aq) + OH^-(aq)$$

2.9 Neutralization

When an acid and an alkali are mixed in the correct proportions a neutral substance can be produced. This process is called **neutralization**. The subject of salt formation from acids and alkalis is dealt with in full in Chapter 32.

There are many everyday examples of neutralization.

1. Soil testing. A soil with a pH between 6.5 and 7.0 is suitable for growing most plants. If the pH drops below 6.0, the soil becomes too acidic for growing some plants. Above a pH of 8 the soil becomes too alkaline and vital minerals are missing from the soil.

   Excess acidity is caused by rainwater washing alkali out of the soil. Limestone (calcium carbonate) or hydrated lime (calcium hydroxide) can be added to the soil to reduce the acidity (Chapter 31).

2. The digestive system. Every person has hydrochloric acid in the gastric juices in the stomach. This is used, together with enzymes, in the digestion of food. Digestion involves the breaking down of complex substances into simpler substances which can be used by the body. Indigestion is caused by an excess of hydrochloric acid in the gastric juices in the stomach. The excess acidity can be controlled by swallowing a mild alkali to neutralize some of the hydrochloric acid. Bicarbonate of soda or magnesium hydroxide are suitable alkalis.

3. Insect bites and stings. Insect bites and stings involve the injection of a small amount of chemical into the skin. This causes irritation. Nettle stings, bee stings and ant bites inject methanoic acid into the skin. These can be treated with calamine lotion (containing zinc carbonate) or bicarbonate of soda. Both of these are mild alkalis. Wasp stings involve injection of an alkali and are therefore treated with a mild acid, vinegar. Neutralization of the sting removes the irritation.

4. Neutralization of acidic water in inland lakes. Acid rain, produced by sulphur dioxide escaping into the atmosphere, can make inland lakes acidic. This can affect organisms living in the lake, e.g. killing fish. Blocks of limestone put into the water can reduce the acidity of the water.

5. Desulphurization in coal-fired power stations. Coal-fired power stations produce sulphur dioxide, which can produce acid rain. The sulphur dioxide can be removed from the waste gases before they escape into the atmosphere. Limestone removes the sulphur dioxide from the waste gases and neutralizes the waste gases.

Neutralization reactions can be summarized by the ionic equation

$$H^+(aq) + OH^-(aq) \rightarrow H_2O(l)$$

Summary

An aqueous solution with a pH less than 7 contains an excess of H^+ ions and contains an acid. The three common mineral acids are sulphuric acid H_2SO_4, nitric acid HNO_3 and hydrochloric acid HCl.

Acids will:

1. Produce hydrogen gas with a reactive metal such as magnesium or zinc.
2. Produce a salt and water with a metal oxide or hydroxide.
3. Produce carbon dioxide with a metal carbonate.
4. Turn indicators to the acid colour.

A strong acid is an acid which is completely ionized in solution. A weak acid is an acid which is only partly ionized in solution. Acids cannot be ionized and show acid properties unless water is present.

A base is a metal oxide, e.g. copper(II) oxide. A base which is soluble in water forms an alkali. Common alkalis include sodium hydroxide $NaOH$, potassium hydroxide KOH and calcium hydroxide $Ca(OH)_2$. All alkali solutions contain an excess of hydroxide ions OH^-.

The reaction between an acid and an alkali is called a neutralization reaction:

$$H^+(aq) + OH^-(aq) \rightarrow H_2O(l)$$

Chapter 3
Metals and nonmetals

3.1 Introduction

3.6a be able to distinguish between metallic and non-metallic elements, mixtures and compounds using simple chemical and physical properties.

We talk quite commonly about metallic properties and differences between metals and nonmetals. In this chapter we are going to consider the physical and chemical properties of metals and how they differ from nonmetals. There are some elements such as silicon which are difficult to classify as metals or nonmetals because they have properties between the two. These elements are called **metalloids**.

Also, we are going to consider the advantages of mixtures of metals called **alloys** compared with pure metals.

3.2 Physical properties of metals

Table 3.1 compares the physical properties of metals and nonmetals.

Table 3.1 Comparison of properties of typical metals and nonmetals

Metals	Nonmetals
Solid at room temperature	Solid, liquid or gas at room temperature
Shiny	Dull
High density	Low density
Good conductor of heat and electricity	Poor conductor of heat and electricity
Can be beaten into thin sheets (malleable) and drawn into wire (ductile)	Brittle

There are many exceptions to the generalizations in Table 3.1. For example, mercury is a metal but is a liquid at room temperature. Carbon (in the form of graphite) is a nonmetal but conducts electricity. Silicon is a grey solid with a metallic appearance and could be mistaken for a metal if only physical properties are considered.

3.3 Chemical properties of metals

Many metals react with dilute hydrochloric or sulphuric acid to produce hydrogen gas.

3.8a know the major characteristics of metals and non-metals as reflected in the properties of a range of their compounds.

E.g.

$$Mg(s) + H_2SO_4(aq) \rightarrow MgSO_4(aq) + H_2(g)$$
magnesium + sulphuric acid → magnesium sulphate + hydrogen
$$Mg(s) + 2HCl(aq) \rightarrow MgCl_2(aq) + H_2(g)$$
magnesium + hydrochloric acid → magnesium chloride + hydrogen

However, not all metals will produce hydrogen in this way.

A better method of distinguishing metals from nonmetals is to burn the element in air or oxygen and form the oxide. The oxide is then tested with Universal Indicator to find the pH of the oxide. If the oxide is pH 7 or above (neutral or alkaline) the element was a metal. If the oxide has a pH less than 7 (acid) the element was a nonmetal. This is a very reliable way of distinguishing between a metal and a nonmetal.

3.4 Alloys

Pure metals have a wide range of uses. Table 3.2 lists some of the uses of pure metals and the reasons for their use. For many purposes, however, mixtures of metals called alloys are preferred. An alloy is usually less malleable and ductile than a pure metal. A copper alloy is much stronger than pure copper and more suitable for coinage. Alloys also have lower melting points than pure metals.

Table 3.2 Uses of pure metals

Metal	Use	A reason for use
Copper	Electricity cables	Excellent conductor of electricity/v. ductile
Tin	Coating tin cans	Not poisonous
Aluminium	Kitchen foil	Very malleable
Iron	Wrought iron gates	Easy to forge and resists corrosion
Lead	Flashing on roofs	Soft, easy to shape, does not corrode

An alloy is made by weighing out correctly the different constituent metals and melting them together to form the alloy.

Steel is undoubtedly the most important alloy. It is an alloy of iron containing between 0.15 and 1.5 per cent of carbon with other metals possibly present.

Table 3.3 includes some of the common alloys and their uses.

Table 3.3 Examples of common alloys

Alloy	Constituent elements	Uses
Steel	Iron + between 0.15% and 1.5% carbon. The properties of steel depend on the percentage of carbon. Other metals may be present, e.g. chromium in stainless steel	Wide variety of uses including cars, ships, tools, reinforced concrete, tinplate (coated with tin)
Brass	Copper and zinc	Ornaments, buttons, screws
Duralumin	Aluminium, magnesium, copper and manganese	Lightweight uses, e.g. aircraft, bicycles
Solder	Tin and lead	Joining metals (N.B. importance of low melting point)
Coinage bronze	Copper, zinc and tin	1p and 2p coins
Bronze	Copper and tin	Ornaments

Summary

Metals are usually solids with a shiny appearance and a silver or gold colour. They usually have a high density and conduct heat and electricity well. However, physical properties can be misleading. An element can sometimes look like a metal but, in fact, be a nonmetal.

A very reliable method of distinguishing a metal from a nonmetal involves forming the oxide and testing the oxide to find its pH with Universal Indicator. If the oxide is neutral or alkaline, the element is a metal. If the oxide is acid, the element is a nonmetal.

An alloy is a mixture of metals which is more useful, for some reason, than a pure metal. Common alloys include brass, bronze, solder, duralumin and steel.

Chapter 4
Atomic structure

4.1 Particles in atoms

3.8b understand the structure of the atom in terms of protons, neutrons and electrons and how this can explain the existence of isotopes.

All elements are made up from **atoms**. An atom is the smallest part of an element that can exist.

It has been found that the atoms of all elements are made up from three basic particles and that the atoms of different elements contain different numbers of these three particles. These particles are:

proton	p	mass 1 u (u = atomic mass unit)	charge +1
electron	e	mass $\frac{1}{1800}$ u (negligible)	charge −1
neutron	n	mass 1 u	neutral

Because an atom has no overall charge, the number of protons in any atom is equal to the number of electrons.

Atomic number

The atomic number is the number of protons in an atom.

Mass number

The mass number is the total number of protons and neutrons in an atom.

E.g. The mass number of carbon-12 is 12, and the atomic number is 6. Therefore a carbon-12 atom contains 6 protons (i.e. atomic number = 6), 6 electrons and 6 neutrons. This is sometimes written as $^{12}_{6}C$ (the atomic number is written under the mass number).

For sodium-23:

mass number = 23   atomic number = 11   (i.e. $^{23}_{11}Na$)
p = 11, e = 11, n = 23 − 11 = 12

It is possible, with many elements, to get more than one type of atom. For example, there are three types of oxygen atom:

oxygen-16	8p, 8e, 8n
oxygen-17	8p, 8e, 9n
oxygen-18	8p, 8e, 10n

These different types of atom of the same element are called **isotopes**. They are different because they contain different numbers of neutrons. (If they did not contain the same number of protons and the same number of electrons they would not be isotopes of oxygen.) Isotopes of the same element have the same chemical properties but slightly different physical properties.

There are two isotopes of chlorine − chlorine-35 and chlorine-37. An ordinary sample of chlorine contains approximately 75 per cent chlorine-35 and 25 per cent chlorine-37. This explains the fact that the relative atomic mass of chlorine is approximately 35.5 (The relative atomic mass of an element is the mass of an 'average atom' compared with the mass of a $_6^{12}$C carbon atom – see Unit 25.1).

4.2 Arrangement of particles in an atom

The protons and neutrons are tightly packed together in the **nucleus** of an atom. The electrons move rapidly around the nucleus in distinct energy levels. Each energy level is capable of accommodating only a certain number of electrons. This is represented in a simplified form in Fig. 4.1.

Make sure you can draw diagrams of simple atoms, e.g. carbon.

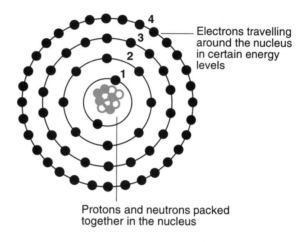

Electrons travelling around the nucleus in certain energy levels

Protons and neutrons packed together in the nucleus

Fig. 4.1 Arrangement of particles in an atom

1. The first energy level (sometimes called the K shell and labelled 1 in Fig. 4.1) can hold only two electrons. This energy level is filled first.

2. The second energy level (sometimes called the L shell and labelled 2 in Fig. 4.1) can hold only eight electrons. This energy level is filled after the first energy level and before the third energy level.

3. The third energy level (sometimes called the M shell and labelled 3 in Fig. 4.1) can hold a maximum of 18 electrons. However, when eight electrons are in the third energy level there is a degree of stability and the next two electrons added go into the fourth energy level (labelled 4 in Fig. 4.1). Then extra electrons enter the third energy level until it contains the maximum of 18 electrons.

4. There are further energy levels, each containing a larger number of electrons than the preceding energy level.

Table 4.1 gives the number of protons, neutrons and electrons in the principal isotopes of the first 20 elements. The electronic structure 2,8,1 denotes 2 electrons in the first energy level, 8 in the second, and 1 in the third. This is sometimes called the **electron configuration** of an atom.

Table 4.1 Numbers of protons, neutrons and electrons in the principal isotopes of the first 20 elements

Element	Atomic number	Mass number	Number of p	Number of n	Number of e	Arrangement of electrons
Hydrogen	1	1	1	0	1	1
Helium	2	4	2	2	2	2
Lithium	3	7	3	4	3	2,1
Beryllium	4	9	4	5	4	2,2
Boron	5	11	5	6	5	2,3
Carbon	6	12	6	6	6	2,4
Nitrogen	7	14	7	7	7	2,5
Oxygen	8	16	8	8	8	2,6
Fluorine	9	19	9	10	9	2,7
Neon	10	20	10	10	10	2,8
Sodium	11	23	11	12	11	2,8,1
Magnesium	12	24	12	12	12	2,8,2
Aluminium	13	27	13	14	13	2,8,3
Silicon	14	28	14	14	14	2,8,4
Phosphorus	15	31	15	16	15	2,8,5
Sulphur	16	32	16	16	16	2,8,6
Chlorine	17	35	17	18	17	2,8,7
Argon	18	40	18	22	18	2,8,8
Potassium	19	39	19	20	19	2,8,8,1
Calcium	20	40	20	20	20	2,8,8,2

You will find that properties of elements and the position in the Periodic Table are related to electronic structure.

Summary

All elements are made up of atoms. Atoms are made up of three types of particle – protons (positive charge), neutrons (neutral) and electrons (negative charge).

In any atom the number of protons and the number of electrons are the same. Atoms of the same element may, however, contain different numbers of neutrons. Atoms of the same element containing different numbers of neutrons are called isotopes.

In an atom the protons and neutrons are packed together in a positively charged nucleus. The negatively charged electrons move around the nucleus in certain energy levels.

Chapter 5
Chemical families and the Periodic Table

5.1 Chemical families

The 105 known elements can be divided into different groups in several ways. All elements can be classified as metals or nonmetals and, from their appearance, it is easy to classify elements as solids, liquids or gases at room temperature. From a chemical point of view, it is useful to group elements together because they have similar chemical behaviour. These groups of elements are sometimes called **families** of elements. Elements in the same family are not identical but usually show marked similarities with other members of the same family.

5.2 The alkali metal family

This is a group of very reactive metals. The most common members of the family are lithium, sodium and potassium and some of their properties are shown in Table 5.1.

Table 5.1 Alkali metals

Element	Symbol	Appearance	Melting point (°C)	Density (g/cm^3)
Lithium	Li	Soft grey metal	181	0.54
Sodium	Na	Soft light grey metal	98	0.97
Potassium	K	Very soft blue/grey metal	63	0.86

These metals have to be stored in oil to exclude air and water. They do not look much like metals, at first sight, but when freshly cut they all have a typical shiny metallic surface.

They are also very good conductors of electricity. Note, however, that they have melting points and densities that are low compared with other metals.

Reaction of alkali metals with water

When a small piece of an alkali metal is put into a trough of water, the metal reacts immediately, floating on the surface of the water and evolving hydrogen.

With sodium and potassium, the heat evolved from the reaction is sufficient to melt the metal.

The hydrogen evolved by the reaction of potassium with cold water is usually ignited and burns with a pink flame.

Sodium reacts more quickly than lithium, and potassium reacts more quickly than sodium.

In each case the solution remaining at the end of the reaction is an alkali.

Learn these reactions –
they come up very
frequently.

$$2Li(s) + 2H_2O(l) \rightarrow 2LiOH(aq) + H_2(g)$$
lithium + water $\rightarrow$ lithium hydroxide + hydrogen
$$2Na(s) + 2H_2O(l) \rightarrow 2NaOH(aq) + H_2(g)$$
sodium + water $\rightarrow$ sodium hydroxide + hydrogen
$$2K(s) + 2H_2O(l) \rightarrow 2KOH(aq) + H_2(g)$$
potassium + water $\rightarrow$ potassium hydroxide + hydrogen

N.B. These three equations are basically the same and, if the alkali metal is represented by M, these equations can be represented by:

$$2M(s) + 2H_2O(l) \rightarrow 2MOH(aq) + H_2(g)$$

Reaction of alkali metals with oxygen

When heated in air or oxygen, the alkali metals burn to form white solid oxides. The colour of the flame is characteristic of the metal:

lithium – red
sodium – orange
potassium – lilac

E.g.
$$4Li(s) + O_2(g) \rightarrow 2Li_2O(s)$$
lithium + oxygen $\rightarrow$ lithium oxide
or
$$4M(s) + O_2(g) \rightarrow 2M_2O(s)$$

The alkali metal oxides all dissolve in water to form alkali solutions.

E.g.
$$Li_2O(s) + H_2O(l) \rightarrow 2LiOH(aq)$$
lithium oxide + water $\rightarrow$ lithium hydroxide
or
$$M_2O(s) + H_2O(l) \rightarrow 2MOH(aq)$$

Reaction of alkali metals with chlorine

When a piece of burning alkali metal is lowered into a gas jar of chlorine, the metal continues to burn forming a white smoke of the metal chloride.

E.g.
$$2K(s) + Cl_2(g) \rightarrow 2KCl(s)$$
potassium + chlorine $\rightarrow$ potassium chloride
or
$$2M(s) + Cl_2(g) \rightarrow 2MCl(s)$$

It is because of these similar reactions that these metals are put in the same family. In each reaction the order of reactivity is the same, i.e. lithium is least reactive and potassium is the most reactive.

There are three more members of this family – rubidium (Rb), caesium (Cs) and francium (Fr). They are all more reactive than potassium.

5.3 The halogen family

This is a family of nonmetals. In the alkali metal family, the members of the family all have similar appearances. In the halogen family, the different members have different appearances but they are put in the same family on the basis of their similar chemical reactions. Their appearances are compared in Table 5.2.

Make sure you
spell fluorine
correctly – not
'flourine'!

Table 5.2 Halogens

Element	Symbol	Appearance at room temperature
Fluorine	F	Pale yellow gas
Chlorine	Cl	Yellow/green gas
Bromine	Br	Red/brown volatile liquid
Iodine	I	Dark grey crystalline solid

There is another member of the family called astatine (At). It is radioactive and a very rare element.

Fluorine is a very reactive gas and is too reactive to handle in normal laboratory conditions.

Solubility of halogens in water

None of the halogens is very soluble in water. Chlorine is the most soluble. Iodine does not dissolve much in cold water and only dissolves slightly in hot water.

Chlorine solution (sometimes called chlorine water) is very pale green. It turns Universal Indicator red showing the solution is acidic. The colour of the indicator is quickly bleached.

Bromine solution (bromine water) is orange. It is very weakly acidic and also acts as a bleach.

Iodine solution is very weakly acidic and is also a slight bleach. The low solubility of halogens in water (a polar solvent) is expected because halogens are composed of molecules.

Solubility of halogens in hexane (a nonpolar solvent)

The halogens dissolve readily in hexane to give solutions of characteristic colour:

chlorine – colourless
bromine – orange
iodine – purple

Reactions of halogens with iron

The halogens react with metals by direct combination to form salts. The name 'halogen' means salt producer. Chlorine forms chlorides, bromine forms bromides and iodine forms iodides.

If chlorine gas is passed over heated iron wire, an exothermic reaction takes place forming iron(III) chloride, which forms as a brown solid on cooling. Figure 5.1 shows a suitable apparatus for preparing anhydrous iron(III) chloride crystals.

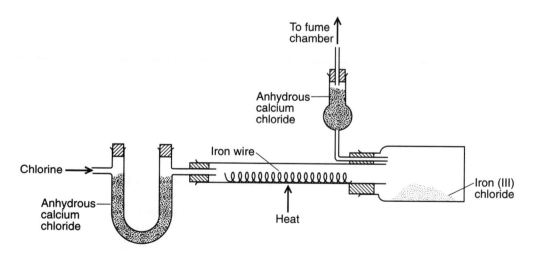

Fig. 5.1 Preparation of iron(III) chloride

$$2Fe(s) + 3Cl_2(g) \rightarrow 2FeCl_3(s)$$
$$\text{iron} + \text{chlorine} \rightarrow \text{iron(III) chloride}$$

The anhydrous calcium chloride tube is to prevent water vapour entering the apparatus.

Bromine vapour also reacts with hot iron wire to form iron(III) bromide. When iodine crystals are heated, they turn to a purple vapour. This vapour reacts with hot iron wire to produce iron(II) iodide.

Order of reactivity of the halogens
From their chemical reactions the relative reactivities of the halogens are:

fluorine	– most reactive
chlorine	
bromine	
iodine	– least reactive

Displacement reactions of the halogens

A more reactive halogen will displace a less reactive halogen from one of its compounds. For example when chlorine is bubbled into a solution of potassium bromide, the chlorine displaces the less reactive bromine. This means the colourless solution turns orange as the free bromine is formed.

$$2KBr(aq) + Cl_2(g) \rightarrow 2KCl(aq) + Br_2(aq)$$
$$\text{potassium bromide} + \text{chlorine} \rightarrow \text{potassium chloride} + \text{bromine}$$

No reaction would take place if iodine solution were added to potassium bromide solution because iodine is less reactive than bromine.

5.4 The noble or inert gas family

This is a family of gases. They are put in the same family because they are all very unreactive. Until about 30 years ago these gases were believed to be completely without chemical reactions. Since then a number of compounds, including xenon tetrafluoride XeF_4, have been produced. Table 5.3 gives some information about the noble gases.

Table 5.3 Noble gases

Element	Symbol	Boiling point (°C)	Density (g/dm³)
Helium	He	– 269	0.17
Neon	Ne	– 246	0.84
Argon	Ar	– 185	1.66
Krypton	Kr	– 153	3.46
Xenon	Xe	– 109	5.45
Radon	Rn	– 62	8.9

The noble gases are important because of their lack of reactions and they form the basis of theories of bonding.

Uses of the noble gases

Helium is used in balloons and airships. Although it is denser than hydrogen it has the advantage of being non-flammable.

Neon is used in advertising signs and **argon** is used to fill electric light bulbs. **Krypton** and **xenon** are used in lighthouse and projector bulbs.

Radon is radioactive and can be used to detect leaks in pipes.

5.5 The Periodic Table

The Periodic Table is an arrangement of all the chemical elements in order of increasing atomic number with elements having similar properties (i.e. of the same chemical family) in the same vertical column. The Periodic Table is shown in Fig. 5.2 in a modern form.

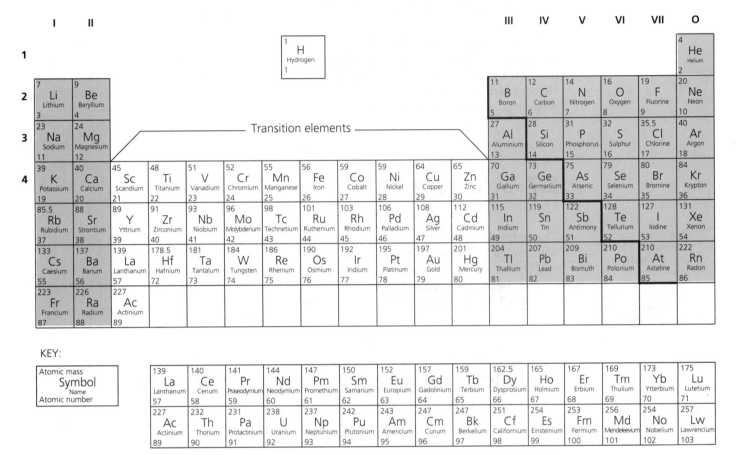

Fig. 5.2 The Periodic Table of elements

5.6 Brief history of the development of the Periodic Table

In the early 19th century many new elements were being discovered and chemists were looking for similarities between these new elements and existing elements.

Döbereiner (1829) suggested that elements could be groups in three (triads). Each member of the triad has similar properties.

E.g. lithium, sodium, potassium
chlorine, bromine, iodine

Newlands (1863) arranged the elements in order of increasing relative atomic mass. He noticed that there was some similarity between each eighth element.

Li   Be   B   C   N   O   F
Na   Mg   Al   Si   P   S   Cl   etc.

These were called **Newlands' Octaves**. Unfortunately the pattern broke down with the heavier elements and because he left no gaps for undiscovered elements. His work did not receive much support at the time.

Meyer (1869) looked at the relationship between relative atomic mass and the density of an element. He then plotted a graph of atomic volume (mass of 1 mole of atoms divided by density) against the relative atomic mass for each element. The curve he obtained showed periodic variations.

Mendeleef arranged the elements in order of increasing relative atomic mass but took into account the patterns of behaviour of the elements. He found it was necessary to leave gaps in the table and said that these were for elements not known at that time. His table enabled him to predict the properties of the undiscovered elements. His work was proved correct by the accurate prediction of the properties of gallium and germanium. The Periodic Table we use today closely resembles the table drawn up by Mendeleef.

A modification of the Periodic Table was made following the work of **Rutherford** and **Moseley**. It was realized that the elements should be arranged in order of atomic number, i.e. the number of protons in the nucleus. In the modern Periodic Table the elements are arranged in order of increasing atomic number with elements with similar properties in the same vertical column.

5.7 Structure of the Periodic Table

3.7b know that the periodic table groups contain families of elements with similar properties, which depend on their electronic structure.

The vertical columns in the table are called **groups**. A group will contain elements with similar properties. The groups are given roman numbers as shown in Fig. 5.2.

The horizontal rows of elements are called **periods**.

The 'main block' elements are shaded in Fig. 5.2 and between the two parts of the main block are the heavy or transition metals.

5.8 Electron arrangement and reactivity in a group

In Chapter 4 the arrangement of electrons within an atom was explained. The chemical properties of an element are controlled by the number of electrons in the outer energy level.

As elements in the same group have similar properties, we should expect some similarity in their electronic arrangement.

Table 5.4 shows the arrangement of electrons in the alkali metal family (group I of the Periodic Table).

3.9a understand how the properties of elements depend on their electronic structure and their position in the periodic table.

Table 5.4 Electron arrangement in group I

Element	Atomic number	Arrangement of electrons
Li	3	2,1
Na	11	2,8,1
K	19	2,8,8,1
Rb	37	2,8,18,8,1
Cs	55	2,8,18,18,8,1

Note that, in each case, the outer energy level contains just one electron. When an element reacts it attempts to obtain a full outer energy level.

Group I elements will lose one electron when they react and form a positive ion.

$$Na \rightarrow Na^+ + e^-$$

We can explain the order of reactivity within the group. The electrons are held in position by the electrostatic attraction of the positive nucleus. This means that the closer the electron is to the nucleus, the harder it will be to remove it.

As we go down the group, the outer electron gets further away from the nucleus and so becomes easier to take away. This means as we go down the group, the reactivity should increase.

Table 5.5 shows the arrangement of electrons in the alkaline earth metal family (group II of the Periodic Table).

Table 5.5 Electron arrangement in group II

Element		Atomic number	Arrangement of electrons
Beryllium	Be	4	2,2
Magnesium	Mg	12	2,8,2
Calcium	Ca	20	2,8,8,2
Strontium	Sr	38	2,8,18,8,2
Barium	Ba	56	2,8,18,18,8,2
Radium	Ra	88	2,8,18,32,18,8,2

As the atoms all have two electrons in their outer energy level, they will lose two electrons to form positive ions.

$$Mg \rightarrow Mg^{2+} + 2e^-$$

More energy will be required to remove two electrons and so they will not be as reactive as the group I metals. As with group I, the reactivity will increase down the group.

E.g. Reaction of group II metals with water

Magnesium will react rapidly with steam.

$$Mg(s) + H_2O(g) \rightarrow MgO(s) + H_2(g)$$
$$\text{magnesium + water (steam)} \rightarrow \text{magnesium oxide + hydrogen}$$

Calcium reacts with cold water.

$$Ca(s) + 2H_2O(l) \rightarrow Ca(OH)_2(aq) + H_2(g)$$
$$\text{calcium + water} \rightarrow \text{calcium hydroxide + hydrogen}$$

Barium is stored in oil because it reacts rapidly with cold water.

$$Ba(s) + 2H_2O(l) \rightarrow Ba(OH)_2(aq) + H_2(g)$$
$$\text{barium + water} \rightarrow \text{barium hydroxide + hydrogen}$$

Table 5.6 shows the arrangement of electrons in the halogen family (group VII of the Periodic Table).

Table 5.6 Electron arrangement in group VII

Element	Atomic number	Arrangement of electrons
F	9	2,7
Cl	17	2,8,7
Br	35	2,8,18,7
I	53	2,8,18,18,7

Note that each member of the group has seven electrons in the outer energy level. This is just one electron short of the full energy level.

When halogen elements react, they gain an electron to complete that outer energy level. This will form a negative ion.

$$Cl + e^- \rightarrow Cl^-$$

As an electron is being gained in the reaction, the most reactive member of the family will be the one where the extra electron is closest to the nucleus, i.e. fluorine. The reactivity decreases down the group.

5.9 Trends within a period

We have already seen that metallic elements form positive ions and that nonmetals form negative ions. The metallic elements will then be those with only a few electrons in their outer energy level. The most metallic elements will be on the extreme left-hand side of the table, i.e. group I.

The nonmetallic elements will be on the right-hand side of the table. The heavy line in Fig. 5.2 divides metals from nonmetals. In any period of the Periodic Table, there is a gradual change from metallic to nonmetallic from left to right.

E.g. third period:

    Na   Mg   Al   Si   P   S   Cl   Ar

Also, from left to right in any period the atoms gradually decrease in size. This surprises many people because, going from left to right, each element has one more electron than the previous element. However, this electron goes into the same energy level and the extra positive charge on the nucleus, caused by the extra proton, increases the attraction on the electrons and makes the atom slightly smaller.

5.10 Heavy or transition metals

See Chapter 33.

Summary

The chemical elements can be divided into groups in various ways. In a simple way they could be divided into:

            metals and nonmetals

or   solids, liquids and gases.

A better way of dividing the elements is into chemical families with elements having similar but not identical properties.

Lithium, sodium and potassium are members of the alkali metal family. Chlorine, bromine and iodine are members of the halogen family. Helium, neon, argon, krypton and xenon are the unreactive gases called noble gases.

The Periodic Table is an arrangement of elements in order of increasing atomic number with elements with similar properties, i.e. in the same family, in the same vertical column. The vertical columns are called groups and the horizontal rows are called periods.

The position of an element in the Periodic Table can tell you a great deal about its properties. Elements on the left-hand side of the table are metals and those on the right-hand side are nonmetals. There is a relationship between the position in the Periodic Table and the arrangement of electrons in an atom of the element.

Much of the chemistry you learn can be understood from the Periodic Table.

Chapter 6
States of matter

6.1 Introduction

There are three states of matter – **solid**, **liquid** and **gas**. Any substance can exist in each of these three states depending on the conditions of temperature and pressure. Figure 6.1 shows the relationship between these states of matter.

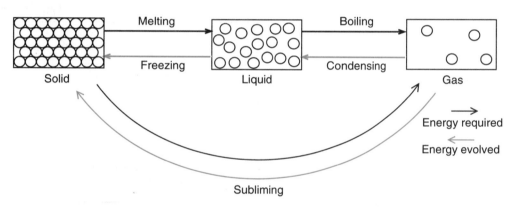

Fig. 6.1 States of matter and their interconversion

When a solid is heated it **melts** and forms a liquid. The temperature at which both solid and liquid can exist is called the **melting point** (or freezing point). When a liquid is heated to its **boiling point**, it **boils** and forms a gas (or vapour).

A simple two-dimensional representation of the particles in a solid, liquid and gas is shown in Fig. 6.1.

In the solid state the particles are usually **regularly** arranged and **rigidly** held in position. The particles can only vibrate. The particles vibrate more as the temperature is increased.

In the liquid state the particles are able to move much more than in the solid. Liquids are usually less dense than their corresponding solids because the particles are more widely spaced. Ice is, however, exceptional because it is less dense than water at 0°C and therefore floats on water. When a solute is dissolved in a liquid, the solute particles fill the spaces between the particles of the liquid. In a liquid there are still forces holding the particles together.

In the ideal gas state the particles are completely independent and are moving randomly in all directions. As temperature increases the particles move faster and therefore collide more often. Gases are very compressible because of the large spaces between particles and this also causes the density to be low.

The properties of solids, liquids and gases are summarized in Table 6.1.

Table 6.1 Comparison of solids, liquids and gases

Property	Solid	Liquid	Gas
Volume	Definite	Definite	Variable – expands or contracts to fill container
Shape	Definite	Takes up shape of bottom of container	Takes up the shape of the whole container
Density	High	Medium	Low
Expansion when heated	Low	Medium	High
Effect of applied pressure	Very slight	Slight decrease in volume	Large decrease in volume
Movement of particles	Very slow	Medium	Fast

Water can exist in these three states – ice (solid), water (liquid) and steam (gas). Figure 6.2 shows the graph obtained when a sample of ice is heated with a steady source of energy. When a change of state is taking place, e.g. solid → liquid or liquid → gas, the temperature remains constant despite a continuing supply of energy. This energy, which is not being used to raise the temperature, is called **latent heat**. Latent heat is used to supply the particles with the extra energy they require as the state changes. It is evolved when the reverse changes take place, e.g. when steam condenses to form water.

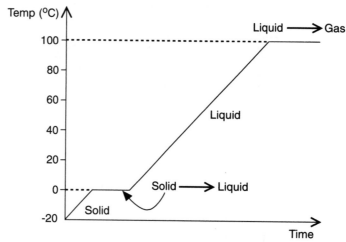

Fig. 6.2 Heating water

6.2 Sublimation

Certain substances (e.g. ammonium chloride and solid carbon dioxide) do not melt when they are heated but change directly from a solid to a gas. As the gas cools it returns directly to the solid state. The reformed solid is chemically the same as the substance heated and is called the **sublimate**. This process is called **sublimation**, and it is a useful method for separating a mixture of two substances where only one of the substances sublimes, e.g. ammonium chloride and sodium chloride. Iodine is frequently quoted as an example of a substance that sublimes. However, when iodine crystals are heated they are usually seen to melt.

6.3 Kinetic theory

The fact that all particles in a solid, liquid or gas are in a state of constant motion is called the kinetic theory. It explains two fundamental concepts – **diffusion** and **Brownian motion**.

6.4 Diffusion

If a drop of liquid bromine is dropped into a gas jar containing air and the gas jar is covered, the liquid bromine vaporizes and, after a while, the bromine vapour has spread evenly throughout the gas jar. The bromine particles and the constituent particles of the air have mixed thoroughly together. This movement of particles to spread out to fill the whole container is called **diffusion**.

Diffusion also takes place in liquids and solids but it is much slower because the particles are moving more slowly in liquids and solids. If a crystal of purple potassium permanganate is dropped into water, the colour spreads throughout the water after about a week.

If a piece of cotton wool soaked in concentrated hydrochloric acid (giving off hydrogen chloride fumes) and a piece of cotton wool soaked in concentrated ammonia solution (giving off ammonia fumes) are put in the opposite ends of a dry 100 cm long glass tube, a ring forms after about five minutes as shown in Fig. 6.3.

$$NH_3(g) + HCl(g) \rightleftharpoons NH_4Cl(s)$$
ammonia + hydrogen chloride $\rightleftharpoons$ ammonium chloride

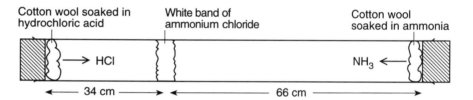

Fig. 6.3 Diffusion of ammonia and hydrogen chloride

The ring does not form immediately because:

1 the particles are not moving in just one direction.

2 the tube is filled with air.

The ammonia particles are moving about twice as fast as the hydrogen chloride particles and so the ring of ammonium chloride formed when the gases meet is nearer the piece of cotton wool soaked in concentrated hydrochloric acid.

Generally, smaller (or lighter) particles move faster than larger (or heavier) particles.

6.5 Brownian motion

In 1827, **Robert Brown** observed that fine pollen grains on the surface of water were not stationary but were in a state of constant random motion. The movement of these pollen grains is caused by collisions between water particles (these are too small to be seen) and pollen grains. Three facts are worth noting:

1 The water particles must be moving rapidly in order to move the larger pollen grains.

2 The direction of movement of a pollen grain is determined by the frequency and direction of these collisions.

3 There is no pattern in the movement of pollen grains or water particles.

Summary

All substances are made up of tiny particles which are constantly moving.

All substances can exist in three states of matter depending upon temperature and pressure. These states of matter are solid, liquid and gas. In the solid state the particles are close together and can only vibrate. When energy is given to melt the solid and turn it to a liquid, the particles move more. Further energy will make the liquid boil and form a gas. In the gas the particles are much more widely spaced and are moving much faster.

Diffusion is evidence for the movement of particles: a few drops of perfume can soon be smelt throughout a room.

Chapter 7
Elements, mixtures and compounds

7.1 Elements

3.7e understand the difference between elements, compounds and mixtures in terms of atoms, ions and molecules.

An **element** is a pure substance which cannot be split up by chemical reaction.

There are 105 chemical elements; most of these occur naturally but a few are man-made. Most of the elements are *solid* and *metallic*. However, bromine and mercury are *liquids* at room temperature and pressure, while hydrogen, helium, nitrogen, oxygen, fluorine, neon, chlorine, argon, krypton, xenon and radon are *gases* at room temperature and pressure.

Elements that have been mixed together can still be separated. For example, a mixture of iron and sulphur can be separated with a magnet.

7.2 Symbols

Each element is represented by a symbol. This is either one or two letters and is a shorthand that all chemists understand:

e.g.		
hydrogen	H	the first letter of the name
carbon	C	
calcium	Ca	the first two letters of the name
helium	He	
chlorine	Cl	the first letter and one other letter in the name
magnesium	Mg	
iron	Fe	two letters coming from the Latin name
sodium	Na	

(N.B. The first letter is a capital letter and the second letter is a small letter.) A full list of the elements and their symbols will be found in Fig. 5.2 on page 43.

7.3 Compounds

Certain mixtures of elements react together or combine (usually when heated) to form **compounds**. The formation of a compound from its constituent elements is called **synthesis**, and energy is usually liberated or released during this process. The compounds thus formed have very different properties from the elements of which they are composed. Splitting up a compound into its constituent elements is not an easy process. The proportions of the different elements in a compound are fixed.

7.4 Comparison of mixtures and compounds

Mixture	Compound
Proportions of the different elements can be varied	Different elements have to be present in fixed proportions
Elements can be separated by simple methods, e.g. iron using a magnet	Difficult to separate into the elements which make it up
Properties of the mixture are those of the elements making it up.	Properties of the compound are different from the properties of the elements.
No energy gained or lost when the mixture is made.	Energy is usually given out or taken in when the compound is formed.

7.5 Examples of compound formation

1. When a mixture of powdered iron and sulphur is heated, a reaction takes place, with the evolution of energy, forming iron(II) sulphide.

$$Fe(s) + S(s) \rightarrow FeS(s)$$
iron + sulphur $\rightarrow$ iron(II) sulphide

2. When a mixture of the gaseous elements hydrogen and oxygen is exploded, a reaction takes place forming water (a liquid). The properties of water are different from the properties of hydrogen and oxygen.

$$2H_2(g) + O_2(g) \rightarrow 2H_2O(l)$$
hydrogen + oxygen $\rightarrow$ water

7.6 Naming compounds

1. Compounds ending in –**ide** contain two elements.

E.g. copper(II) oxide is a compound of copper and oxygen;
calcium chloride is a compound of calcium and chlorine.

(Exceptions are compounds such as sodium hydroxide, which contains the elements sodium, hydrogen and oxygen.)

2 Compounds ending in **-ate** or **-ite** contain oxygen. There is a greater proportion of oxygen in the compound ending in –ate.

E.g.   sodium sulphate Na_2SO_4
           sodium sulphite Na_2SO_3

3 Compounds with a prefix **per-** contain extra oxygen.

E.g.   sodium oxide Na_2O
           sodium peroxide Na_2O_2

4 Compounds with a prefix **thio-** contain a sulphur atom in place of an oxygen atom.

E.g.   sodium sulphate Na_2SO_4
           sodium thiosulphate $Na_2S_2O_3$

7.7 Formulae

Each compound is represented by a formula which gives the proportions of the different elements in the compound by mass. The formula of any compound could be found by carrying out a suitable experiment. The formulae of many compounds can be found by use of the list of ions in Table 7.1.

If you are going to study Chemistry beyond GCSE you will need to write formulae correctly and confidently.

Table 7.1 List of common ions

Positive ions		Negative ions	
Sodium	Na^+	Chloride	Cl^-
Potassium	K^+	Bromide	Br^-
Silver	Ag^+	Iodide	I^-
Copper(II)	Cu^{2+}	Hydroxide	OH^-
Lead	Pb^{2+}	Nitrate	NO_3^-
Magnesium	Mg^{2+}	Nitrite	NO_2^-
Calcium	Ca^{2+}	Hydrogencarbonate	HCO_3^-
Zinc	Zn^{2+}	Sulphate	SO_4^{2-}
Barium	Ba^{2+}	Sulphite	SO_3^{2-}
Iron(II)	Fe^{2+}	Carbonate	CO_3^{2-}
Iron(III)	Fe^{3+}	Oxide	O^{2-}
Aluminium	Al^{3+}	Sulphide	S^{2-}
Ammonium	NH_4^+	Phosphate	PO_4^{3-}
Hydrogen	H^+		

In forming the compound the number of ions used is such that the number of positive charges equals the number of negative charges.

Sodium chloride is made up from Na^+ and Cl^- ions. Since a sodium ion has a single positive charge and a chloride ion has a single negative charge, the formula of sodium chloride is $NaCl$.

Sodium sulphate is made up from Na^+ and SO_4^{2-} ions. Twice as many sodium ions as sulphate ions are necessary in order to have equal numbers of positive and negative charges. The formula of sodium sulphate is Na_2SO_4. Table 7.2 contains further examples.

Table 7.2 Further examples of formulae

Compound	Ions present	Formula
Copper(II) oxide	$Cu^{2+}O^{2-}$	CuO
Ammonium chloride	$NH_4^+Cl^-$	NH_4Cl
Silver nitrate	$Ag^+NO_3^-$	$AgNO_3$
Magnesium chloride	$Mg^{2+}Cl^-$	$MgCl_2$
Magnesium hydroxide	$Mg^{2+}OH^-$	$Mg(OH)_2$
Aluminium nitrate	$Al^{3+}NO_3^-$	$Al(NO_3)_3$
Aluminium oxide	$Al^{3+}O^{2-}$	Al_2O_3
Hydrochloric acid	H^+Cl^-	HCl
Sulphuric acid	$H^+SO_4^{2-}$	H_2SO_4
Nitric acid	$H^+NO_3^-$	HNO_3

N.B.

1. Acids contain H^+ ions.

2. A small number after a bracket multiplies everything inside the bracket. E.g. $Mg(OH)_2$ is composed of one magnesium, two oxygen and two hydrogen atoms. These are formed into three ions – one Mg^{2+} ion and two OH^- ions.

All of the compounds above are composed of ions. However, many compounds are not ionized. The formulae of some of these compounds are shown in Table 7.3.

Table 7.3 Formulae of some common compounds

Compound	Formula	Compound	Formula
Water	H_2O	Sulphur dioxide	SO_2
Carbon dioxide	CO_2	Sulphur trioxide	SO_3
Carbon monoxide	CO	Ammonia	NH_3
Nitrogen monoxide	NO	Hydrogen chloride	HCl
Nitrogen dioxide	NO_2	Methane	CH_4

Summary

An element is a pure substance which cannot be split up by chemical reaction. Elements can be represented by symbols composed of one or two letters.

Most elements are solid at room temperature and most are metallic.

Elements can be combined together in fixed proportions to form compounds. The properties of a compound are different from the properties of the elements which make it up. Each compound can be represented in shorthand by writing a formula. It is most important to be able to write formulae correctly.

Chapter 8
Bonding

8.1 Introduction

3.7e understand the difference between elements, compounds and mixtures in terms of atoms, ions and molecules.

The joining of atoms together is called **bonding**. There are several types of bonding found in common chemicals. An arrangement of particles bonded together is called a **structure**.

Three methods of bonding will be discussed below.

8.2 Ionic (or electrovalent) bonding

This involves a **complete transfer of electrons** from one atom to another. Two examples are given below:

1 Sodium chloride

A sodium atom has an electronic structure of 2,8,1 (i.e. one more electron than the stable inert gas electronic arrangement of 2,8). A chlorine atom has an electronic arrangement of 2,8,7 (i.e. one electron less than the stable electronic arrangement 2,8,8).

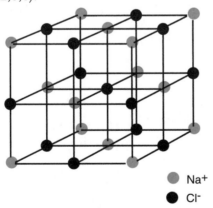

Na⁺

Cl⁻

Fig. 8.1 Structure of sodium chloride

If each sodium atom loses one electron (and forms a sodium ion Na^+) and each chlorine atom gains one electron (and forms a chloride ion Cl^-), both the ions formed have **stable electronic arrangements**. The ions are held together by strong electrostatic forces.

It is incorrect to speak of a 'sodium chloride *molecule*'. A sodium chloride *crystal* consists of a regular arrangement of equal numbers of sodium and chloride ions. This is called a **lattice** (Fig. 8.1).

2 Magnesium oxide

Electronic arrangement in magnesium atom	2,8,2
Electronic arrangement in oxygen atom	2,6

Two electrons are lost by each magnesium atom to form Mg^{2+} ions. Two electrons are gained by each oxygen atom to form O^{2-} ions.

Loss of one or two electrons by a metal during ionic bonding is common, e.g. NaCl or MgO. If three electrons are lost by a metal the resulting compound shows some covalent character, e.g. $AlCl_3$.

8.3 Covalent bonding

Covalent bonding involves the **sharing of electrons** rather than complete transfer. Two examples are given below:

❶ Chlorine molecule (Cl_2)

A chlorine atom has an electronic arrangement of 2,8,7. When two chlorine atoms bond together they form a chlorine molecule. If one electron was transferred from one chlorine atom to the other, only one atom could achieve a stable electronic arrangement.

Instead, one electron from each atom is donated to form a pair of electrons which is shared between both atoms, holding them together. This is called a **single covalent bond**. Figure 8.2 shows a simple representation of a chlorine molecule. This is often shown as Cl—Cl.

❷ Oxygen molecule (O_2)

An oxygen atom has an electronic arrangement of 2,6. In this case each oxygen atom donates two electrons and the four electrons (two pairs) are shared between both atoms. This is called a **double covalent bond**. Figure 8.3 shows a simplified representation of an oxygen molecule. This is usually shown as O=O.

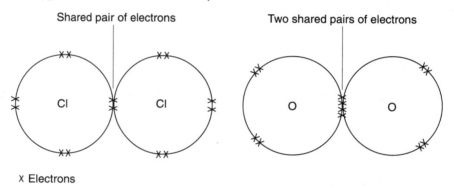

Fig. 8.2 Chlorine molecule   **Fig. 8.3** Oxygen molecule

Other common examples of covalent bonding and the different molecular shapes are shown in Fig. 8.4.

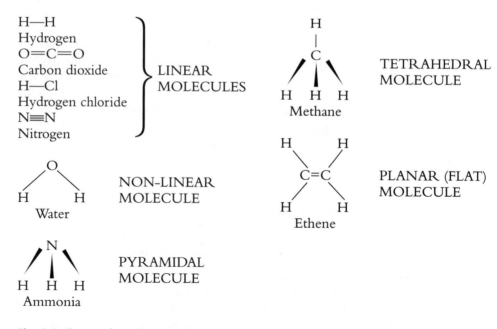

Fig. 8.4 Shapes of simple molecules

8.4 Metallic bonding

Metallic bonding is found only in metals. A metal consists of a close-packed regular arrangement of positive ions, which are surrounded by a 'sea' of electrons that bind the ions together. Figure 8.5 shows the arrangement of ions in a single layer. There are two alternative ways of stacking these layers. The arrows in Fig. 8.5 indicate that the layer shown continues in all directions. Around any one ion in a layer there are six ions arranged hexagonally.

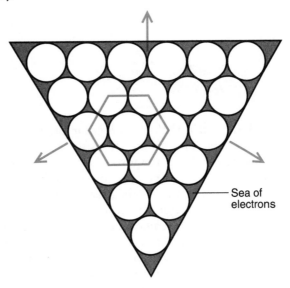

Sea of electrons

Fig. 8.5
Arrangement of ions in a metal layer

8.5 Effects of bonding on properties of substances

Compounds containing ionic bonds have certain properties in common – they have high melting and boiling points, and as a result are solids at room temperature. The ions are tightly held together in a regular lattice and energy (called **lattice energy**) is required to break up the lattice and melt the substance. The melting point of magnesium oxide is very high, making it suitable for use as a **refractory** (i.e. for lining furnaces).

Substances containing ionic bonding usually dissolve in water (a **polar solvent**) but not in a nonpolar solvent. If they do not dissolve in water it is often because they have very high lattice energy.

Electricity passes through substances containing ionic bonds when the substances are molten or in solution in water but not when solid. These substances are called **electrolytes**.

Substances containing covalent bonding may be solid, liquid or gas at room temperature. They are usually insoluble in polar solvents but more soluble in nonpolar solvents. Generally they do not conduct electricity in any state.

Metals generally have high densities because the ions are close packed in the lattice. Because of the strong bonds between the ions caused by the **free electrons**, the melting points of most metals are high. The free electrons explain why metals are good conductors of heat and electricity.

8.6 Structures of substances

The different types of structure found in pure materials are summarized in Fig. 8.6.

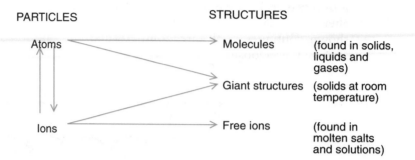

Fig. 8.6 Summary of structures

A substance with a **molecular structure** contains separate groups of atoms called **molecules**. The groups of atoms are tightly held together within the molecules by covalent bonds but the forces between the molecules are much weaker. If the molecules are small, the substance is usually a liquid or a gas. A few solids do contain small molecules, but these solids have low melting points, e.g. sulphur and iodine. If the molecules are large the substance will be a solid with a high melting point. Large molecules are sometimes called **macromolecules** (e.g. polythene) or **giant molecular structures** (e.g. silicon dioxide). Substances with a molecular structure do not conduct electricity in any state because there are no free ions or electrons. They are usually not very soluble in water but dissolve in nonpolar solvents. Examples include sulphur, iodine, chlorine and carbon dioxide.

A substance with an ionic structure contains many ions bonded together into a **giant structure** of ions. Thus these substances always have high melting points as a large amount of energy is needed to break up the structure. Ionic substances conduct electricity when molten or dissolved in water because the ions are free to move. An example is sodium chloride.

Metals consist of giant structures (high melting points) – except mercury, which is a liquid. Carbon is a nonmetal that has a giant atomic structure, and in the form of graphite it is also the only nonmetal that conducts electricity. Most other nonmetallic elements exist as small molecules, which is why many of them are gases under normal conditions. The noble gases exist as single atoms in a gaseous state.

8.7 Allotropy

Allotropy is the existence of two or more forms of an element in the same physical state. These different forms are called **allotropes**. Allotropy is caused by the possibility of more than one arrangement of atoms. For example carbon can exist in allotropes including diamond and graphite. Sulphur can exist in two allotropes – α-sulphur and β-sulphur.

8.8 Allotropy of carbon

The two most commonly mentioned allotropes of carbon are diamond and graphite. Another allotrope of carbon is fullerine which is a crystalline form of carbon made of clusters of carbon atoms.

1 Diamond

In the diamond structure each carbon atom is strongly bound (covalent bonding) to four other carbon atoms tetrahedrally. A large giant structure (three dimensional) is built up. All bonds between carbon atoms are the same length (0.154 nm). It is the strength and uniformity of the bonding which make diamond very hard, nonvolatile and resistant to chemical attack. Figure 8.7 shows the arrangement of particles in diamond.

2 Graphite

Graphite has a layer structure. In each layer the carbon atoms are bound covalently. The bonds within the layers are very strong. The bonds between the layers, however, are very weak, which enables layers to slide over one another. This makes the graphite soft and flaky. Figure 8.8 shows the arrangement of particles in graphite.

—— Strong bond
--- Weak bond

Fig. 8.7 Structure of diamond   **Fig. 8.8** Structure of graphite

Table 8.1 compares the properties of diamond and graphite.

Table 8.1 Comparing the properties of diamond and graphite

Property	Diamond	Graphite
Appearance	Transparent, colourless crystals	Black, opaque, shiny solid
Density (g/cm³)	3.5	2.2
Hardness	Very hard	Very soft
Electrical conductivity	Nonconductor	Good electrical conductor
Burning in oxygen	Burns only with difficulty when heated to high temperature. Carbon dioxide produced. No residue	Burns readily to produce carbon dioxide. No residue

Summary

There are different methods of joining or bonding atoms together.

Ionic bonding involves complete transfer of electrons from a metal to a nonmetal. Positive and negative ions are formed which are held together by strong electrostatic forces. Sodium chloride is an example of a substance with ionic bonding. Substances with ionic bonding have high melting and boiling points, are usually soluble in water (a polar solvent) and insoluble in organic (nonpolar) solvents such as hexane.

Covalent bonding involves a sharing of electrons. A single covalent bond involves one pair of shared electrons. Methane, CH_4, is a compound with covalent bonding.

Compounds with covalent bonding often have low melting and boiling points, are often insoluble in water and soluble in hexane.

Metallic bonding is found in metals. A metal consists of a regular arrangement of positive ions which are surrounded by a 'sea' of electrons that bind the ions together.

The existence of two or more forms of the same element in the same physical state is called allotropy. The different forms are called allotropes.

Allotropes of carbon include diamond and graphite. The difference in the physical properties of diamond and graphite can be explained by the different arrangements of carbon atoms in the two allotropes.

Chapter 9
Radioactivity

9.1 Introduction

The nuclei of some heavier atoms are unstable and tend to split up with the emission of certain types of radiation and the formation of new elements. This decay is called **radioactive decay**.

It is also possible for lighter atoms containing a large proportion of neutrons to undergo radioactive decay, e.g. ^3_1H (tritium) is a radioactive isotope of hydrogen.

9.2 Types of radiation emitted

The radiation emitted can be of three types:

- **α-particles.** These are positively charged particles identical to the nucleus of a helium atom, i.e. two protons and two neutrons but no electrons. They are comparatively heavy and slow moving and have little penetrating power. For example, they are unable to penetrate a piece of paper. They are deflected by magnetic and electrostatic fields. Because of their low penetrating power they cannot be detected by the usual apparatus used in the laboratory.

- **β-rays.** These are negatively charged particles. They are in fact electrons. They have greater penetrating power than α-particles and are deflected by magnetic and electric fields. They are detected by the apparatus used in the laboratory.

- **γ-rays.** These are high energy electromagnetic waves with zero charge. They are very penetrating and are unaffected by electric and magnetic fields. Although they penetrate the apparatus, they are not recorded on laboratory apparatus.

9.3 Apparatus used for radioactivity measurements

In experiments in the laboratory, radioactivity measurements are made using a **Geiger counter** attached to a suitable counting tube. The sample is placed in the counting tube and the measurements are made on the Geiger counter.

Because radioactive decay is taking place in the atmosphere and surroundings, it is necessary to correct for **background radiation**. In an experiment, if the reading on the Geiger counter is 512 counts per second (c.p.s.) when the sample is in place but 10 c.p.s. in the absence of any radioactive sample, the corrected reading would be 502 c.p.s. (i.e. 512 − 10).

9.4 Half-life $t_{1/2}$

3.9b understand the nature of radioactive decay, relating half-life to the use of radioactive materials.

The rate of decay of a radioactive isotope is independent of temperature. The time taken for half the mass of a radioactive isotope to decay is called the **half-life** and is a characteristic of the isotope. It is the time taken for the corrected reading on the Geiger counter to fall to half of its original value.

$$\text{Half-life of } ^{214}_{84}\text{Po} = 1.5 \times 10^{-4} \text{ s}$$
$$\text{Half-life of } ^{226}_{88}\text{Ra} = 1620 \text{ years}$$

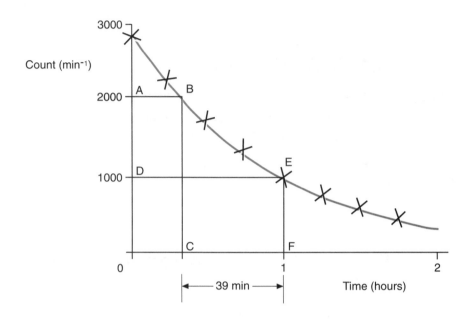

Fig. 9.1
Radioactive decay and half-life

A graph can be plotted as in Fig. 9.1 if regular readings are taken at intervals and then corrected. If a convenient reading is taken (say 2000) and the lines AB and BC drawn, then the lines DE and EF are drawn at a reading which is half of the original reading. The time difference between BC and EF is called the half-life.

9.5 Changes that accompany radioactive decay

Radioactive decay can change the number of protons and neutrons in the nucleus of an atom.

When an isotope loses an α-particle, it loses two protons and two neutrons. For example, α-decay of uranium-238:

$$^{238}_{92}\text{U} \rightarrow {}^{4}_{2}\text{He} + {}^{234}_{90}\text{Th}$$
$$\text{uranium-238} \rightarrow \alpha\text{-particle} + \text{thorium-234}$$

(N.B. In $^{238}_{92}\text{U}$, 238 is the mass number and 92 is the atomic number)

The product of α-decay contains two fewer protons and, therefore, is two places to the left of uranium in the Periodic Table.

When an isotope undergoes β-decay, a neutron in the nucleus changes to a proton and an electron, which is emitted. The product, therefore, has one more proton than the starting isotope, and is therefore one place to the right in the Periodic Table. Thorium-234 undergoes β-decay:

$$^{234}_{90}\text{Th} \rightarrow {}^{234}_{91}\text{Pa} + \text{electron}$$
$$\text{thorium-234} \rightarrow \text{protactinium-234} + \text{electron}$$

The emission of γ-rays does not change the number of protons or neutrons in the isotope. Gamma radiation usually accompanies other types of emission.

9.6 Uses of radioactivity

Radioactivity has a large number of uses in industry. These include:

1. Treating cancer by subjecting a patient to controlled amounts of γ-radiation from a cobalt-60 source.
2. Sterilizing instruments and equipment using γ-radiation.
3. Controlling the thickness of paper, rubber, metals and plastic accurately.
4. Controlling the filling of packets and containers.
5. Tracing the movement of a substance by following a radioactive isotope.
6. The energy produced by radioactive fission of uranium-235 is used within a nuclear power station to provide electricity.
7. Irradiation of food with γ-radiation from cobalt-60 to kill bacteria and ensure that the food remains fit to eat for longer.

The uses of a radioactive isotope depend upon its half-life. If the half-life is too short or too long it can have little practical application.

9.7 Disposal of radioactive waste

Radioactive waste, because of its very dangerous nature and its very long life, is extremely difficult to dispose of.

Used rods from power stations contain a whole range of radioactive materials, including plutonium. At Sellafield, in Cumbria, much of this waste is treated.

Waste with only low levels of radioactivity can be pumped into the sea. Waste containing higher levels of radioactivity can be set in concrete and stored. Investigations are going on to find suitable sites for dumping radioactive waste inland.

Disposal of radioactive waste will always be a problem.

Summary

Radioactive materials can emit α-, β- or γ-radiation. The rate of this emission or decay does not depend upon temperature. The time taken for half of a radioactive sample to decay is called its half-life. Half-lives can vary between a fraction of a second and millions of years.

Emission of α- and β-particles changes the number of protons or neutrons in an atom, and therefore changes the isotope.

Radioactive isotopes have a wide range of uses. Apart from the production of atomic bombs and generation of electricity in a nuclear power station, there are many other industrial, medical and scientific uses.

Chapter 10
Gas laws

10.1 Introduction

Solids and liquids do not change their volume appreciably with changes in external pressure. Also their expansion on heating, although significant in bridge construction or in the mercury thermometer, is relatively small. In contrast, a gas alters its volume considerably with changes in temperature and/or pressure. In this chapter we are going to look quantitatively at the changes in volume of a fixed mass of gas when pressure and temperature change.

10.2 The effect of pressure on the volume of a gas

The effect of pressure on the volume of a fixed mass of gas is expressed by **Boyle's law**. This law was attributed to Robert Boyle (1627–91), who is often regarded as the father of chemistry.

Boyle's law states that **the volume (V) of a fixed mass of gas is inversely proportional to the pressure (p) providing the temperature remains constant**. Expressed mathematically, that is

$$pV \text{ is a constant.}$$

Table 10.1 shows the pressure and volume of a fixed mass of gas.

Table 10.1

Pressure (kPa)	Volume (cm³)
100	100
50	200
200	50
10	1000

Looking at these figures you will notice that as the pressure increases so the volume decreases. Similarly, as the volume decreases the pressure increases. This is what is meant by **inversely proportional** – as one variable goes up the other goes down to compensate. In every case the number obtained when multiplying the pressure and the volume is the same (10 000). You should be able to work out the volume of the gas if the pressure was 250 kPa. Your answer should be 40 cm³ because 250 × 40 = 10 000.

Another way of expressing this relationship which is useful for calculating changes in volume when pressure changes is:

$$p_1 V_1 = p_2 V_2$$

where p_1 is the original pressure
V_1 is the original volume
p_2 is the final pressure
V_2 is the final volume

Sample calculation

100 cm³ of air is trapped in a gas syringe at a pressure of 100 kPa. Calculate the volume of the same mass of gas at a pressure of 133.3 kPa assuming the temperature remains constant.

Using $p_1 V_1 = p_2 V_2$
where $p_1 = 100$ kPa, $V_1 = 100$ cm³ and $p_2 = 133.3$ kPa
Substitute $V_2 = \dfrac{100 \times 100}{133.3}$
$= 75$ cm³

When you have carried out a calculation like this, spend a few seconds making a check to see if your answer is reasonable. Here you have increased the pressure, so you should expect therefore a smaller volume, because increasing pressure decreases the volume – they are inversely proportional.

10.3 The effect of temperature on the volume of a gas

When a fixed mass of gas is heated at constant pressure the gas expands. This relationship is summarized by **Charles' law**. Jacques Charles (1746–1823) was a French scientist whose interest in the properties of gases was probably increased by an interest in balloons and ballooning.

Charles' law states that **the volume (V) of a fixed mass of gas is directly proportional to its absolute temperature (T) (that is its temperature on the kelvin scale), providing pressure is constant**.

This is expressed mathematically by the relationship.

$$V/T \text{ is a constant}$$

In the same way as we saw a constant value when we multiplied p and V together in Table 10.1, we would get a constant value if we divided volume by absolute temperature for each set of results. Alternatively, if we plotted volume against absolute temperature we should get a straight-line graph. You will notice this time that as the absolute temperature increases, the volume increases by the same amount. This is called **directly proportional**.

Remember we must use absolute temperatures. To convert a temperature from degrees Celsius to kelvin, you just add 273,

so 100 °C is the same as 373 K (note no °)

Again this relationship can be expressed mathematically, at constant pressure, as

$$V_1 T_2 = V_2 T_1 \text{ where }$$

V_1 is the initial volume
T_1 is the initial absolute temperature
V_2 is the final volume
T_2 is the final absolute temperature

Sample calculation

100 cm³ of a gas at 27 °C is heated to 127 °C at a pressure of 100 kPa. Calculate the volume at 127 °C.

The temperature change is from 300 K to 400 K

Substituting in the equation

$$100 \times 400 = V_2 \times 300$$
$$= 133 \text{ cm}^3$$

Again, check your answer. Is it reasonable? Increasing the temperature should increase the volume.

10.4 General gas equation

You must learn the general gas equation. It cannot be given to you on the paper.

Boyle's law and Charles' law can be combined together in the **general gas equation**. This is

$$\frac{p_1 V_1}{T_1} = \frac{p_2 V_2}{T_2}$$

Sample calculation

A fixed mass of gas has a volume of 100 cm^3 at a pressure of 100 kPa and temperature of 27 °C (300 K). The gas is heated to 227 °C (500 K) at 200 kPa. Calculate the volume. Substituting in the general gas equation.

$$V_2 = \frac{100 \times 100 \times 500}{300 \times 200}$$
$$= 83.3 \text{ cm}^3$$

Look at your answer. Increasing the temperature increases the volume. Increasing the pressure decreases the volume. These two effects do not exactly cancel each other out but the answer is not much different from the original value. If the answer had been 833 cm^3 you would look for your mistake.

It is important to keep your units consistent throughout. Inconsistency in units is the major source of mistakes. For example, pressure could be used in kPa or atmospheres, but you must use the same throughout.

Summary

The volume of a gas changes significantly with changes in external pressure and temperature. The mathematical relationships are summarized by Boyle's law and Charles' law. These two laws are combined in the general gas equation.

$$\frac{p_1 V_1}{T_1} = \frac{p_2 V_2}{T_2}$$

Chapter 11
Oxidation and reduction

11.1 Oxidation

Oxidation can be defined in various ways. Two simple definitions are where:

① Oxygen is added to a substance.

② Hydrogen is lost by a substance.

3.6f understand oxidation processes, including combustion, as reactions with oxygen to form oxides.

   E.g. 1. If magnesium is burnt in oxygen, the magnesium is oxidized.

$$2Mg(s) + O_2(g) \rightarrow 2MgO(s)$$
$$\text{magnesium} + \text{oxygen} \rightarrow \text{magnesium oxide}$$

When any substance is burnt it is oxidized.

   E.g. 2. If concentrated hydrochloric acid is oxidized, chlorine gas is produced.

$$MnO_2 + 4HCl(aq) \rightarrow MnCl_2(aq) + 2H_2O(l) + Cl_2(g)$$
$$\text{manganese(IV) oxide} + \text{hydrochloric acid} \rightarrow \text{manganese(II) chloride} + \text{water} + \text{chlorine}$$

The concentrated hydrochloric acid loses hydrogen when being changed to chlorine and is therefore oxidized.

11.2 Reduction

Reduction is the reverse of oxidation. Reduction can be simply defined as reactions where:

① Oxygen is lost by a substance.

② Hydrogen is gained by a substance.

   E.g. 1. If hydrogen is passed over heated copper(II) oxide, the copper(II) oxide is reduced to copper. The copper(II) oxide loses oxygen.

$$CuO(s) + H_2(g) \rightarrow Cu(s) + H_2O(g)$$
$$\text{copper(II) oxide} + \text{hydrogen} \rightarrow \text{copper} + \text{water}$$

   E.g. 2. If hydrogen and ethene are passed over a heated catalyst, the ethene is reduced to ethane. Ethene gains hydrogen.

$$C_2H_4(g) + H_2(g) \rightarrow C_2H_6(g)$$
$$\text{ethene} + \text{hydrogen} \rightarrow \text{ethane}$$

11.3 Redox reactions

Oxidation and reduction processes occur together. If one substance is oxidized, another is reduced. A process where oxidation and reduction are taking place may be called a **redox** (reduction–oxidation) reaction.

E.g. If a mixture of lead(II) oxide and carbon are heated together, the following reaction takes place:

$$PbO(s) + C(s) \rightarrow Pb(s) + CO(g)$$
lead(II) oxide + carbon → lead + carbon monoxide

In this reaction, lead(II) oxide is losing oxygen and forming lead. Lead(II) oxide is, therefore, being reduced. Carbon is gaining oxygen when it forms carbon monoxide: carbon is being oxidized when it forms carbon monoxide: carbon is being oxidized. Oxidation and reduction are both taking place. This is a redox reaction.

No reaction would take place if the lead(II) oxide was heated alone. Carbon is the substance which is necessary for the reduction to take place because it removes the oxygen. Carbon is called the **reducing agent**. A reducing agent is a substance which reduces some other substances but is itself oxidized.

Similarly, lead(II) oxide is the **oxidizing agent**. It supplies oxygen, which is used to oxidize the carbon. An oxidizing agent is a substance which oxidizes some other substance but is itself reduced.

Common reducing agents include hydrogen, carbon, carbon monoxide and metals.

Common oxidizing agents include oxygen, chlorine, concentrated sulphuric acid and concentrated nitric acid.

11.4 Further oxidation and reduction

3.8f be able to use symbolic equations to describe and explain a range of reactions including ionic interactions and those occurring in electrolytic cells.

The definitions of oxidation and reduction in Units 11.1 and 11.2 are not complete. It is often better to define oxidation and reduction in terms of electron loss and gain.

Oxidation is any process where electrons are lost and reduction is any process where electrons are gained.

Remember:

loss of electrons – oxidation (leo)

E.g. 1. If chlorine is bubbled into a solution of iron(II) chloride (containing Fe^{2+} ions), the iron(II) chloride is oxidized to iron(III) chloride (containing Fe^{3+} ions). The solution changes from pale green to yellow-brown.

$$2FeCl_2(aq) + Cl_2(g) \rightarrow 2FeCl_3(aq)$$
iron(II) chloride + chlorine → iron(III) chloride
or $\quad\quad 2Fe^{2+}(aq) + Cl_2(g) \rightarrow 2Fe^{3+}(aq) + 2Cl^-(aq)$

E.g. 2. During the electrolysis of lead(II) bromide (see Chapter 16), oxidation and reduction are taking place.

At the cathode, lead ions are reduced to lead:

$$Pb^{2+}(l) + 2e^- \rightarrow Pb(s)$$

At the anode bromide ions are oxidized to bromine:

$$2Br^-(l) \rightarrow Br_2(g) + 2e^-$$

11.5 Common oxidizing agents

These are substances that, by their presence, cause other substances to be oxidized.

Oxygen

During the reaction oxygen molecules (O_2) gain electrons and form oxide (O^{2-}) ions.

E.g. $$2Mg(s) + O_2(g) \rightarrow 2MgO(s)$$
magnesium + oxygen → magnesium oxide

Chlorine

During the reaction chlorine molecules (Cl_2) gain electrons and form chloride (Cl^-) ions.

E.g. $$Cl_2(g) + 2FeCl_2(aq) \rightarrow 2FeCl_3(aq)$$
chlorine + iron(II) chloride → iron(III) chloride

Potassium manganate(VII) (potassium permanganate) KMnO$_4$
(acidified with dilute sulphuric acid)

During the reaction the solution turns from purple to become colourless as the manganate(VII) ions (MnO_4^-) are reduced to manganese(II) ions.

E.g. with iron(II) sulphate solution

$$MnO_4^-(aq) + 8H^+(aq) + 5e^- \rightarrow Mn^{2+}(aq) + 4H_2O(l)$$
$$\underline{Fe^{2+}(aq) \rightarrow Fe^{3+}(aq) + e^-}$$
$$MnO_4^-(aq) + 8H^+(aq) + 5Fe^{2+}(aq) \rightarrow Mn^{2+}(aq) + 4H_2O(l) + 5Fe^{3+}(aq)$$

Potassium dichromate(VI) (potassium dichromate) K$_2$Cr$_2$O$_7$
(acidified with dilute sulphuric acid)

During the reaction the solution turns from orange to green as the $Cr_2O_7^{2-}$ ions are reduced to Cr^{3+}.

E.g. with iron(II) sulphate solution

$$Cr_2O_7^{2-}(aq) + 14H^+(aq) + 6e^- \rightarrow 2Cr^{3+}(aq) + 7H_2O(l)$$
$$\underline{Fe^{2+}(aq) \rightarrow Fe^{3+}(aq) + e^-}$$
$$Cr_2O_7^{2-}(aq) + 14H^+(aq) + 6Fe^{2+}(aq) \rightarrow 2Cr^{3+}(aq) + 7H_2O(l) + 6Fe^{3+}(aq)$$

Concentrated sulphuric acid H$_2$SO$_4$ (usually hot)

When concentrated sulphuric acid acts as an oxidizing agent, sulphur dioxide is always produced.

E.g. with copper

$$Cu(s) + 2H_2SO_4(l) \rightarrow CuSO_4(aq) + 2H_2O(l) + SO_2(g)$$
copper + sulphuric acid → copper(II) sulphate + water + sulphur dioxide

Concentrated nitric acid HNO$_3$ (usually hot)

When concentrated nitric acid acts as an oxidizing agent, nitrogen dioxide is produced.

E.g. with copper

$$Cu(s) + 4HNO_3(l) \rightarrow Cu(NO_3)_2(aq) + 2H_2O(l) + 2NO_2(g)$$
copper + nitric acid → copper(II) nitrate + water + nitrogen dioxide

11.6 Common reducing agents

These are substances that, by their presence, cause other substances to be reduced.

Hydrogen H$_2$

E.g. $$C_2H_4(g) + H_2(g) \rightarrow C_2H_6(g)$$
ethene + hydrogen → ethane

Hydrogen sulphide H_2S

When hydrogen sulphide acts as a reducing agent, sulphur is always produced.

E.g. with chlorine

$$H_2S(g) + Cl_2(g) \rightarrow 2HCl(g) + S(s)$$
hydrogen sulphide + chlorine → hydrogen chloride + sulphur

Carbon C

E.g. with lead(II) oxide

$$PbO(s) + C(s) \rightarrow Pb(s) + CO(g)$$
lead(II) oxide + carbon → lead + carbon monoxide

Carbon monoxide CO

When carbon monoxide acts as a reducing agent, carbon dioxide is produced.

E.g. with iron(III) oxide (Unit 15.6).

$$Fe_2O_3(s) + 3CO(g) \rightarrow 2Fe(l) + 3CO_2(g)$$
iron(III) oxide + carbon monoxide → iron + carbon dioxide

Metals

E.g. iron acts as a reducing agent with copper(II) sulphate solution.

$$Cu^{2+}(aq) + Fe(s) \rightarrow Fe^{2+}(aq) + Cu(s)$$
copper(II) ions + iron → iron(II) ions + copper

11.7 Fuels

A **fuel** is a substance which can be used to produce energy. Most fuels produce energy on combustion or burning. They use up oxygen in the air and produce waste gases.

Fuels can be classified as solid fuels (coal, wood, coke), liquid fuels (petrol, paraffin) or gaseous fuels (natural gas, butane).

Fuels can also be classified as **fossil fuels** and **renewable fuels**. Fossil fuels such as coal, oil and natural gas were produced in the Earth over millions of years and they cannot be replaced when they are used up. Ethanol, hydrogen and wood are renewable fuels. New supplies can be made or grown to replace the supplies used up.

Most of these fuels contain carbon and hydrogen in compounds. They may also contain other elements such as oxygen, sulphur and nitrogen. Combustion of a fuel containing carbon and hydrogen is complex. In a plentiful supply of air or oxygen, carbon dioxide and water are produced. In a limited supply of air or oxygen, carbon monoxide can be produced. This is highly poisonous and causes many deaths. Air pollution (Chapter 35) is produced when waste products from the combustion of fuels escape into the atmosphere and build up.

Summary

A reaction where oxygen is added or hydrogen is removed is called an **oxidation reaction**. Combustion reactions are oxidations. The opposite, where oxygen is lost or hydrogen is added, is called a **reduction reaction**. Where both oxidation and reduction occur, a **redox reaction** is said to take place.

Oxidation can also be defined as a loss of electrons and reduction as a gain in electrons.

A fuel is a substance which can be used to produce energy. Usually a fuel burns using up oxygen to produce energy and waste products. Fuels can be classified as solid fuels, liquid fuels and gaseous fuels. Fossil fuels are fuels produced in the Earth and, unlike renewable fuels, they cannot be replaced.

Chapter 12
The reactivity series of metals

12.1 Introduction

3.6d be able to recognise variations in the properties of metals and make predictions based on the reactivity series.

In this chapter the comparative reactivity of different pure metals is considered. Table 12.1 summarizes the reactivity of common metals.

Table 12.1 Reactions of some metals

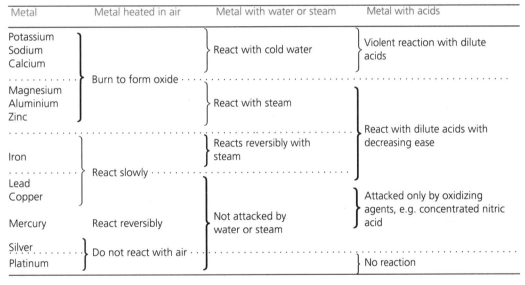

Metal	Metal heated in air	Metal with water or steam	Metal with acids
Potassium Sodium Calcium		React with cold water	Violent reaction with dilute acids
	Burn to form oxide		
Magnesium Aluminium Zinc		React with steam	React with dilute acids with decreasing ease
Iron		Reacts reversibly with steam	
	React slowly		
Lead Copper			Attacked only by oxidizing agents, e.g. concentrated nitric acid
Mercury	React reversibly	Not attacked by water or steam	
Silver Platinum	Do not react with air		No reaction

Following the detailed consideration of these reactions and other similar reactions, it is possible to arrange metals in a **reactivity** (or activity) **series**. This is a list of metals in order of reactivity with the most reactive metal at the top of the list and steadily decreasing reactivity down the list. The list is:

potassium	K
sodium	Na
calcium	Ca
magnesium	Mg
aluminium	Al
zinc	Zn
iron	Fe
lead	Pb
copper	Cu
mercury	Hg
silver	Ag
platinum	Pt

N.B. This is the same order as in Table 12.1. This list could be shorter or longer depending upon the number of metals you wish to consider. Do not try to learn this list. It will be given to you when you need it.

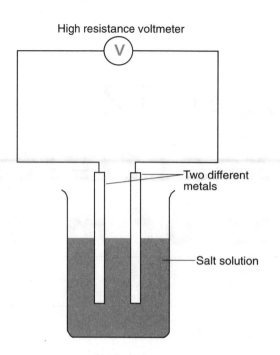

High resistance voltmeter

Two different metals

Salt solution

Fig. 12.1
Measuring voltages of simple cells

A similar list could be obtained by measuring voltages. If two rods of different metals are dipped into salt solution, a small voltage is produced which can be measured by means of a high resistance voltmeter (Fig. 12.1).

By comparing voltages of these cells it is possible to come up with the same list but, strictly speaking, this is called the **electrochemical series** and the elements are in order of decreasing standard electrode potentials. In this book, the term 'reactivity series' will be used.

12.2 Use of the reactivity series

The reactivity series is very useful to the chemist in making predictions. It can be used to:

1 Explain the stability of compounds when heated.
2 Predict possible reactions involving metals.
3 Explain the corrosion of certain metals (Chapter 14).
4 Explain the method used to extract a metal from its ore (Chapter 15).

12.3 Stability of compounds containing metals

Compounds of metals high in the reactivity series are not easily split up by heating. Compounds of metals low in the reactivity series are split up by heating.

Examples of this can be seen by comparing the action of heat on carbonates (Table 12.2). Sodium and potassium carbonates are not split up on heating. Table 12.3 compares the action of heat on metal nitrates. The lower the metal is in the reactivity series, the more readily and completely the nitrate of the metal splits up.

Table 12.2 Important properties of carbonates

Carbonate	Formula	Colour	Solubility in water	Action of heat
Potassium	K_2CO_3	White	Soluble	Not decomposed
Sodium	Na_2CO_3	White	Soluble	
Calcium	$CaCO_3$	White	Insoluble	
Magnesium	$MgCO_3$	White	Insoluble	
Zinc	$ZnCO_3$	White	Insoluble	Decomposed to the oxide of
Iron	$FeCO_3$	Light brown	Insoluble	the metal and carbon dioxide
Lead	$PbCO_3$	White	Insoluble	$PbCO_3(s) \rightarrow PbO(s) + CO_2(g)$
Copper	$CuCO_3$	Bluish-green	Insoluble	

Table 12.3 Action of heat on metal nitrates

Nitrate	Formula	Colour	Equation	Colour of the solid residue
Potassium nitrate	KNO_3	White	$2KNO_3(s) \rightarrow 2KNO_2(s) + O_2(g)$ potassium nitrate → potassium nitrite + oxygen	White
Sodium nitrate	$NaNO_3$	White	$2NaNO_3(s) \rightarrow 2NaNO_2(s) + O_2(g)$ sodium nitrate → sodium nitrite + oxygen	White
Calcium nitrate	$Ca(NO_3)_2$	White	$2Ca(NO_3)_2(s) \rightarrow 2CaO(s) + 4NO_2(g) + O_2(g)$ calcium nitrate → calcium oxide + nitrogen dioxide + oxygen	White
Magnesium nitrate	$Mg(NO_3)_2$	White	$2Mg(NO_3)_2(s) \rightarrow 2MgO(s) + 4NO_2(g) + O_2(g)$ magnesium nitrate → magnesium oxide + nitrogen dioxide + oxygen	White
Zinc nitrate	$Zn(NO_3)_2$	White	$2Zn(NO_3)_2(s) \rightarrow 2ZnO(s) + 4NO_2(g) + O_2(g)$ zinc nitrate → zinc oxide + nitrogen dioxide + oxygen	Yellow when hot, white when cold
Iron(III) nitrate	$Fe(NO_3)_3$	Brown	$4Fe(NO_3)_3(s) \rightarrow 2Fe_2O_3(s) + 12NO_2(g) + 3O_2(g)$ iron(III) nitrate → iron(III) oxide + nitrogen dioxide + oxygen	Reddish-brown
Lead nitrate	$Pb(NO_3)_2$	White	$2Pb(NO_3)_2(s) \rightarrow 2PbO(s) + 4NO_2(g) + O_2(g)$ lead nitrate → lead oxide + nitrogen dioxide + oxygen	Yellow
Copper(II) nitrate	$Cu(NO_3)_2$	Blue	$2Cu(NO_3)_2(s) \rightarrow 2CuO(s) + 4NO_2(g) + O_2(g)$ copper(II) nitrate → copper(II) oxide + nitrogen dioxide + oxygen	Black
Silver nitrate	$AgNO_3$	White	$2AgNO_3(s) \rightarrow 2Ag(s) + 2NO_2(g) + O_2(g)$ silver nitrate → silver + nitrogen dioxide + oxygen	Silvery

12.4 Predicting chemical reactions involving metals

A knowledge of the order of the metals in the reactivity series can be used to predict and explain chemical reactions involving metals.

The reactivity series can also be written:

> potassium
> sodium
> calcium
> magnesium
> aluminium
> (carbon)
> zinc
> iron
> lead
> (hydrogen)
> copper
> mercury
> silver
> platinum

You don't need to memorize the reactivity series. It will be given to you in the question or in a data book.

The inclusion of carbon and hydrogen in their correct places, although they are not metals, extends the usefulness of the reactivity series.

Metals above hydrogen will displace hydrogen from acids. The metals below will not displace hydrogen from dilute acids. For example, copper does not react with dilute hydrochloric acid.

Metals above carbon in the reactivity series are not produced by reduction of metal oxides with carbon. Metals below carbon can be produced by reduction of metal oxides with carbon.

If iron(III) oxide and aluminium powder are heated together, a reaction takes place because aluminium is more reactive than iron.

$$Fe_2O_3(s) + 2Al(s) \rightarrow 2Fe(s) + Al_2O_3(s)$$
iron(III) oxide + aluminium → iron + aluminium oxide

No reaction would take place if zinc oxide and copper were heated together because copper is less reactive than zinc.

If an iron nail is put into copper(II) sulphate solution, a reaction takes place. The blue solution turns almost colourless and brown copper is deposited.

$$Fe(s) + CuSO_4(aq) \rightarrow FeSO_4(aq) + Cu(s)$$
iron + copper(II) sulphate → iron(II) sulphate + copper

The reaction takes place because iron is more reactive than copper.

No reaction would take place if a piece of lead were put into a solution of magnesium sulphate.

Reactions of this type are called **displacement reactions** and it is important that the metal being added is more reactive than the metal already present in the compound if a reaction is to take place.

Summary

Metals can be arranged in order of decreasing reactivity (or activity) in a reactivity (or activity) series. For many purposes a short form of the reactivity series is useful:

sodium
calcium
magnesium
aluminium
zinc
iron
lead
copper

The reactivity series can be used to explain stability of compounds, i.e. how easily they are split up. It can also be used to understand and predict displacement reactions, where a reactive metal replaces a less reactive metal in a compound.

Chapter 13
Chemical equations

13.1 Introduction

Writing word equations is level 6.

Chemical equations are widely used in textbooks and examination papers. An equation is a useful summary of a chemical reaction, and it is always theoretically possible to obtain an equation from the results of an experiment. It is advisable, however, to be able to write important equations in an examination.

The steps in writing a chemical equation are as follows:

1 Write down the equation as a word equation using either the information given or your memory. Include all the reacting substances and products.

E.g. calcium hydroxide + hydrochloric acid $\rightarrow$ calcium chloride + water

Often the information you require is given to you in a jumbled form in the question; e.g. iron(II) chloride is produced when dry hydrogen chloride gas is passed over heated iron. The other product is hydrogen. The word equation for this reaction is:

iron + hydrogen chloride $\rightarrow$ iron(II) chloride + hydrogen

2 Fill in the correct formulae for all the reacting substances and products.

$$Ca(OH)_2 + HCl \rightarrow CaCl_2 + H_2O$$

3 The equation then needs to be balanced. During any chemical reaction, atoms cannot be created or destroyed. There must be the same number of atoms before and after the reaction. Only the proportions of the reacting substances and products can be altered to balance the equation – not the formulae.

$$Ca(OH)_2 + 2HCl \rightarrow CaCl_2 + 2H_2O$$

4 Finally, the states of reacting substances and products can be included in small brackets after the formulae. Thus:

(s) for solid – though sometimes (c) is seen for representing a crystalline solid
(l) for liquid
(g) for gas
(aq) for a solution with water as solvent

These state symbols are not given or expected by all examination boards.

$$Ca(OH)_2(aq) + 2HCl(aq) \rightarrow CaCl_2(aq) + 2H_2O(l)$$

Writing equations requires a great deal of practice. As you work through this book you will find many equations.

3.8f be able to use symbolic equations to describe and explain a range of reactions including ionic interactions and those occuring in electrolytic cells.

13.2 Information provided by an equation

$$2Mg(s) + O_2(g) \rightarrow 2MgO(s)$$
$$\text{magnesium} + \text{oxygen} \rightarrow \text{magnesium oxide}$$

This equation gives the following information:

2 moles of magnesium atoms (48 g) combine with 1 mole of oxygen molecules (32 g) to produce 2 moles of magnesium oxide (80 g). It also tells us that magnesium and magnesium oxide are solids and oxygen is a gas.

A chemical equation gives:

1. the chemicals reacting together (called reactants) and the chemicals produced (called products).
2. the physical states of reactants and products.
3. the quantities of chemicals reacting together and produced.

The equation does not, however, give information about energy changes in the reaction, the rate of the reaction and the conditions needed for the reaction to take place.

Calculating quantities of chemicals reacting together and produced in a reaction is considered in Chapter 25.

13.3 Ionic equations

Ionic equations are useful because they emphasize the important changes taking place in a chemical reaction. For example, the (unbalanced) equation for the neutralization reaction between sodium hydroxide and hydrochloric acid is:

$$NaOH(aq) + HCl(aq) \rightarrow NaCl(aq) + H_2O(l)$$
$$\text{sodium hydroxide} + \text{hydrochloric acid} \rightarrow \text{sodium chloride} + \text{water}$$

Since all of the reactants and products (except water) are composed of ions, this equation could be written:

$$Na^+(aq)OH^-(aq) + H^+(aq)Cl^-(aq) \rightarrow Na^+(aq)Cl^-(aq) + H_2O(l)$$

An equation should show change and therefore anything present before and after the reaction can be deleted. The simplest ionic equation, deleting $Na^+(aq)$ and $Cl^-(aq)$, is therefore:

$$OH^-(aq) + H^+(aq) \rightarrow H_2O(l)$$

The same ionic equation also applies to similar reactions, e.g. calcium hydroxide and nitric acid.

In addition to balancing in the usual way, the sum of the charges on the left-hand side must equal the sum of the charges on the right-hand side.

Other common ionic equations include:

$$2Fe^{2+}(aq) + Cl_2(g) \rightarrow 2Fe^{3+}(aq) + 2Cl^-(aq)$$
$$2Br^-(aq) + Cl_2(g) \rightarrow Br_2(aq) + 2Cl^-(aq)$$
$$Zn(s) + 2H^+(aq) \rightarrow Zn^{2+}(aq) + H_2(g)$$

Summary

A chemical equation is a useful way of summarizing a chemical reaction which takes place. A word equation is simpler to write but is not as useful as a symbol equation.

Word equation:

Copper(II) oxide + hydrochloric acid → copper(II) chloride + water

Symbol equation:

$$CuO(s) + 2HCl(aq) \rightarrow CuCl_2(aq) + H_2O(l)$$

A symbol equation, apart from summarizing the reaction, can provide information about the reaction.

Chapter 14
Rusting of iron and steel

14.1 Introduction

Iron and steel react in the atmosphere to produce reddish-brown rust. Rust flakes off the surface producing a fresh surface for rusting. A piece of iron or steel therefore completely rusts away. It has been estimated that rusting costs at least £2 000 000 000 in Great Britain each year.

The chemical composition of rust is complicated. It is probably best regarded as a hydrated iron(III) oxide, $Fe_2O_3 \cdot xH_2O$. The rusting process is perhaps better summarized by the ionic equation

$$Fe \rightarrow Fe^{3+} + 3e^-$$

Rusting is an oxidation process. Why does iron oxidize much faster than aluminium although aluminium is higher in the reactivity series and therefore more reactive? This can be explained by the thin coating of aluminium oxide which forms on the aluminium and prevents further oxidation. It does not flake off like rust.

14.2 Conditions necessary for rusting

Figure 14.1 shows an experiment frequently used to show the conditions necessary for rusting.

If three test tubes are set up as shown in Fig. 14.1 and left for a few days, rusting takes place only in test tube C. From this we can conclude that both air and water are necessary for rusting to take place. In fact, it is the oxygen in the air which, along with water, is vital. Rusting is speeded up by the presence of acid (carbon dioxide or sulphur dioxide are examples) or salt.

14.3 Ways of preventing rusting

Rusting can be prevented by excluding air and/or water. It can be prevented by the following methods:

● Iron can be painted by spraying, dipping or brushing. Providing the paint surface is not broken, rusting will not take place. The paint coating prevents oxygen and water from coming into contact with the iron. When the paint coating is broken rusting will take place. This type of protection is used to protect cars from rusting and for protecting large bridges (e.g. Forth Bridge) and iron railings.

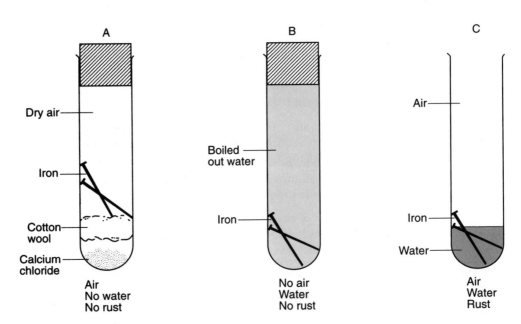

Fig. 14.1 Rusting of iron

2. Iron can be coated with a layer of plastic. This layer again prevents oxygen and water from coming into contact with the iron. This type of protection is used for draining racks in the kitchen. However, eventually the plastic coating starts to split and rapid rusting occurs.

3. Iron can be coated with oil or grease. Again oxygen and water cannot come into contact with the iron and rusting does not take place. This form of protection is very easy and very effective. A smearing of oil onto a saw blade will prevent its rusting. It is a very good method for treating moving parts.

4. Iron can be coated with a layer of zinc in a process called **galvanizing**. The zinc coating can be put on by dipping or spraying. If the zinc coating is deeply scratched to expose bare iron rusting will not take place.

   If a car body repair is being carried out, rust has first to be removed. The bare steel may then be treated with a zinc-based primer paint before spraying with the coloured paint.

   Zinc coating cannot be used for food cans because zinc compounds are poisonous.

5. Iron can be coated with a thin coating of tin to make tinplate. This can be used for making food cans. If the tin coating is scratched to show the bare steel, rusting of the steel will take place.

   Aluminium is being used more and more to replace tinplate in making food cans.

   Modern processes of refuse disposal are now removing tinplate from household refuse, then removing the tin from the cans. The tin obtained is purified by electrolysis and re-used for tin can manufacture.

6. Iron can be protected by **sacrificial protection**. This is used for protecting steel hulls of ships and steel piers. Rusting takes place even faster in the presence of carbon dioxide or salt water. To prevent a steel hull from rusting, blocks of a suitable metal are strapped to the steel hull. The metal used must be more reactive than iron. Zinc or magnesium would be suitable metals to use as they are higher than iron in the reactivity series.

   The zinc or magnesium blocks corrode in preference to iron. As long as they remain no rusting will take place. These blocks can be easily replaced when they have corroded away.

7. Steel can be protected by **electroplating**. Using electrolysis a thin coating of nickel is deposited on the steel to prevent rusting. Finally a very thin coating of chromium is electroplated on top of the nickel. The chromium gives a nice shiny surface. Chromium plating of bicycle handlebars, car bumpers and electric kettles is a very expensive process and is being replaced by aluminium alloys or stainless steel. Stainless steel is an alloy of iron which is less inclined to rust than iron or other types of steel.

14.4 Further explanation of rusting

Two factors seem to start the rusting process.

1. Impurities and mechanical strains cause imperfections in the iron. The rusting of a nail takes place around the head and the point, both places where the metal was strained during manufacture.

2. A large amount of dissolved oxygen in contact with the surface of the iron will encourage rusting to start.

Some areas of the iron become **anodic**, where there is a lower oxygen concentration and some areas become **cathodic**, where there is a high oxygen concentration.

In the anodic area, iron atoms are oxidized by losing electrons to the cathodic area.

$$Fe(s) \rightarrow Fe^{2+}(aq) + 2e^-$$

These ions are further oxidized by dissolved oxygen to form iron(III) ions.

$$Fe^{2+}(aq) \rightarrow Fe^{3+}(aq) + e^-$$

In the cathodic area, dissolved oxygen takes up the electrons from the anodic area. The oxygen is reduced in the presence of water to form hydroxide ions.

$$O_2(aq) + 2H_2O(l) + 4e^- \rightarrow 4OH^-(aq)$$

The iron(III) ions combine with the hydroxide ions to form iron(III) hydroxide, which then loses some of the water.

$$2Fe(OH)_3(s) \rightarrow Fe_2O_3 \cdot xH_2O(s) + (3-x)H_2O(l)$$

Summary

Rusting of iron and steel requires both oxygen and water to be present. Other substances such as salt, carbon dioxide and sulphur dioxide speed up the reaction.

There are many ways of reducing the rusting. Painting, greasing and coating with other metals, etc., provide mechanical methods of reducing rusting. Rusting can also be reduced by electrochemical processes. Making the metal negatively charged reduces the rusting.

Chapter 15
Extraction of metals

15.1 Introduction

Metals are widely used in everyday life. Very rarely are pure metals found free in the ground. Usually they are found in compounds with other materials in the form of ores. This chapter is concerned with methods of extracting metals from their ores. It is important to relate this section to the reactivity series (Chapter 12).

15.2 Recycling of metals

Since the Second World War there has been a threefold increase in the amount of copper used each year and a sixfold increase in the amount of aluminium. Obviously with this increasing use of metals, supplies of suitable metal ores will eventually run out. It has been estimated that all aluminium ores will be used up by the year 2100 and all supplies of copper ores will be used up by the year 2000!

One way of making these ores last is to reuse or recycle metals. Copper is being recovered from scrap copper wires and pipes. Aluminium is being recovered from soft drink cans and kitchen foil. Tin is being removed from scrap food cans to be reused in making new food cans. As metals become more expensive recycling becomes more likely.

15.3 Treatment of ores

Some of the least reactive metals, e.g. gold, can be found in the form of the unreacted metal in the earth. Other metals can be found as compounds with other unwanted material in the form of an **ore**. Table 15.1 shows the ores of some common metals and the chief chemical constituent of the ore. (The examples in bold type are the ones most frequently asked for by examiners.)

Before the metal is extracted from the ore, the ore is frequently concentrated or purified.

Bauxite (aluminium oxide) is purified by adding the ore to sodium hydroxide solution. The aluminium oxide reacts and forms soluble sodium aluminate. Impurities such as iron(III) oxide can be removed by filtration. The aluminium oxide is then precipitated in a pure form (in fact aluminium hydroxide is precipitated and this is heated to give the pure oxide).

Table 15.1 Common ores

Metal	Ore	Chief chemical constituent
Sodium	Rock salt	Sodium chloride
Calcium	Chalk, limestone, marble	Calcium carbonate
Magnesium	Magnesite (also in sea water)	Magnesium carbonate magnesium chloride
Aluminium	**Bauxite**	**Aluminium oxide**
Zinc	**Zinc blende**	**Zinc sulphide**
Iron	**Haematite**	**Iron(III) oxide**
Copper	Malchite	Basic copper(II) carbonate
Mercury	Cinnabar	Mercury(II) sulphide

Zinc blende and galena (lead sulphide) can be concentrated by froth flotation. The ore is added to a detergent bath that is agitated. By careful control of the conditions in the bath it is possible to cause the metallic sulphide to float and the impurities to sink.

The method used to extract the metal from the ore depends on the position of the metal in the reactivity series. If a metal is high in the reactivity series its ores are stable and the metal can be obtained only by electrolysis. Metals that can be obtained by electrolysis include potassium, sodium, calcium, magnesium and aluminium.

Metals in the middle of the reactivity series do not form very stable ores and they can be extracted by reduction, often with carbon. Examples of metals extracted by reduction are zinc, iron and lead.

Metals low in the reactivity series, if present in ores, can be extracted simply by heating because the ores are unstable. For example, mercury can be extracted by heating cinnabar.

Questions on extraction of metals often appear on examination papers and common examples are detailed below.

15.4 Extraction of sodium

Sodium is extracted by the electrolysis of molten sodium chloride in the Downs cell. Calcium chloride is added to the sodium chloride to lower the melting point to about 600 °C. A Downs cell is shown in Fig. 15.1.

The cathode (negative electrode) is made of iron and the cylindrical anode (positive electrode) is made of graphite (carbon).

During the electrolysis the following reactions take place at the electrodes:

cathode $\qquad$ $Na^+(l) + e^- \rightarrow Na(l)$

anode $\qquad$ $2Cl^-(l) \rightarrow Cl_2(g) + 2e^-$

The sodium and chlorine produced are kept apart to prevent them reacting and reforming sodium chloride. The chlorine produced is a valuable by-product.

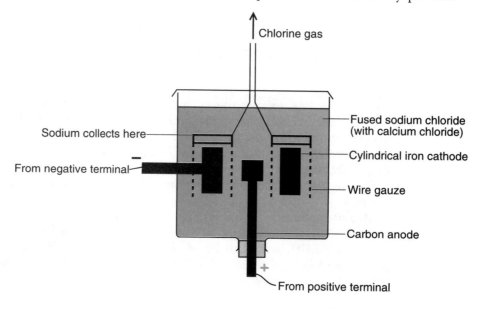

Fig. 15.1 Extraction of sodium

15.5 Extraction of aluminium

Extraction of
aluminium and
iron come up very
frequently in GCSE
papers.

Aluminium is extracted from purified aluminium oxide by electrolysis. However, aluminium oxide has a high melting point and is not readily soluble in water, but it does dissolve in molten cryolite (Na_3AlF_6) and this produces a suitable electrolyte. An appropriate cell (Hall's cell) is shown in Fig. 15.2.

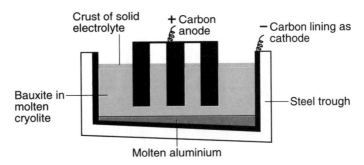

Fig. 15.2 Extraction of aluminium

The electrodes are made of carbon. The reactions taking place at the electrodes are as follows:

cathode	$Al^{3+} + 3e^- \rightarrow Al$	overall reaction
anode	$2O^{2-} \rightarrow O_2 + 4e^-$	$4Al^{3+} + 6O^{2-} \rightarrow 4Al + 3O_2$

At the working temperature of the cell, the oxygen reacts with the carbon of the anode to produce carbon dioxide. The anode has, therefore, to be replaced frequently. As this process requires a large amount of electricity, an inexpensive source, e.g. hydroelectric power, is an advantage.

15.6 Extraction of iron

Iron is extracted from iron ore, in large quantities, by reduction in a blast furnace (Fig. 15.3). The furnace is loaded with iron ore, coke and limestone and is heated by blowing hot air into the base from the tuyères. Inside the furnace the following reactions take place, raising the temperature to about 1500 °C:

1 The burning of the coke in the air:

$$C(s) + O_2(g) \rightarrow CO_2(g)$$
carbon + oxygen → carbon dioxide

2 The reduction of the carbon dioxide to carbon monoxide:

$$CO_2(g) + C(s) \rightarrow 2CO(g)$$
carbon dioxide + carbon → carbon monoxide

3 The reduction of the iron ore to iron by carbon monoxide:

$$Fe_2O_3(s) + 3CO(g) \rightarrow 2Fe(l) + 3CO_2(g)$$
iron(III) oxide + carbon monoxide → iron + carbon dioxide

4 The decomposition of the limestone produces extra carbon dioxide:

$$CaCO_3(s) \rightarrow CaO(s) + CO_2(g)$$
calcium carbonate → calcium oxide + carbon dioxide

5 The removal of impurities by the formation of slag:

$$CaO(s) + SiO_2(s) \rightarrow CaSiO_3(l)$$
calcium oxide + silicon dioxide → calcium silicate ('slag')

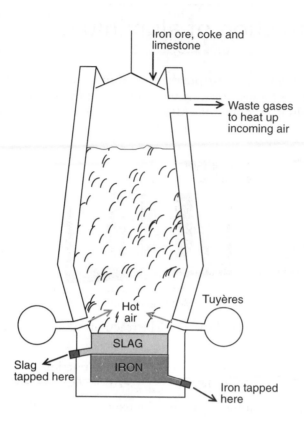

Iron ore, coke and limestone

Waste gases to heat up incoming air

Tuyères

Hot air

SLAG

IRON

Slag tapped here

Iron tapped here

Fig. 15.3
Extraction of iron in a blast furnace

The molten iron sinks to the bottom of the furnace and the slag floats on the surface of the molten iron. The iron and slag can be tapped off separately at intervals. The iron produced is called **pig iron** and contains about 4 per cent carbon. The slag, once discarded, is used as a phosphorus fertilizer and for road building.

Most of the pig iron produced is converted into the alloy, steel. The pig iron is melted and scrap steel is added (another example of recycling). Air or oxygen is bubbled through the molten iron. All impurities are oxidized and pure iron remains. The required amounts of carbon are added together with any other metals necessary.

15.7 Extraction of zinc

Following the concentration of the ore (see Unit 15.3), the ore is heated strongly in air to convert the zinc sulphide to zinc oxide.

$$2ZnS(s) + 3O_2(g) \rightarrow 2ZnO(s) + 2SO_2(g)$$
zinc sulphide + oxygen → zinc oxide + sulphur dioxide

(The sulphur dioxide can be used to manufacture sulphuric acid, see Chapter 24).

The zinc oxide and coke are mixed together in a cylindrical furnace and heated strongly. The carbon reduces zinc oxide to zinc.

$$ZnO(s) + C(s) \rightarrow Zn(g) + CO(g)$$
zinc oxide + carbon → zinc + carbon monoxide

At the temperature of the furnace, zinc distils off and is condensed. The carbon monoxide produced is used to heat the furnace.

15.8 Extraction of titanium

Titanium occurs as titanium(IV) oxide in the ore rutile. Titanium is above carbon in the reactivity series and cannot, therefore, be reduced with carbon.

Titanium is extracted by reduction using the metal sodium as the reducing agent.

Titanium(IV) oxide is mixed with carbon and heated in a stream of chlorine to produce titanium(IV) chloride.

$$TiO_2(s) + 2C(s) + 2Cl_2(g) \rightarrow TiCl_4(l) + 2CO(g)$$
titanium(IV) oxide + carbon + chlorine → titanium(IV) chloride + carbon monoxide

Titanium(IV) chloride is then heated with sodium to produce titanium.

$$TiCl_4(l) + 4Na(l) \rightarrow Ti(s) + 4NaCl(s)$$
titanium(IV) chloride + sodium → titanium + sodium chloride

Because sodium is very expensive, the metal titanium will be very expensive.

Summary

The method used to extract a metal from its ore depends upon the position of the metal in the reactivity series.

Metals high in the reactivity series, e.g. sodium and aluminium, form stable compounds (Chapter 12) and the metal must be extracted by electrolysis. This will be expensive because of the large quantities of electricity required.

Metals lower in the reactivity series, e.g. iron, can be extracted by reduction using carbon as a reducing agent.

Metals low in the reactivity series may be found uncombined or 'native' in the earth. If they are in compounds, the compounds will be easy to split up.

Shortage of suitable deposits of ores will encourage:

1. Recycling of metals.
2. Exploitation of low quality deposits.
3. The use of alternative materials.

Chapter 16

The effect of electricity on chemicals

16.1 Conductors and insulators

A substance which allows electricity to pass through it is called a **conductor**. Of the solid elements at room temperature, only metals and graphite (a form of carbon) are good conductors. They conduct electricity because electrons pass freely through the solid.

Substances which do not allow electricity to pass through are called **insulators**. Some substances, e.g. germanium, conduct electricity slightly and are called **semiconductors**. They are important for making transistors.

16.2 Electrolytes

Certain substances do not conduct electricity when solid but do when molten or dissolved in water. They are called **electrolytes**. However, the passage of electricity through the melt or solution is accompanied by a chemical decomposition. The splitting up of an electrolyte, when molten or in aqueous solution, is called **electrolysis**.

Electrolytes include:

acids, metal oxides, metal hydroxides and salts

Electrolytes are composed of **ions** (i.e. ionic bonding, see Unit 8.2) but in the solid state the ions are rigidly held in regular positions and are unable to move to an electrode. Sodium chloride is composed of a regular lattice of sodium Na^+ and chloride Cl^- ions.

Melting the electrolyte breaks down the forces between the ions. The ions are, therefore, free to move in a molten electrolyte. In molten sodium chloride the sodium and chloride ions are able to move freely.

Dissolving an electrolyte in water (or other polar solvent) also causes the breakdown of the lattice and again the ions are free to move.

16.3 Electrolysis of molten lead(II) bromide

3.6f know about the readily observable effects of electrolysis.

Lead(II) bromide is an electrolyte. The apparatus in Fig. 16.1 could be used for the electrolysis of molten lead(II) bromide.

The bulb does not light up while the lead(II) bromide is solid, showing that no electric current is passing through the solid lead(II) bromide. As soon as the lead(II) bromide melts, the bulb lights up. After a while, bromine is seen escaping and, at the end of the experiment, lead can be found inside the crucible.

The reaction is, therefore

$$PbBr_2(l) \rightarrow Pb(l) + Br_2(g)$$
lead(II) bromide → lead + bromine

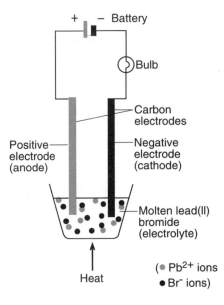

Fig. 16.1 Electrolysis of molten lead bromide

The carbon rods are called **electrodes**. The electrode attached to the positive terminal of the battery is the positive electrode (sometimes called the **anode**). The electrode attached to the negative terminal of the battery is the negative electrode (sometimes called the **cathode**). The positive electrode has a shortage of electrons and the negative electrode a surplus of electrons. Electrons are constantly flowing through the wire.

Lead(II) bromide is composed of lead ions Pb^{2+} and bromide ions Br^-. When the lead bromide is molten, the ions move (or migrate) towards the electrode of opposite charge, i.e. Pb^{2+} ions move to the negative electrode and Br^- ions to the positive electrode.

When the ions reach the oppositely charged electrode they are discharged. At the positive electrode (anode), bromide ions lose electrons to the electrode and form bromine molecules.

$$2Br^- \rightarrow Br_2 + 2e^- \quad \text{(oxidation)}$$

At the negative electrode (cathode), lead ions gain electrons from the electrode and form lead atoms.

$$Pb^{2+} + 2e^- \rightarrow Pb \quad \text{(reduction)}$$

The electrolysis of a molten electrolyte is comparatively easy to understand because only one type of positive ion and one type of negative ion are present. In a solution it is possible to have two types of positive ions and then these ions can compete to be discharged at the cathode.

16.4 Electrolysis of aqueous solutions

In pure water about 1 in every 600 000 000 water molecules ionize to form hydrogen and hydroxide ions:

$$H_2O(l) \rightleftharpoons H^+(aq) + OH^-(aq)$$

This very slight ionization of water molecules explains the very slight electrical conductivity of pure water.

A solution of sodium chloride in water contains the following ions:

| $H^+(aq)$ | $OH^-(aq)$ | from the water |
| $Na^+(aq)$ | $Cl^-(aq)$ | from the sodium chloride |

Both positive ions migrate to the negative electrode and both negative ions move to the positive electrode. At each electrode one or both of the ions may be discharged.

Table 16.1 below summarizes the results of some electrolysis experiments.

Table 16.1 Examples of electrolysis of solutions

Solution	Electrodes	Ion discharged at positive electrode	Ion discharged at negative electrode	Product at positive electrode	Product at negative electrode
Dilute sulphuric acid	Carbon	$OH^-(aq)$	$H^+(aq)$	Oxygen	Hydrogen
Dilute sodium hydroxide	Carbon	$OH^-(aq)$	$H^+(aq)$	Oxygen	Hydrogen
Copper sulphate	Carbon	$OH^-(aq)$	$Cu^{2+}(aq)$	Oxygen	Copper
Copper sulphate	Copper	None	$Cu^{2+}(aq)$	None	Copper
Copper(II) chloride	Carbon	$Cl^-(aq)$	$Cu^{2+}(aq)$	Chlorine	Copper
Very dilute sodium chloride	Carbon	$OH^-(aq)$	$H^+(aq)$	Oxygen	Hydrogen
Concentrated sodium chloride	Carbon	$Cl^-(aq)$	$H^+(aq)$	Chlorine	Hydrogen
Concentrated sodium chloride	Mercury cathode	$Cl^-(aq)$	$Na^+(aq)$	Chlorine	Sodium (amalgam)
Potassium iodide	Carbon	$I^-(aq)$	$H^+(aq)$	Iodine	Hydrogen

The apparatus that could be used for the electrolysis of a solution and the collection of the gaseous products is shown in Fig. 16.2.

The following points about the electrolysis of solutions are worth remembering:

1. Metals, if produced, are discharged at the negative electrode.

2. Hydrogen is produced at the negative electrode only.

3. Nonmetals, apart from hydrogen, are produced at the positive electrode.

4. Reactive metals are not formed at the cathode during electrolysis of aqueous solutions. An exception is during the electrolysis of sodium chloride using a mercury cathode.

5. The products obtained can depend upon the concentration of the electrolyte in the solution. For example, electrolysis of concentrated sodium chloride produces chlorine at the anode but electrolysis of dilute sodium chloride can produce oxygen at the anode.

6. Providing the concentrations of the negative ions in solution are approximately the same, the order of discharge is

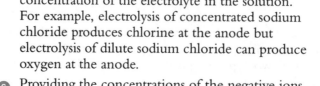

Fig. 16.2 Electrolysis of solutions

Gaseous product from anode
Gaseous product from cathode
Electrolyte solution
Negative electrode (cathode)
Positive electrode (anode)
Bulb

$$OH^-(aq)$$
$$I^-(aq)$$
$$Br^-(aq)$$
$$Cl^-(aq) \qquad \text{ease of discharge decreases}$$
$$NO_3^-(aq)$$
$$SO_4^{2-}(aq)$$

16.5 Uses of electrolysis

3.7g be able to relate knowledge and understanding of chemical principles to manufacturing processes and everyday effects.

1 Electroplating
Electrolysis can be used to form a very thin coating of a metal on the surface of another metal. This can be used for decorative purposes or to prevent corrosion.
   If a piece of copper is to be nickel plated the surface must be clean and grease free. The copper is made to be the cathode and a piece of nickel is the anode in an electrolysis experiment with nickel(II) sulphate solution as the electrolyte. A nickel coating is deposited on the negative electrode (the copper) and the nickel anode goes into solution as nickel(II) ions.

2 Extraction of metals (Chapter 15)

3 Purification of copper

4 Manufacture of sodium hydroxide (Chapter 23)

16.6 Quantitative electrolysis

3.10d be able to interpret electrolytic processes quantitatively.

If the bulb in Fig. 16.1 is replaced by an ammeter, it is possible to measure the current passing in the circuit (in amperes, A) and to calculate the quantity of electricity passed in a certain time.
   If a current of **1 A** flows for **1 second, s**, the quantity of electricity passed is **1 coulomb, C**. During an experiment it is found that, because a large number of coulombs are passed, it is better to work in units of faradays.

$$\textbf{1 faraday (F) = 96 500 coulombs}\ \text{(approximately)}$$

$$\text{quantity of electricity passed} = \frac{\text{current (in A)} \times \text{time (in s)}}{96\ 500}\ \text{F}$$

It is found, by experiment, that the quantity of electricity passed determines the mass of products formed.

Faraday's first law of electrolysis states that **the mass of a given element liberated during electrolysis is directly proportional to the quantity of electricity consumed during the electrolysis.**

16.7 Quantity of different elements deposited by the same quantity of electricity

Faraday's second law states that **the masses of different elements liberated by the same quantity of electricity form simple whole number ratios when divided by their relative atomic masses.**
   For example, during an electrolysis experiment 1.08 g of silver are deposited and 0.32 g of copper. The relative atomic masses (A_r) of silver and copper are 108 and 64 respectively. Therefore dividing the mass deposited by the appropriate relative atomic mass gives:

$$\begin{array}{cc} \textit{Silver} & \textit{Copper} \\ \dfrac{1.08}{108} = 0.01 & \dfrac{0.32}{64} = 0.005 \end{array}$$

The answers obtained are in a simple ratio of 2:1. This is in accordance with Faraday's second law of electrolysis.

It is found that the discharge of one mole of atoms of an element from an ion with a single positive or negative charge requires 1 F of electricity.

$$\therefore \text{ 1 F produces 108 g of silver from } Ag^+ \text{ ions}$$
$$\text{or} \qquad 35.5 \text{ g of chlorine from } Cl^- \text{ ions}$$

In a similar way, the discharge of one mole of atoms of an element from an ion with a double positive or negative charge requires 2 F of electricity.

$$\therefore \text{ 2 F produces 64 g of copper from } Cu^{2+} \text{ ions}$$
$$\text{or} \qquad 16 \text{ g of oxygen from } O^{2-} \text{ ions}$$

Sample calculation

Calculate the mass of calcium atoms produced when a current of 5 A is passed for 32 min 10 s through molten calcium bromide ($Ca^{2+}.2Br^-$) ($A_r(Ca) = 40$).

$$\text{quantity of electricity passed} = 5 \times 1930 \text{ C}$$
$$= \frac{5 \times 1930}{96\,500} \text{ F}$$
$$= 0.1 \text{ F}$$

Since calcium ions are Ca^{2+}, when 2 F are passed, the number of moles of calcium atoms formed = 1.

$$\therefore 0.1 \text{ F produces } \frac{0.1}{2}\text{mol of calcium atoms}$$

$$= \frac{0.1}{2} \times 40 \text{ g of calcium}$$

$$= 2 \text{ g of calcium}$$

N.B. One faraday of electricity contains 1 mole of electrons.

Summary

Metals and carbon conduct electricity well because electrons can pass freely through them. They are called conductors. Substances which will not let electrons pass through are insulators.

Some substances, called electrolytes, do not conduct electricity when solid but do when they are molten or dissolved in water. This passing of electricity splits up the electrolyte to produce new products. Common electrolytes are metal oxides, acids, alkalis and salts. They are all composed of ions. The ions are not free to move in the solid but become free to move on melting or dissolving in water.

Electrolysis of lead(II) bromide produces lead metal at the negative electrode (cathode) and bromine gas at the positive electrode (anode).

Electrolysis of aqueous solutions can produce a greater variety of products. Hydrogen gas is commonly produced at the cathode and oxygen is commonly produced at the anode. Reactive metals such as sodium and potassium are never produced during electrolysis of aqueous solutions.

Electrolysis is an important industrial process but it is expensive because of the large quantities of electricity needed.

The quantity of products formed during electrolysis depends upon the quantity of electricity used. The quantity of electricity used is measured in coulombs or faradays.

Chapter 17
Rates of reaction

17.1 Introduction

3.7f understand the factors which influence the rate of a chemical reaction.

The **rate** of a chemical reaction is a measure of how fast the reaction takes place. It is important to remember that a rapid reaction is completed in a short time. Some reactions are very fast, e.g. the formation of silver chloride precipitate when silver nitrate and hydrochloric acid solutions are mixed. Other reactions are very slow, e.g. the rusting of iron. For practical reasons, reactions used in the laboratory for studying rates of reaction must not be too fast or too slow.

17.2 Finding suitable measurable changes

Having selected a suitable reaction it is necessary to find a change that can be observed during the reaction. An estimate of the rate of the reaction can be obtained from the time taken for the measurable change to take place. Suitable changes include:

1. Colour.
2. Formation of precipitate.
3. Change in mass (e.g. a gas evolved causing a loss of mass).
4. Volume of gas evolved.
5. Time taken for a given mass of reagent to disappear.
6. pH.
7. Temperature.

17.3 Studying rates of reaction

Some of the easiest reactions to study in the laboratory are those in which a gas is evolved. The reaction can be followed by measuring the volume of gas evolved over a period of time using the apparatus in Fig. 17.1

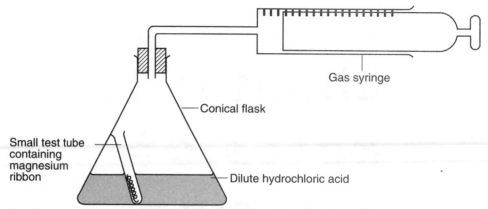

Fig. 17.1 Studying the reaction between magnesium and dilute hydrochloric acid

A suitable reaction is:

$$Mg(s) + 2HCl(aq) \rightarrow MgCl_2(aq) + H_2(g)$$
magnesium + hydrochloric acid → magnesium chloride + hydrogen

It is important to keep the reactants separate whilst setting up the apparatus so that the starting time of the reaction can be measured accurately.

Figure 17.2 shows a typical graph obtained for the reaction between dilute hydrochloric acid and magnesium. The dotted line shows the graph for a similar experiment using the same quantities of magnesium and hydrochloric acid but with conditions changed so that the reaction is slightly faster. The rate of the reaction is greatest when the graph is steepest, i.e. at the start of the reaction. The reaction is complete when the graph becomes horizontal, i.e. there is no further increase in the volume of hydrogen.

N.B. If you are carrying out an experiment all of the points may not lie on the curve. This is because of experimental error. You should draw the best graph through as many points as possible. It is often possible to follow the course of similar reactions by measuring the loss of mass during the reaction due to escape of gas. However, in this case the loss of mass is very small.

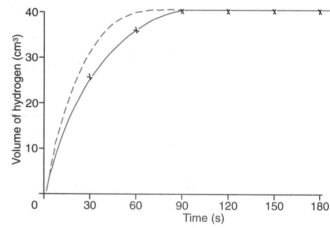

Fig. 17.2 A graph of volume of hydrogen collected at intervals

17.4 Collision theory for rates of reaction

Before looking at the factors that can alter the rate of reaction, we must consider what happens when a reaction takes place.

First of all, the particles of the reacting substances must **collide** with each other and, secondly, a fixed amount of energy called the **activation energy** (E_a) must be reached if the reaction is to take place (Fig. 17.3). If a collision between particles can produce sufficient energy (i.e. if they collide fast enough and in the right direction) a reaction will take place. Not all collisions will result in a reaction.

A reaction is speeded up if the number of suitable collisions is increased.

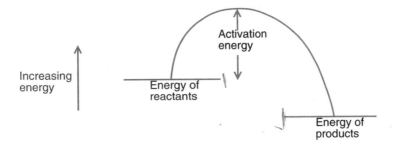

Fig. 17.3 Activation energy

17.5 Effect of concentration on the rate of reaction

The more concentrated the reactants, the greater will be the rate of reaction. This is because increasing the concentration of the reactants increases the number of collisions between particles and, therefore, increases the rate of reaction.

This also explains why the greatest rate of reaction is usually as soon as the reactants are mixed, i.e. they are both at their highest concentrations. As the reaction proceeds the concentrations of the reacting substances decrease and the rate of reaction decreases.

The effect of concentration can be shown by doing several experiments using equal masses of magnesium ribbon and hydrochloric acid of different concentrations.

Alternatively, a series of experiments can be carried out using a standard solution of sodium thiosulphate and hydrochloric acid solutions of different concentrations. The time is taken until the solution goes so cloudy that a cross disappears when viewed through the solution.

$$Na_2S_2O_3(aq) + 2HCl(aq) \rightarrow 2NaCl(aq) + S(s) + H_2O(l) + SO_2(g)$$
sodium thiosulphate + hydrochloric acid → sodium chloride + sulphur + water
                                                                        + sulphur dioxide

The cloudiness is due to the precipitation of sulphur.

17.6 Effect of pressure on the rate of reaction

When one or more of the reactants are gases an increase in pressure can lead to an increased rate of reaction. The increase in pressure forces the particles closer together. This causes more collisions and increases the rate of reaction.

17.7 Effect of temperature on the rate of reaction

An increase in temperature produces an increase in the rate of reaction. A rise of 10°C approximately doubles the rate of reaction.

When a mixture of substances is heated, the particles move faster. This has two effects. Since the particles are moving faster they will travel a greater distance in a given time and so will be involved in more collisions. Also, because the particles are moving faster a larger proportion of the collisions will exceed the activation energy and so the rate of reaction increases.

The reaction between standard sodium thiosulphate and standard hydrochloric acid solutions at different temperatures can be used to examine the effect of temperature on the rate of reaction.

17.8 Effect of particle size on the rate of reaction

When one of the reactants is a solid, the reaction must take place on the surface of the solid. By breaking up the solid into smaller pieces, the surface area is increased, giving a greater area for collisions to take place and so causing an increase in the rate of reaction. This explains why mixtures of coal dust and air can cause explosions.

This effect can be examined by reacting equal masses of calcium carbonate with different particle sizes (e.g. chalk and marble chips) with equal volumes of the same hydrochloric acid solution.

$$CaCO_3(s) + 2HCl(aq) \rightarrow CaCl_2(aq) + H_2O(l) + CO_2(g)$$
calcium carbonate + hydrochloric acid → calcium chloride + water + carbon dioxide

17.9 Effect of light on the rate of reaction

The rates of some reactions are increased by exposure to light. Light has a similar effect, therefore, to increasing temperature.

Silver chloride, precipitated by mixing silver nitrate and hydrochloric acid solutions, turns from white to greyish-purple on exposure to sunlight due to the partial decomposition of silver chloride. The effects of light on hydrogen peroxide and concentrated nitric acid explain why they are stored in dark glass bottles.

A mixture of hydrogen and chlorine does not react if kept in the dark but in the presence of light an explosive reaction takes place.

17.10 Effect of catalysts on the rate of reaction

A **catalyst** is a substance which can alter the rate of a reaction but remains chemically unchanged at the end of the reaction. Catalysts usually speed up reactions. A catalyst which slows down a reaction is called a negative catalyst or **inhibitor**.

Catalysts speed up reactions by providing an alternative pathway for the reaction, i.e. one that has a much lower activation energy. More collisions will, therefore, have enough energy for this new pathway (Fig. 17.4).

In the laboratory the catalysed decomposition of hydrogen peroxide is usually studied:

$$2H_2O_2(aq) \rightarrow 2H_2O(l) + O_2(g)$$
hydrogen peroxide → water + oxygen

Catalysts for this reaction include manganese(IV) oxide and certain enzymes. **Enzymes** are biological catalysts.

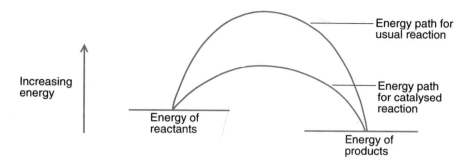

Fig. 17.4 Energy diagram for a catalysed reaction

Catalysts are important in many industrial processes. They do not increase the yield of the products but they do increase the rate of production.

Examples include:

1. Iron in the Haber process to produce ammonia (see Unit 22.3).

2. Vanadium(V) oxide in the Contact process to produce sulphuric acid (see Unit 24.2).

3. Platinum in the industrial conversion of ammonia to nitric acid (see Unit 22.6).

Catalysts are usually heavy (transition) metals or compounds of heavy (transition) metals.

Summary

The factors which affect the rate of a chemical reaction include:

1. Concentration.
2. Particle size.
3. Pressure (for reactions involving gases).
4. Temperature.
5. Light.
6. Presence of a catalyst.

The differences in rates of reaction can be explained in terms of a simple collision theory.

Chapter 18
Reversible reactions and equilibrium

18.1 Introduction

Most chemical reactions can only go in one direction. For example, when magnesium is reacted with dilute hydrochloric acid, the products are hydrogen and magnesium chloride.

$$Mg(s) + 2HCl(aq) \rightarrow MgCl_2(aq) + H_2(g)$$
magnesium + hydrochloric acid $\rightarrow$ magnesium chloride + hydrogen

There is no way that the reverse reaction will take place. Hydrogen will not react with magnesium chloride, under any conditions, to produce magnesium and hydrochloric acid.

Some reactions, however, are reversible. A reversible reaction is a reaction that can go in either direction depending on the conditions of the reaction. There are a number of common examples of reversible reactions. The sign $\rightleftarrows$ in an equation shows that the reaction is reversible. Also, it is possible for an equilibrium to be established with a reversible reaction. The sign $\rightleftharpoons$ shows that a system is in equilibrium.

18.2 Heating copper(II) sulphate crystals

When copper(II) sulphate crystals are heated, water vapour is driven off causing the blue crystals to turn to a white powder (anhydrous copper(II) sulphate). When a few drops of water are added to the cold white powder, the blue colour returns and heat is given out, showing the reversible nature of the reaction.

$$CuSO_4 \cdot 5H_2O(s) \rightleftarrows CuSO_4(s) + 5H_2O(l)$$
copper(II) sulphate crystals $\rightleftarrows$ anhydrous copper(II) sulphate + water

18.3 Heating ammonium chloride crystals

When ammonium chloride crystals are heated, the ammonium chloride dissociates into ammonia gas and hydrogen chloride gas. As the gases cool, they recombine to form solid ammonium chloride.

Similarly, if the stopper from a bottle of concentrated ammonia solution is held near a stopper from a bottle of concentrated hydrochloric acid (evolving hydrogen chloride fumes), a dense white smoke of ammonium chloride is formed.

$$NH_4Cl(s) \rightleftharpoons NH_3(g) + HCl(g)$$
ammonium chloride $\rightleftharpoons$ ammonia + hydrogen chloride

18.4 Formation of calcium hydrogencarbonate

Another readily reversible reaction involves the formation of calcium hydrogencarbonate.

If carbon dioxide is bubbled through a solution of calcium hydroxide (limewater), a cloudy white suspension of calcium carbonate is produced. This mixture goes clear again when more carbon dioxide is bubbled through, due to the formation of soluble calcium hydrogencarbonate.

Heating calcium hydrogencarbonate solution causes the reverse reaction and the cloudiness returns as insoluble calcium carbonate is reformed.

$$CaCO_3(s) + H_2O(l) + CO_2(g) \rightleftharpoons Ca(HCO_3)_2(aq)$$
calcium carbonate + water + carbon dioxide $\rightleftharpoons$ calcium hydrogencarbonate

18.5 Reaction of iron with steam

When steam is passed over heated iron, a slow reaction takes place producing hydrogen and an iron oxide. The apparatus suitable for this experiment is shown in Fig. 18.1.

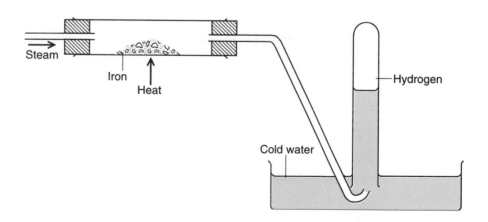

Fig. 18.1
Reaction of iron with steam

$$3Fe(s) + 4H_2O(g) \rightarrow Fe_3O_4(s) + 4H_2(g)$$
iron + water (steam) $\rightarrow$ iron(II) di-iron(III) oxide + hydrogen

In a second experiment dry hydrogen gas is passed over heated iron(II) di–iron(III) oxide (Fig. 18.2). This time the reverse reaction takes place and the iron oxide is reduced to iron.

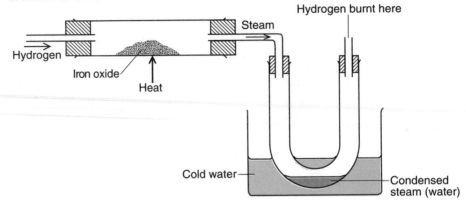

Fig. 18.2 Reaction of hydrogen and iron oxide

$$Fe_3O_4(s) + 4H_2(g) \rightarrow 3Fe(s) + 4H_2O(g)$$

An interesting consideration now is what would happen if the four chemicals were present together in a sealed container.

The iron would react with the steam to form hydrogen and iron oxide, but at the same time hydrogen would be reacting with the iron oxide to produce iron and steam.

After a time a state of balance would be set up where the rate of the forward reaction would be equal to the rate of the reverse reaction. This is called a state of **chemical equilibrium**.

$$Fe_3O_4(s) + 4H_2(g) \rightleftharpoons 3Fe(s) + 4H_2O(g)$$

Note that although there will appear to be no overall change in the concentrations of any of the chemicals, the equilibrium is a **dynamic** process, i.e. both forward and reverse reactions are taking place but at the same rate.

An equilibrium can be established only in a sealed system, where no chemicals can enter or leave the system. A system in equilibrium is very delicately balanced. Any disturbance of the system, e.g. a change in temperature, may disturb the equilibrium by favouring the forward or reverse reaction.

18.6 Factors affecting an equilibrium

In any equilibrium, the position of the equilibrium can be altered by changing the conditions.

Le Chatelier, a French chemist, stated a principle that governs the behaviour of equilibria. The principle states that **for a system in equilibrium, if any change is made to the conditions, the equilibrium will alter so as to oppose the change.**

Changes in conditions include temperature, pressure (if gases are involved) and concentration.

Effect of temperature

If the temperature of the system in equilibrium is lowered, the reaction will move in a direction to produce more heat, i.e. the exothermic reaction is favoured.

Effect of pressure

This applies to reactions involving gases. If the pressure is increased, the reaction will move to reduce the pressure by reducing the number of particles present.

Effect of concentration

If the concentration of one substance is increased, the reaction will move in a direction to use up the substance whose concentration was increased. If one substance is removed from the system, the reaction will move in a direction to produce more of the substance being removed.

18.7 Equilibrium in important industrial processes

3.7g be able to relate knowledge and understanding of chemical principles to manufacturing processes and everyday effects.

In any industrial process it is important to get the best conversion of reactants to products that is possible without excessive expense. Several important processes involve reversible reactions. The conditions of the reaction chamber can greatly affect the position of the equilibrium and hence the economics of the process.

The Contact process for the production of sulphuric acid is considered in Unit 24.2. The Haber process for the production of ammonia is considered in Unit 22.3. In both cases there is a consideration of the best way of achieving a good yield of products economically.

Summary

A reversible reaction, shown by the sign $\rightleftarrows$ in the equation, is a reaction that can go either forwards or backwards depending upon the conditions.

If a reversible reaction is carried out so that the products cannot escape, it is impossible to turn the reactants completely into the products. You will finish up with an equilibrium. In the equilibrium, all reactants and products are present and their concentrations are not changing. The rate of the forward reaction is equal to the rate of the reverse reaction. An equilibrium reaction is shown by the sign $\rightleftharpoons$.

Chapter 19
Energy changes in chemistry

19.1 Introduction

A consideration of energy, and more particularly energy change, is a fundamental aspect of a chemistry course. In this chapter the distinction between physics and chemistry becomes blurred.

A change in energy content of chemicals will be recognized by a change in temperature of the surroundings. There are different forms of energy. The most important forms of energy to a chemist are heat energy and electrical energy.

Energy can neither be created nor destroyed in any process. It is just changed from one form to another. This is called the Law of Conservation of Energy, which is related to the Law of Conservation of Mass. The work of Einstein has shown that mass and energy can be interconverted.

19.2 Energy possessed by chemicals

All substances are composed of small particles. At any temperature above absolute zero ($-273\,^{\circ}\text{C}$) the particles are in motion. These particles can possess two types of energy:

1 Kinetic energy
Particles that are moving possess kinetic energy (energy of movement). As the temperature rises, the particles move faster and possess more kinetic energy.

2 Chemical energy (or bonding energy)
When bonds are formed energy is released. If the bonds holding particles together are to be broken, energy has to be supplied.

It is not possible to measure the total energy possessed by any chemical in the laboratory. It is only possible to measure energy changes.

The energy change that accompanies a chemical reaction is due to changes in chemical or bonding energy between reactant and product.

19.3 Exothermic processes

There are many examples where energy is liberated during the reaction and the temperature of the system rises.

*3.6e know that
some chemical
reactions are
exothermic, while
others are
endothermic.*

For example, the burning of carbon produces energy. Such a reaction is called an **exothermic reaction**. The quantity of energy produced depends on the quantity of carbon burnt.

$$C(s) + O_2(g) \rightarrow CO_2(g)$$
carbon + oxygen → carbon dioxide ($\Delta H = -393.5$ kJ)

This information tells a chemist that if 1 mole of carbon atoms (12 g) is burnt in an adequate supply of oxygen, 393.5 kJ of energy are liberated. ΔH is called the **enthalpy** (or heat) of reaction and is **negative** if the reaction is exothermic.

This process can be summarized in Fig. 19.1.

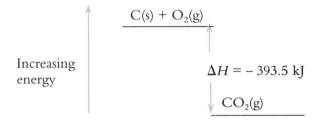

Fig. 19.1 Energy diagram for the complete combustion of carbon

During an exothermic reaction, more energy is produced from the formation of new bonds than the energy required to break existing bonds, and therefore there is a surplus of energy, which is lost to the surroundings.

19.4 Endothermic processes

There are a few reactions where energy is absorbed from the surroundings during the reaction and the temperature falls.

For example, the formation of hydrogen iodide from hydrogen and iodine is an **endothermic reaction**.

$$H_2(g) + I_2(g) \rightleftharpoons 2HI(g)$$
hydrogen + iodine $\rightleftharpoons$ hydrogen iodide ($\Delta H = 52$ kJ)

ΔH is **positive**, in this case, because the reaction is endothermic. This process is summarized in Fig. 19.2.

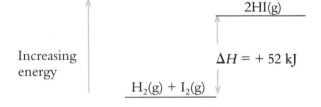

Fig. 19.2 Energy diagram for the synthesis of hydrogen iodide

During an endothermic reaction, more energy is required to break bonds than is liberated when new bonds are formed. This deficiency in energy has to be made up from the surroundings.

19.5 Activation energy

If the products contain less energy than the reactants, it might be expected that the exothermic changes would always occur spontaneously. This is not the case. Before the reaction can take place energy, called the activation energy, has to be supplied to start the reaction off (Fig. 19.3).

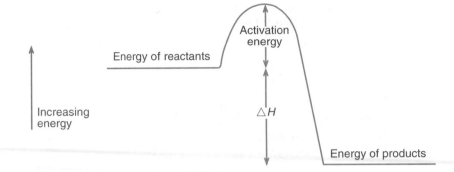

Fig. 19.3 Energy changes during a reaction

The function of a catalyst is usually to speed up a reaction by lowering the activation energy barrier (see Unit 17.10).

19.6 Fundamental definitions

Heat of formation

The heat liberated or absorbed when 1 mole of a substance is formed from its constituent elements.

Heat of combustion

The heat liberated when 1 mole of a substance is completely burnt in excess oxygen.

Heat of neutralization

The heat liberated when 1 mole of hydrogen ions $H^+(aq)$ reacts with 1 mole of hydroxide ions $OH^-(aq)$.

$$H^+(aq) + OH^-(aq) \rightarrow H_2O(l)$$

The heat of neutralization of many acids and alkalis is −58 kJ/mol.

19.7 To find the heat of combustion of an alcohol

A small spirit lamp containing the alcohol is weighed accurately. During the weighing the spirit lamp should be covered to prevent evaporation of the alcohol.

A known mass of water is placed in a metal can (see Fig. 19.4). The temperature of the water is recorded. The spirit lamp is lit and placed underneath The can is heated until the temperature has risen by about 30 °C. The final temperature is recorded. The spirit lamp is then reweighed to find the mass of alcohol burnt.

Sample results

mass of spirit lamp + ethanol before burning = 21.94 g
mass of spirit lamp + ethanol after burning = 21.10 g
mass of ethanol burnt = 0.84 g
mass of water in the can = 100 g

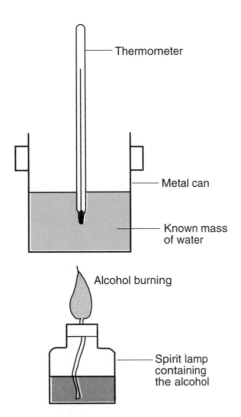

Thermometer

Metal can

Known mass of water

Alcohol burning

Spirit lamp containing the alcohol

Fig. 19.4 Experiment to find the heat of combustion of an alcohol

(You can ignore the heat required to raise the temperature of the can.)

Specific heat capacity of the water $= 4.2$ kJ/kg/°C
temperature rise $= 30$ °C

heat gained by water = mass (in kg) × temp. rise × specific heat capacity

$$= \frac{1}{10} \times 30 \times 4.2 \text{ kJ}$$

$$= 12.6 \text{ kJ}$$

It is assumed that all the heat produced when the ethanol burns is used to heat up the water.

12.6 kJ is produced when 0.84 g of ethanol burns

$\frac{12.6}{0.84}$ kJ is produced when 1 g of ethanol burns

mass of 1 mol of ethanol molecules $C_2H_5OH = 46$ g

heat produced when 46 g of ethanol burns $= \frac{12.6}{0.84} \times 46$ kJ

Since the combustion of ethanol is exothermic, the heat of combustion

$$\Delta H = -690 \text{ kJ/mol}$$

However, the heat of combustion of ethanol in the data book is -1370 kJ/mol.
    The big difference between the theoretical and practical heats of combustion is due to the heat lost to the surroundings.

19.8 Cells and batteries

The energy produced during a chemical reaction can be used in various ways. These include:

❶ Heat (chemical energy $\rightarrow$ heat energy).
❷ To do work (chemical energy $\rightarrow$ mechanical energy).
❸ To produce electricity (chemical energy $\rightarrow$ electrical energy).

Not all the energy produced, ΔH, can be converted to electricity. The maximum amount of energy that can be converted to electricity is ΔG. The rest of the energy is wasted.

A simple cell is produced when rods of zinc and copper are dipped into a solution of copper(II) sulphate.

The reaction taking place is:

$$Zn(s) + CuSO_4(aq) \rightarrow ZnSO_4(aq) + Cu(s)$$
zinc + copper(II) sulphate $\rightarrow$ zinc sulphate + copper

A simple cell does not operate well and can be improved as shown in Fig. 19.5.

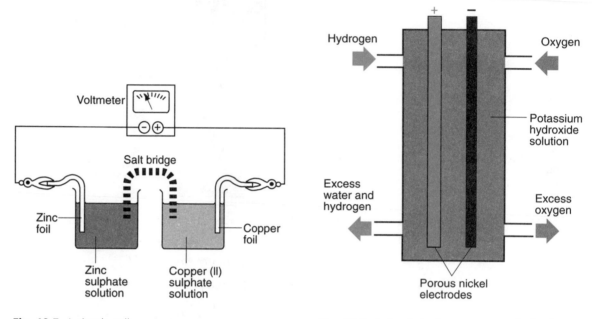

Fig. 19.5 A simple cell

Fig. 19.6 A simple hydrogen–oxygen fuel cell

19.9 Fuel cells

A fuel cell is an efficient means of converting chemical energy into electrical energy. A continuous supply of electrical energy can be obtained if there is a continuous supply of fuel.

In a hydrogen-oxygen fuel cell (Fig. 19.6), hydrogen and oxygen combine to form water. The energy is released as electricity.

Fuel cells have been used in vehicles and space rockets. They produce electricity without pollution.

19.10 Energy changes due to bond making and bond breaking

3.10b understand chemical reactions in terms of the energy transfers associated with making and breaking chemical bonds.

In Unit 19.2 it was stated that energy is required to break bonds and energy is evolved when bonds form. The net overall energy change in a chemical reaction is the difference between the energy liberated on forming bonds and the energy required to break bonds. In this section we are going to look at some examples quantitatively. Table 19.1 gives the average bond lengths and bond energies for some common covalent bonds.

Table 19.1 Bond lengths and bond energies for some common covalent bonds

Bond	Bond length (nm)	Bond energy (kJ/mol)
H–H	0.074	436
C–C	0.154	348
C=C	0.134	612
N≡N	0.110	944
O=O	0.121	496
O–H	0.096	463
N–H	0.101	388
F–F	0.142	158
Cl–Cl	0.199	242
Br–Br	0.228	193
I–I	0.267	151
H–F	0.092	562
H–Cl	0.128	431
H–Br	0.141	366
H–I	0.160	299
C–H	0.109	412
C–F	0.138	484
C–Cl	0.177	338
C–Br	0.193	276
C–I	0.214	238

The bond energy is the energy change for the process

$$X–Y(g) \rightarrow X(g) + Y(g)$$

The first thing you should note is that there is no correlation between the bond length and the bond energies.

If we take a reaction, for example between hydrogen and chlorine

$$H_2(g) + Cl_2(g) \rightarrow 2HCl(g)$$

we can represent this as

$$
\begin{array}{ccc}
 & & H–Cl \\
H–H \quad Cl–Cl & \rightarrow & \\
 & & H–Cl
\end{array}
$$

The energy required to break one mole of H–H bonds is +436 kJ (the positive sign because we are using the convention that supplying energy, to break bonds, is positive).

The energy required to break one mole of Cl–Cl bonds is +242 kJ.

The energy produced when two moles of H–Cl bonds are formed is 2×431 kJ = −862 kJ.

The energy change is + 436 + 242 − 862 = −184 kJ.

The negative value tells us that the reaction is exothermic.

Summary

Energy changes are often noticed during chemical reactions.

A reaction where energy is given out to the surroundings is called an **exothermic** reaction. In an exothermic reaction, the substances produced (called products) contain less energy than the reacting substances (called reactants).

In an **endothermic** reaction, energy is taken in from the surroundings. The reactants contain less energy than the products.

There are many examples of exothermic reactions but few endothermic reactions.

A cell is a means of producing the energy from a chemical reaction in an efficient way. The chemical energy is converted into electrical energy.

Calculations can be carried out using bond energies to find the energy change during a reaction. It is necessary to add up the energies for the bonds being broken and the energies for the bonds being formed. The difference will be the energy change.

Chapter 20
Chemicals from petroleum

20.1 Petroleum

Petroleum (also called **crude oil**) is a most important mineral. It is found in various parts of the world, including the Middle East, USA (including Alaska and Texas), Venezuela and the North Sea. Apart from producing valuable fuels, it is also the source of a wide range of chemicals and useful everyday materials.

Petroleum was formed by the decomposition of animal and plant material over millions of years. It is a fossil fuel (see Unit 11.7). It is found trapped in permeable rock layers between layers of impermeable rock (Fig. 20.1). It is extracted by drilling deep holes into the earth. Often the oil will escape from the ground under its own pressure at first but pumping may be required later. Petroleum is a complex mixture of hydrocarbons. **Hydrocarbons** are compounds of carbon and hydrogen only. Most of the compounds present in petroleum are alkanes.

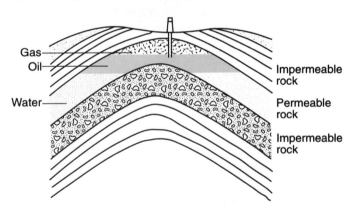

Fig. 20.1 Formation of petroleum

20.2 Alkanes

The **alkanes** are a series of hydrocarbons (compounds of carbon and hydrogen) with the general formula C_nH_{2n+2} where $n = 1, 2, 3, ...,$ for successive members of the series.

The first member of the series ($n = 1$) is methane CH_4 and the second member ($n = 2$) is ethane C_2H_6.

Table 20.1 summarizes some information about the simplest alkanes.

Table 20.1 The simplest alkanes

Alkane	Molecular formula	Structural formula	Melting point (°C)	Boiling point (°C)	State at room temperature and pressure
Methane	CH_4	$H-\overset{\displaystyle H}{\underset{\displaystyle H}{C}}-H$	−183	−162	Gas
Ethane	C_2H_6	$H-\overset{\displaystyle H}{\underset{\displaystyle H}{C}}-\overset{\displaystyle H}{\underset{\displaystyle H}{C}}-H$	−183	−89	Gas
Propane	C_3H_8	$H-\overset{\displaystyle H}{\underset{\displaystyle H}{C}}-\overset{\displaystyle H}{\underset{\displaystyle H}{C}}-\overset{\displaystyle H}{\underset{\displaystyle H}{C}}-H$	−188	−42	Gas
Butane	C_4H_{10}	$H-\overset{\displaystyle H}{\underset{\displaystyle H}{C}}-\overset{\displaystyle H}{\underset{\displaystyle H}{C}}-\overset{\displaystyle H}{\underset{\displaystyle H}{C}}-\overset{\displaystyle H}{\underset{\displaystyle H}{C}}-H$	−135	−0.5	Gas
Pentane	C_5H_{12}	$H-\overset{\displaystyle H}{\underset{\displaystyle H}{C}}-\overset{\displaystyle H}{\underset{\displaystyle H}{C}}-\overset{\displaystyle H}{\underset{\displaystyle H}{C}}-\overset{\displaystyle H}{\underset{\displaystyle H}{C}}-\overset{\displaystyle H}{\underset{\displaystyle H}{C}}-H$	−130	36	Liquid

Alkanes contain only single bonds and are said to be **saturated**. Organic compounds containing double or triple bonds are said to be **unsaturated**.

A series of compounds which are related to each other (e.g. the alkanes) is called a **homologous series**. Each member is called a **homologue**. In each homologous series, each member has the same general formula but differs from the next in the series by a unit of CH_2.

The physical properties of the members show a gradual change with increasing relative molecular mass. Thus, for example, in the alkanes the melting points and boiling points rise with increasing relative molecular mass. In a similar way, the density increases and the solubility in water decreases with rising relative molecular mass.

Natural gas which is piped to our homes and used for all gas appliances is almost pure methane. Calor gas which is bought in cylinders for camping is propane. Butane is used in gas cigarette lighters. Higher alkanes are used in petrol and other fuels.

20.3 Chemical reactions of methane

1 Methane burns in air or oxygen

Methane forms carbon dioxide in excess air and carbon monoxide in a limited supply of air.

$$CH_4(g) + 2O_2(g) \rightarrow CO_2(g) + 2H_2O(g)$$
methane + oxygen → carbon dioxide + water

$$2CH_4(g) + 3O_2(g) \rightarrow 2CO(g) + 4H_2O(g)$$
methane + oxygen → carbon monoxide + water

2 Reaction with chlorine

In diffused light, methane reacts giving a series of products by the successive replacement of hydrogen atoms. Each of the reactions is a **substitution reaction**.

$$CH_4(g) + Cl_2(g) \rightarrow HCl(g) + CH_3Cl(g)$$
methane + chlorine → hydrogen chloride + chloromethane

$$CH_3Cl(g) + Cl_2(g) \rightarrow HCl(g) + CH_2Cl_2(g)$$
chloromethane + chlorine → hydrogen chloride + dichloromethane

$$CH_2Cl_2(g) + Cl_2(g) \rightarrow HCl(g) + CHCl_3(g)$$
dichloromethane + chlorine → hydrogen chloride + trichloromethane

$$CHCl_3(g) + Cl_2(g) \rightarrow HCl(g) + CCl_4(g)$$
trichloromethane + chlorine → hydrogen chloride + tetrachloromethane

20.4 Isomerism

There is only one possible structure for each of the first three alkanes but the four carbon atoms and the ten hydrogen atoms in a molecule of butane, C_4H_{10}, can be linked in two different ways, as shown in Fig. 20.2

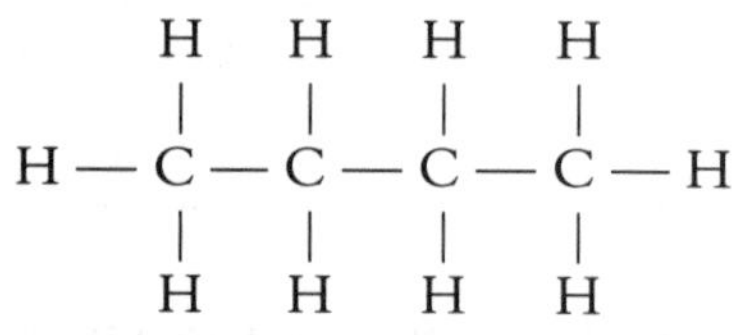

Butane
(or n–butane)

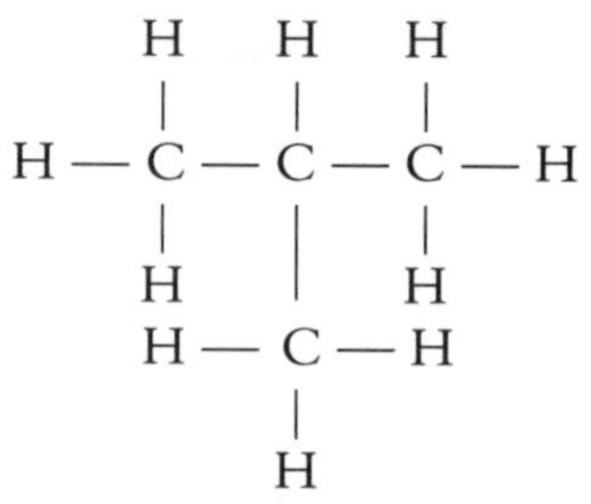

2-methylpropane
(or isobutane)

Fig. 20.2 Isomers of butane

This is an example of **isomerism**, i.e. the existence of two or more compounds (called **isomers**) having the same molecular formula but different structural formulae.

Isomerism becomes more common in the higher alkanes, e.g. there are 75 isomers of decane $C_{10}H_{22}$. Isomerism also occurs within other homologous series and also with compounds in different homologous series, e.g. C_2H_5OH (an alcohol) and CH_3OCH_3 (an ether).

20.5 Alkenes

The **alkenes** are a series of hydrocarbons with the general formula C_nH_{2n}, where $n = 2$, 3, ... Table 20.2 summarizes some information about the simplest alkenes.

Table 20.2 The simplest alkenes

Alkene	Molecular formula	Structural formula	Melting point (°C)	Boiling point (°C)	State at room temperature and pressure
Ethene	C_2H_4	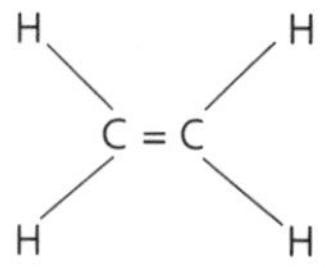	−169	−102	Gas
Propene	C_3H_6	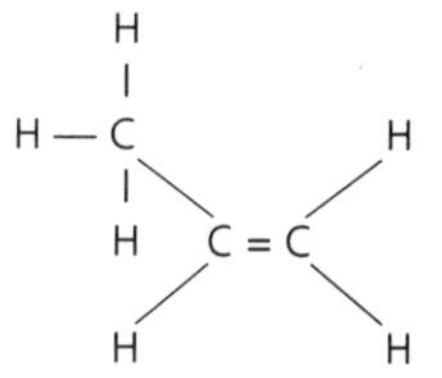	−185	−48	Gas
Butene	C_4H_8	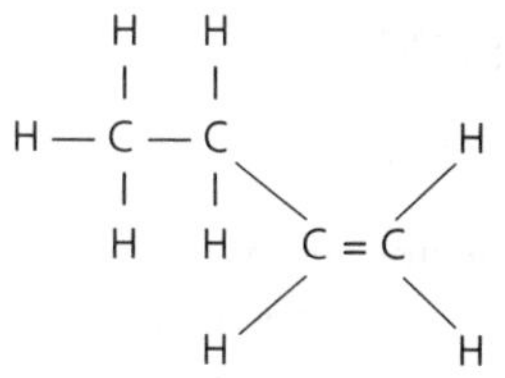	−185	−6	Gas
Pentene	C_5H_{10}	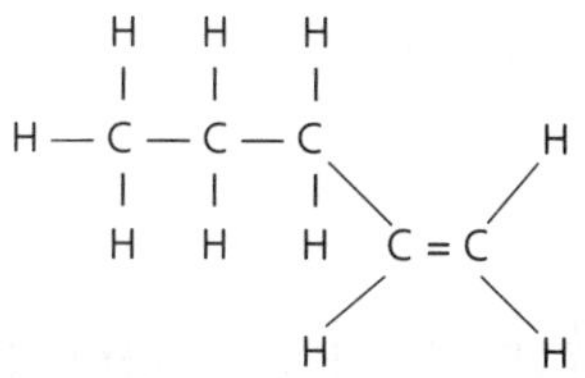	−138	30	Liquid

It should be noted that all alkenes contain a double bond between two carbon atoms. They are, therefore, **unsaturated**. Alkenes with four or more carbon atoms can exist as different isomers.

20.6 Reactions of ethene

Other alkenes react in a similar way.

1 Combustion

Ethene burns in air or oxygen if ignited. In excess air carbon dioxide and water are produced and in a limited supply of air carbon monoxide and water are produced.

2 Addition reactions

Addition reactions are common with all unsaturated compounds. In such a reaction two substances combine to produce a single new substance. The reaction between ethene and bromine is most frequently mentioned. Ethene reacts rapidly with bromine vapour to form colourless oily drops of 1,2–dibromoethane (Fig. 20.3).

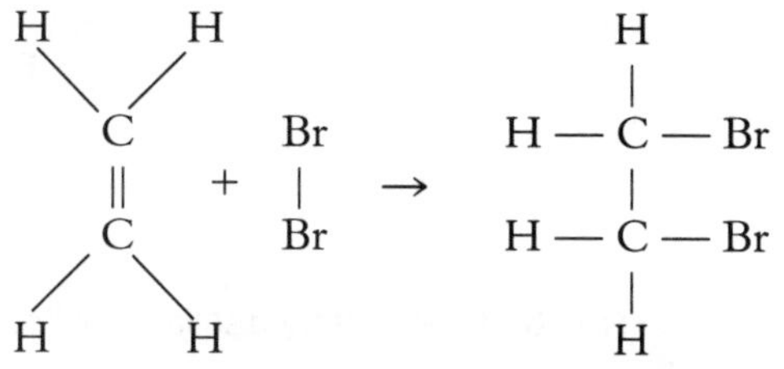

Fig. 20.3 Addition of bromine to ethene

This reaction is used to detect compounds containing double or triple bonds (unsaturated). The compound is shaken with bromine dissolved in a suitable solvent (e.g. tetrachloromethane). Unsaturated compounds remove the reddish colour of the bromine. This test does not, of course, distinguish between compounds containing double and triple bonds.

Ethene also reacts with hydrogen at 200 °C, in the presence of a finely divided nickel catalyst, to form ethane.

$$C_2H_4(g) + H_2(g) \rightarrow C_2H_6(g)$$
ethene + hydrogen $\rightarrow$ ethane

This reaction is similar to the reaction in which natural fats and oils are converted to margarine by the addition of hydrogen at about 5 atmospheres pressure and 180 °C.

20.7 Alkynes

The **alkynes** are a series of hydrocarbons with a general formula C_nH_{2n-2}. The simplest member is ethyne (sometimes called acetylene) C_2H_2, which has the structural formula H–C≡C–H. All alkynes contain a triple bond between two carbon atoms and, like the alkenes, are unsaturated.

20.8 Refining of petroleum

Petroleum consists mainly of a complex mixture of hydrocarbons, the greater proportion of which are alkanes. The petroleum can be split up into various fractions by **fractional distillation**.

Fractional distillation of petroleum may be carried out on a small scale in the laboratory using the apparatus in Fig. 20.4.

Several fractions may be obtained corresponding to different boiling point ranges (e.g. first fraction up to 70 °C, second fraction 70–120 °C, third fraction 120–170 °C, fourth fraction 170–220 °C, etc.). On examining the fractions obtained, certain definite changes in properties of the fractions with increasing boiling point can be seen. In particular, the yellow colour and viscosity (i.e. the ease with which the liquid pours, or stickiness) increase with increasing boiling point whilst the flammability decreases.

Industrially, the fractional distillation of petroleum is carried out on a large scale in an oil refinery. The fractionation is carried out in a fractional distillation column (Fig. 20.5).

The main fractions include:

1. Petrol (6–12 carbon atoms).
2. Paraffin (11–16 carbon atoms).
3. Lubricating oil (more than 20 carbon atoms).

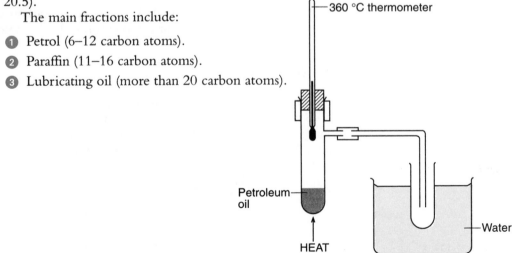

Fig. 20.4 Laboratory distillation of petroleum

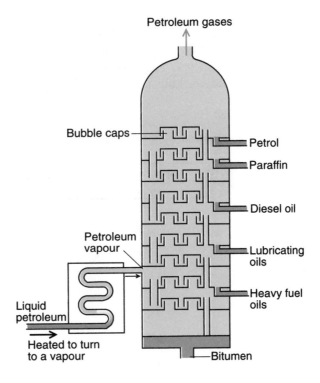

Fig. 20.5 Industrial distillation of petroleum

20.9 Cracking

Petroleum contains a complex mixture of hydrocarbons. After refining, many of the higher boiling point fractions containing long chain molecules are difficult to sell profitably. Oil companies have developed cracking and reforming processes to convert these fractions into shorter chain molecules which are very easy to sell to the chemical industry. They are used for making chemicals and making polymers.

Cracking involves the breaking of long chain alkanes (Fig. 20.6) and can be carried out in two ways:

1. Thermal cracking – carried out simply by heating.
2. Catalytic cracking – carried out using a catalyst.

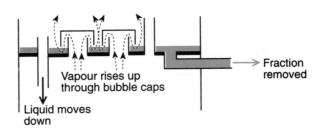

Fig. 20.6 Cracking of hexane

Cracking always produces some unsaturated products.

Reforming involves processes where the shapes of the molecules are changed but the sizes of the molecules are not. It is used, for example, to produce petrol with a high octane rating.

A simple cracking experiment can be carried out in the laboratory using the apparatus in Fig. 20.7. Liquid paraffin vapour is passed over strongly heated broken china where the cracking takes place. The product, ethene gas, can be collected over water.

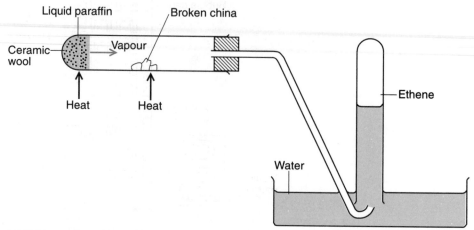

Fig. 20.7 Thermal cracking of liquid paraffin

Summary

Petroleum (crude oil) is a complicated mixture of hydrocarbons produced by the decomposition of plants and animals over millions of years. The petroleum is separated into fractions with different properties by fractional distillation.

Alkanes are a homologous series (family) of saturated hydrocarbons. They all fit the formula C_nH_{2n+2}. The simplest member of the family is methane, CH_4.

Alkanes with more than four carbon atoms can have different arrangements of atoms. These different forms are called isomers (often confused with isotopes).

Alkenes are unsaturated hydrocarbons containing a carbon–carbon double bond. They all fit the general formula C_nH_{2n}. The simples member is ethene, C_2H_4. Bromine dissolved in a suitable solvent is used to test for the presence of a double or triple bond.

Fractional distillation of petroleum produces a larger amount of long chain hydrocarbons than required. These long chain hydrocarbons can be split up by cracking to produce smaller unsaturated molecules which can be used for making polymers (Chapter 21).

Chapter 21
Polymerization

21.1 Introduction

3.8d be able to explain the physical and chemical processes by which different chemicals are made from oil.

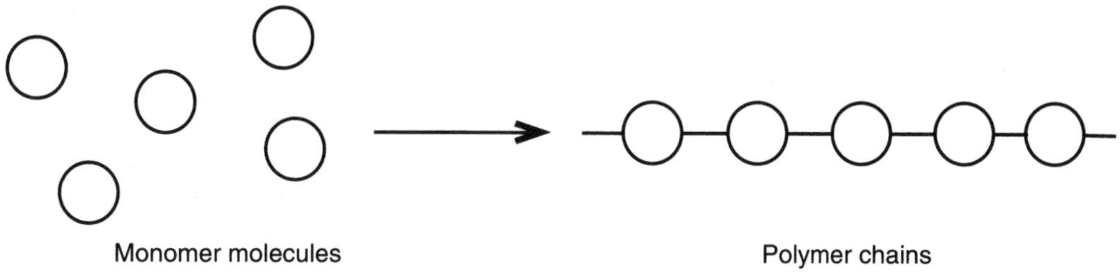

Polymerization is the linking together of relatively small and simple molecules to form large units called **polymers**. The individual small molecules are called **monomers**.

Monomer molecules   Polymer chains

Fig. 21.1 Polymerization

21.2 Addition polymers

Addition polymerization is one type of polymerization. It may be represented as follows:

$$n\text{M} \rightarrow (\text{M})_n$$

where M is a monomer unit.

This type of polymerization can take place only if the monomer is an unsaturated molecule. Many monomers, in fact, contain a double bond between two carbon atoms.

E.g. **Ethene** produces the polymer called **poly(ethene)** (polythene) as shown in Fig. 21.2

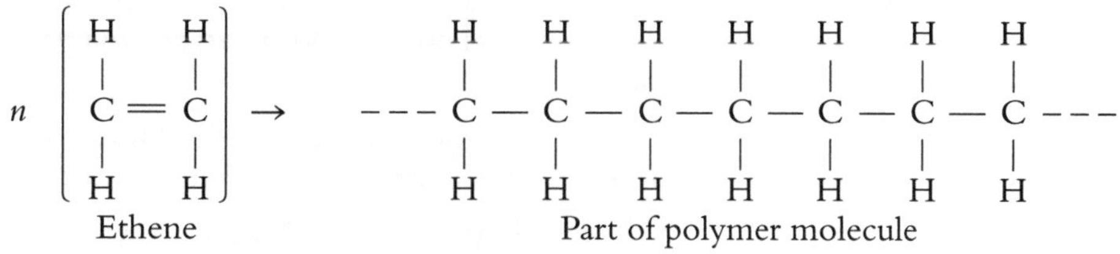

Ethene   Part of polymer molecule

Fig. 21.2 Polymerization of ethene

In the resulting polymer unit there are usually hundreds of ethene units combined together.

The polymer can be produced in two ways:

1 Ethene gas is bubbled into a hydrocarbon solvent containing a complex catalyst. The temperature is below 100 °C and the pressure of the gas is atmospheric. The polythene produced is called high density (HD) polythene.

2 Ethene is heated at high pressure (1000 atmospheres) and a temperature of 180 °C with a little oxygen present as initiator. The polythene produced is called low density (LD) polythene.

Table 21.1 gives details of some common addition polymers and their uses.

21.3 Advantages and disadvantages of addition polymers

Addition polymers are very widely used today. They are usually soft, have low densities and low melting points and do not corrode. It is possible to make addition polymers that are hard or have high melting points.

One advantage of addition polymers is the fact that they can be easily moulded into shape, making the production of complicated items such as a car dashboard easy.

The biggest disadvantage of addition polymers comes from the fact that they do not decompose. They are extremely difficult to dispose of, for example in household refuse. If tipped onto an open tip they do not rot away.

If household rubbish is screened until only a mixture of waste paper and waste polymers remains it is possible to separate the polymers. Thorough wetting with water will make the paper sink to the bottom of a water tank. Polymers are not wetted and continue to float. They can be scooped off. The result is a mixture of polymers which cannot easily be separated into its components. The mixture of polymers can be melted and made into cheap insulation blocks.

Another way of disposing of household rubbish containing polymers is to burn it. In several places household rubbish is made into pellets which can be used for solid fuel boilers.

On heating addition polymers, the polymers melt very easily. When these start to burn they often produce highly poisonous gases, along with carbon dioxide and water vapour that are produced in large quantities. Burning poly(acrylonitrile), for example, can produce highly poisonous hydrogen cyanide.

21.4 Condensation polymerization

There is another type of polymerization possible; this type is called **condensation polymerization**.

When two molecules react together to form a larger molecule and lose a small molecule (e.g. water) this is called a **condensation reaction**. An example is the esterification reaction.

$$CH_3COOH(l) + C_2H_5OH(l) \rightleftharpoons CH_3COOC_2H_5(l) + H_2O(l)$$
ethanoic acid + ethanol $\rightleftharpoons$ ethyl ethanoate + water

ACID + ALCOHOL $\rightleftharpoons$ ESTER + WATER

In condensation polymerization reactions the monomer molecules join together with the elimination of small molecules. Each monomer unit must contain **two reactive groups** otherwise no polymer is possible.

Table 21.1 Examples of addition polymers

Monomer	Polymer			
Formula/name	Name	Trade name	Formula	Uses
ETHENE	Poly(ethene)	Polythene	$\left(-\overset{\displaystyle H}{\underset{\displaystyle H}{C}}-\overset{\displaystyle H}{\underset{\displaystyle H}{C}}-\right)_n$	Plastic sheets, pipes, plastic bags
PROPENE	Poly(propene)	Propathene	$\left(-\overset{\displaystyle H}{\underset{\displaystyle H}{C}}-\overset{\displaystyle H}{\underset{\displaystyle CH_3}{C}}-\right)_n$	Plastic sheets, electric insulators, washing-up bowls
VINYL CHLORIDE (CHLOROETHENE)	Poly(vinyl chloride) or poly(chloroethene)	PVC	$\left(-\overset{\displaystyle H}{\underset{\displaystyle H}{C}}-\overset{\displaystyle H}{\underset{\displaystyle Cl}{C}}-\right)_n$	Records, clothes, electrical wire insulators
STYRENE (PHENYLETHENE)	Polystyrene or poly(phenylethene)	—	$\left(-\overset{\displaystyle H}{\underset{\displaystyle H}{C}}-\overset{\displaystyle H}{\underset{\displaystyle C_6H_5}{C}}-\right)_n$	Packing materials, ceiling tiles, plastic model kits
METHYL METHACRYLATE	Poly(methyl methacrylate)	Perspex	$\left(-\overset{\displaystyle H}{\underset{\displaystyle H}{C}}-\overset{\displaystyle H}{\underset{\displaystyle COOCH_3}{C}}-\right)_n$	Substitute for glass
ACRYLONITRILE	Poly(acrylonitrile)	Orlon, Courtelle, Acrilan	$\left(-\overset{\displaystyle H}{\underset{\displaystyle H}{C}}-\overset{\displaystyle H}{\underset{\displaystyle CN}{C}}-\right)_n$	Synthetic fibre
TETRAFLUOROETHENE	Poly(tetra-fluoroethene)	Teflon PTFE	$\left(-\overset{\displaystyle F}{\underset{\displaystyle F}{C}}-\overset{\displaystyle F}{\underset{\displaystyle F}{C}}-\right)_n$	Coating for nonstick saucepans, bridge bearings

The monomer formulas, shown as $C=C$ structures:

- ETHENE: $H_2C=CH_2$
- PROPENE: $\overset{H}{\underset{H}{C}}=\overset{H}{\underset{CH_3}{C}}$
- VINYL CHLORIDE (CHLOROETHENE): $\overset{H}{\underset{H}{C}}=\overset{H}{\underset{Cl}{C}}$
- STYRENE (PHENYLETHENE): $\overset{H}{\underset{H}{C}}=\overset{H}{\underset{C_6H_5}{C}}$
- METHYL METHACRYLATE: $\overset{H}{\underset{H}{C}}=\overset{H}{\underset{COOCH_3}{C}}$
- ACRYLONITRILE: $\overset{H}{\underset{H}{C}}=\overset{H}{\underset{CN}{C}}$
- TETRAFLUOROETHENE: $\overset{F}{\underset{F}{C}}=\overset{F}{\underset{F}{C}}$

Nylon is an important man-made condensation polymer. Although there are various types of nylon, the commonest is nylon-6,6 (so-called because both starting materials contain six carbon atoms). For nylon-6,6, the starting materials are hexane-1,6-diamine and hexanedioic acid. They may be represented as follows:

H_2N — ▢ — NH_2 $HOOC$ — ● — $COOH$
Hexane-1,6-diamine   Hexanedioic acid
(reactive group — NH_2)   (reactive group — $COOH$)

One of the reactive —NH_2 groups on the hexane-1,6-diamine molecule reacts with one of the reactive —COOH groups on the hexanedioic acid molecule with the elimination of a molecule of water. The product still contains two reactive groups and a series of similar reactions take place resulting in the formation of a polymer (Fig. 21.3).

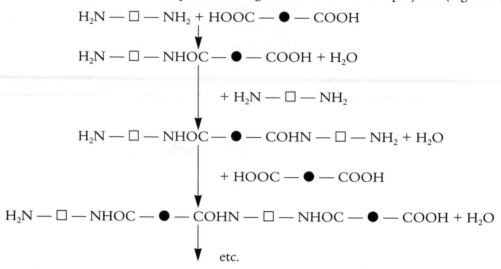

Fig. 21.3 Formation of nylon-6,6 (a condensation polymer)

Another condensation polymer is **polyester**. This is widely used for making clothes and home furnishings.

Many natural products are condensation polymers. These include starch, cellulose and proteins (see Chapter 34).

21.5 Thermosetting and thermoplastic polymers

Polymers can be divided into two groups according to the changes which occur on heating. These changes are related to the structure of the polymer.

Thermoplastics become soft and mouldable on heating without undergoing any significant chemical changes. On cooling they harden again. This melting and hardening can be repeated over and over again. Recycling thermoplastic polymers is relatively simple.

Thermosetting polymers or thermosets are resistant to high temperatures and cannot be melted. They decompose before they melt and, therefore, cannot be softened and remoulded. They are insoluble and swell only slightly in organic solvents. They are usually harder than thermoplastic polymers.

There is a difference in the structure of thermoplastic and thermosetting polymers. A simple representation of the two types of polymer are shown in Fig. 21.4. In a

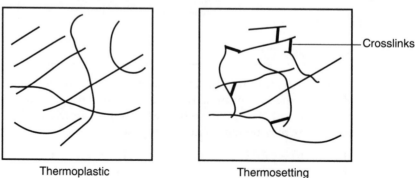

Thermoplastic   Thermosetting

Fig. 21.4 The two types of polymer

thermoplastic polymer the chains are not linked. On melting, the chains are able to move freely over each other. In a thermosetting polymer there are strong links between the polymer chains. The rigid structure is not easily broken down.

Natural rubber consists of chains of polymer molecules. It is naturally soft and sticky. It can be hardened by a process of vulcanization where sulphur atoms link the chains by cross-linking. The vulcanized rubber is now hard.

Summary

Polymerization is the joining together of smaller molecules called monomers to form polymers. There are two types of polymerization – addition polymerization and condensation polymerization.

Addition polymerization involves joining the monomers together without losing any atoms. Making poly(ethene) from ethene is an example of addition polymerization. The monomer contains a double bond between two carbon atoms. This double bond is lost when the polymer is formed.

Condensation polymerization requires a series of condensation reactions. Polyester and nylon are examples of condensation polymerization.

Polymers can be classified as thermoplastic and thermosetting according to the changes which occur on heating. These changes are related to the structure of the polymer.

Chapter 22
Ammonia, nitric acid and fertilizers

22.1 Introduction

Nitrogen is the most important element required for healthy plant growth. It is required to build up plant proteins in stems, leaves, etc. Although about 80% of the atmosphere is nitrogen, this cannot be absorbed by most plants and the nitrogen required comes through the roots in solution. Ammonia (NH_3), ammonium compounds and nitrates formed from nitric acid are important in the nitrogen cycle (Unit 22.9).

In this chapter we will consider ammonia and nitric acid. These are important compounds in the industrial manufacture of many chemicals, including fertilizers.

22.2 Laboratory preparation of ammonia

Ammonia gas is prepared in the laboratory by heating a mixture of an ammonium salt and an alkali. For example, a mixture of ammonium chloride and sodium hydroxide could be used.

$$NH_4Cl(s) + NaOH(s) \rightarrow NaCl(s) + H_2O + NH_3(g)$$
ammonium chloride + sodium hydroxide $\rightarrow$ sodium chloride + water + ammonia

or

$$(NH_4)_2SO_4(s) + Ca(OH)_2(s) \rightarrow CaSO_4(s) + 2H_2O(g) + 2NH_3(g)$$
ammonium sulphate + calcium hydroxide $\rightarrow$ calcium sulphate + water + ammonia

The underlying reaction taking place in each case can be represented by the same ionic equation:

$$NH_4^+ + OH^- \rightarrow NH_3 + H_2O$$

Suitable apparatus for preparing dry ammonia is shown in Fig. 22.1.

Ammonia gas is dried by passing it through a tower containing calcium oxide (quicklime).

$$CaO(s) + H_2O(l) \rightarrow Ca(OH)_2(s)$$
calcium oxide + water $\rightarrow$ calcium hydroxide

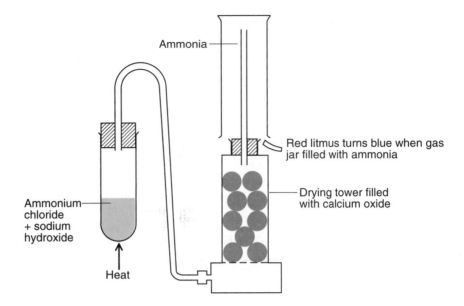

Fig. 22.1 Preparation of ammonia

Concentrated sulphuric acid cannot be used because it reacts with ammonia gas:

$$2NH_3(g) + H_2SO_4(l) \rightarrow (NH_4)_2SO_4(s)$$
ammonia + sulphuric acid $\rightarrow$ ammonium sulphate

Ammonia gas is collected by upward delivery (downward displacement of air) because it is much less dense than air and is readily soluble in water.

22.3 Industrial production of ammonia

Ammonia is produced industrially in large amounts from nitrogen and hydrogen using the **Haber process**.

1 Sources of nitrogen and hydrogen

Nitrogen is obtained by fractional distillation of liquid air (see Unit 35.2). Hydrogen can be obtained from water and also from oil or natural gas (see Chapter 20).

2 Reaction between nitrogen and hydrogen

The mixture of nitrogen (1 part) and hydrogen (3 parts) is compressed to 200 atmospheres and passed through the catalyst chamber at 500 °C. The catalyst chamber contains finely divided iron as the catalyst. About 10 per cent of the nitrogen and hydrogen mixture is converted to ammonia.

$$N_2(g) + 3H_2(g) \rightleftharpoons 2NH_3(g)$$
nitrogen + hydrogen $\rightleftharpoons$ ammonia

(Forward reaction exothermic, i.e. ΔH is negative.)

Effect of temperature

3.7g be able to relate knowledge and understanding of chemical principles to manufacturing processes and everyday effects.

The forward reaction is exothermic. If the system is cooled, the equilibrium will move to oppose this change, i.e. move to the right producing more ammonia.

Effect of pressure

From the equation it can be seen that 1 mole of nitrogen molecules reacts with 3 moles of hydrogen molecules to give 2 moles of ammonia molecules. This means that the formation of ammonia is accompanied by a reduction in the number of molecules. Increasing the pressure favours the conversion to ammonia.

Effect of concentration

If the concentration of one of the chemicals is altered, the equilibrium will move to oppose the change. This means that if the ammonia is removed from the system as it is formed the equilibrium will move to the right to produce more ammonia.

Industrial conditions for the Haber process

1. Very high pressure (about 200 atmospheres although some modern plants use pressures up to 1000 atmospheres).
2. Temperature of about 500 °C. Note that a lower temperature would cause a greater proportion of ammonia to be formed but the rate of reaction is too slow.
3. The iron catalyst enables the equilibrium to be established more quickly but does not produce *more* ammonia.

3 Removal of ammonia from the mixture of gases

When the mixture of gases leaving the catalyst chamber is cooled, only ammonia liquefies and so can be removed. The unreacted nitrogen and hydrogen are recycled.

22.4 Testing for ammonia

1. Ammonia turns red litmus blue and does not burn in air when a lighted splint is applied.
2. Dense white fumes of ammonium chloride are formed when ammonia gas comes into contact with hydrogen chloride gas (e.g. the stopper from a bottle of concentrated hydrochloric acid).

$$NH_3(g) + HCl(g) \rightleftharpoons NH_4Cl(s)$$

22.5 Properties of ammonia

Ammonia is a colourless gas with a pungent and characteristic odour (smelling salts). It turns red litmus blue and is less dense than air.

$$2NH_3(g) + 3CuO(s) \rightarrow 3Cu(s) + 3H_2O(g) + N_2(g)$$
$$\text{ammonia} + \text{copper(II) oxide} \rightarrow \text{copper} + \text{water} + \text{nitrogen}$$
$$\text{(black)} \qquad \text{(pinkish brown)}$$

A similar reaction takes place with oxides of lead and iron. This experiment can be used to demonstrate that ammonia contains nitrogen.

22.6 Industrial manufacture of nitric acid

Nitric acid is manufactured by the catalytic oxidation of ammonia and dissolving the products in water.

1 A mixture of ammonia vapour and excess air is passed over a heated platinum gauze catalyst at 900 °C. An exothermic reaction takes place producing nitrogen monoxide and steam.

$$4NH_3(g) + 5O_2(g) \rightarrow 4NO(g) + 6H_2O(g)$$
ammonia + oxygen → nitrogen monoxide + water

2 The mixture of gases is cooled and nitrogen monoxide reacts with further oxygen in the air to produce nitrogen dioxide.

$$2NO(g) + O_2(g) \rightarrow 2NO_2(g)$$
nitrogen monoxide + oxygen → nitrogen dioxide

3 The mixture of gases is then passed through a tower containing a flow of cold water. Nitric acid is produced by the reaction of nitrogen dioxide with water in the presence of oxygen.

$$4NO_2(g) + O_2(g) + 2H_2O(l) \rightarrow 4HNO_3(l)$$
nitrogen dioxide + oxygen + water → nitric acid

22.7 Properties of concentrated nitric acid

1 Action of heat on concentrated nitric acid

Thermal decomposition of concentrated nitric acid produces a mixture of nitrogen dioxide, steam and oxygen. If the gas produced is collected over water, only oxygen is collected.

$$4HNO_3(l) \rightarrow 2H_2O(g) + 4NO_2(g) + O_2(g)$$
nitric acid → water + nitrogen dioxide + oxygen

2 Oxidizing properties of concentrated nitric acid

Concentrated nitric acid is a strong oxidizing agent. When it acts as an oxidizing agent it is reduced to nitrogen dioxide and water. The following are examples of this property.

Copper

Concentrated nitric acid reacts with copper to form a blue solution of copper(II) nitrate. The nitric acid is reduced to nitrogen dioxide and water. The reaction is exothermic.

$$Cu(s) + 4HNO_3(l) \rightarrow Cu(NO_3)_2(aq) + 2H_2O(l) + 2NO_2(g)$$
copper + nitric acid → copper(II) nitrate + water + nitrogen dioxide

The reaction takes place without heating. Concentrated nitric acid reacts with all common metals except gold and platinum.

Carbon

Carbon is oxidized by warm, concentrated nitric acid producing carbon dioxide. The nitric acid is reduced to nitrogen dioxide and water.

$$C(s) + 4HNO_3(l) \rightarrow CO_2(g) + 4NO_2(g) + 2H_2O(g)$$
carbon + nitric acid → carbon dioxide + nitrogen dioxide + water

22.8 Properties of dilute nitric acid

1 With indicators

Dilute nitric acid turns blue litmus red.

2 With metals

Most dilute acids will react with some metals to produce hydrogen. Hydrogen is only produced using very dilute nitric acid. If magnesium is reacted with cold, very dilute nitric acid hydrogen is produced.

$$Mg(s) + 2HNO_3(aq) \rightarrow Mg(NO_3)_2(aq) + H_2(g)$$
magnesium + nitric acid → magnesium nitrate + hydrogen

In other cases, dilute nitric acid is still a sufficiently strong oxidizing agent to oxidize the hydrogen to water.

$$3Cu(s) + 8HNO_3(aq) \rightarrow 3Cu(NO_3)_2(aq) + 4H_2O(l) + 2NO(g)$$
copper + nitric acid → copper(II) nitrate + water + nitrogen monoxide

The nitrogen monoxide forms nitrogen dioxide in contact with air.

$$2NO(g) + O_2(g) \rightarrow 2NO_2(g)$$
nitrogen monoxide + oxygen → nitrogen dioxide

More reactive metals than copper may produce dinitrogen monoxide (N_2O) or nitrogen (N_2).

3 With metal oxides or hydroxides

Dilute nitric acid reacts with a metal oxide or hydroxide to produce a metal nitrate solution.

E.g.
$$CuO(s) + 2HNO_3(aq) \rightarrow Cu(NO_3)_2(aq) + H_2O(l)$$
copper(II) oxide + nitric acid → copper(II) nitrate + water

$$NaOH(aq) + HNO_3(aq) \rightarrow NaNO_3(aq) + H_2O(l)$$
sodium hydroxide + nitric acid → sodium nitrate + water

4 With metal carbonates

Dilute nitric acid reacts with metal carbonates in a similar way to other dilute acids, producing carbon dioxide and water. With dilute nitric acid the salt produced is a nitrate. It is not necessary to heat the mixture.

E.g.
$$CaCO_3(s) + 2HNO_3(aq) \rightarrow Ca(NO_3)_2(aq) + H_2O(l) + CO_2(g)$$
calcium carbonate + nitric acid → calcium nitrate + water + carbon dioxide

$$Na_2CO_3(s) + 2HNO_3(aq) \rightarrow 2NaNO_3(aq) + H_2O(l) + CO_2(g)$$
sodium carbonate + nitric acid → sodium nitrate + water + carbon dioxide

22.9 Nitrogen fertilizers

Nitrogen is required in large amounts by plants. It is absorbed through the roots in the form of nitrate solutions. These nitrates are required to build up proteins in the plant.

Figure 22.2 explains the circulation of nitrogen in nature, called the **nitrogen cycle**.
Nitrogen in the air is fixed in the soil by three methods:

1. Lightning causes nitrogen and oxygen to react together forming nitrogen monoxide. This nitrogen monoxide finally forms nitrates in the soil.

2. Bacteria in root nodules of certain plants (called leguminous plants, e.g. clover, peas, etc.) are able to absorb nitrogen directly from the air.

2. Certain bacteria in the soil are able to fix nitrogen directly from the air.

Nitrogen also enters the soil from the death and decay of plants and animals, from animal urine and faeces. Bacterial action converts proteins into ammonia and then, via nitrites, into nitrates.

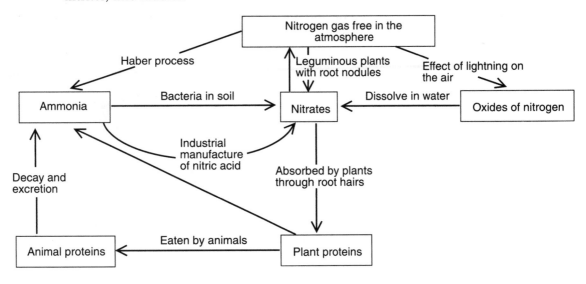

Fig. 22.2 The nitrogen cycle

Because man intervenes in the nitrogen cycle by removing crops from the soil and not allowing them to decay, it becomes necessary to add nitrogen to the soil in the form of fertilizers.

Nitrogen can be supplied to the soil in the form of **manure** or **dried blood**. These natural forms of nitrogen often improve the quality of the soil. There are natural deposits of sodium nitrate in the desert areas of Chile.

Because of the insufficient supply of natural sources of nitrogen, it is necessary to supplement these with artificial fertilizers. These include **calcium nitrate**, **ammonium sulphate**, **ammonium nitrate** and **urea**. If a compound is very soluble in water (e.g. ammonium nitrate) it is readily washed out of the soil by rain, but before it is washed out its effects are rapid. Urea is soluble in cold water but it also reacts very slowly with water to produce ammonium compounds. It is therefore suitable as a long term fertilizer.

When considering which nitrogen fertilizer is most suitable in a particular situation, the following should be considered:

1. Percentage of nitrogen in the fertilizer.
2. Cost of the fertilizer.
3. Solubility in water.

For example, Table 22.1 compares information concerning three fertilizers.

Table 22.1 Comparison of three fertilizers

Compound	Formula	Mass of 1 mole	Price per kg of nitrogen	Solubility in water
Ammonium nitrate	NH_4NO_3	80 g	40 p	Readily soluble
Calcium cyanamide	$CaCN_2$	80 g	60 p	Insoluble but reacting very slowly
Urea	$CO(NH_2)_2$	60 g	30 p	Soluble but reacting very slowly with water

1 Calculate the percentage of nitrogen in ammonium nitrate (Unit 25.9).

2 Which fertilizer is most suitable for applying in spring so that it will continue to act throughout the summer and autumn?

Obviously ammonium nitrate is not suitable because it is too soluble. The choice between the other two depends on price and the percentage of nitrogen. On this basis, urea (which contains a greater percentage of nitrogen) would be chosen.

When nitrogen fertilizers get washed into streams and rivers they can cause serious water pollution problems.

The production of fertilizers is a very large scale business. Ammonium nitrate is the most common nitrogen fertilizer used in Britain. Figure 22.3 summarizes the process used to make ammonium nitrate from ammonia and nitric acid.

In the final stage the solution of ammonium nitrate is evaporated. Solid ammonium nitrate is melted and sprayed down a tall tower. As the droplets fall they meet an upward flow of air. The fertilizer solidifies and forms small, hard pellets called **prills**. These are easy to handle and spread on to fields.

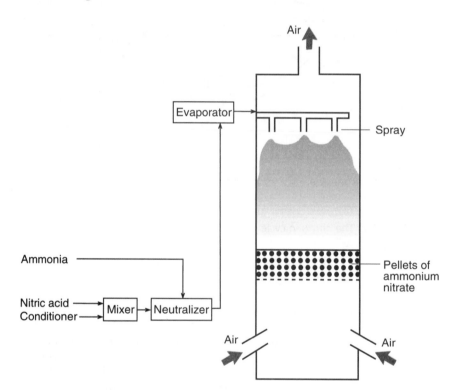

Fig. 22.3 Flow diagram showing ammonium nitrate production

22.10 Phosphorus fertilizers

Plants need phosphorus from the soil in order to produce a good root system. This is necessary before a healthy plant can develop.

Phosphorus can be supplied to the soil by **slag** or **bone meal**. Natural deposits of calcium phosphate $Ca_3(PO_4)_2$ are not very suitable because it is insoluble. However, if calcium phosphate is treated with concentrated sulphuric acid, **calcium superphosphate** is formed.

$$Ca_3(PO_4)_2(s) + 2H_2SO_4(l) \rightarrow Ca(H_2PO_4)_2(s) + 2CaSO_4(s)$$
calcium phosphate + sulphuric acid → calcium superphosphate + calcium sulphate

Calcium superphosphate contains soluble phosphates.

Ammonium phosphate $(NH_4)_3PO_4$ is a suitable phosphorus fertilizer and it also contains nitrogen.

22.11 Potassium fertilizers

Plants need potassium for the production of flowers and seeds. Potassium can be added to the soil in the form of **wood ash** or by the addition of **potassium sulphate**.

22.12 Use of fertilizers

Ready mixed fertilizers are sometimes called **NPK fertilizers** because they supply nitrogen, phosphorus and potassium.

When fertilizers are used, they are sprinkled over the soil or sometimes injected into the soil (e.g. liquid ammonia). It is necessary to monitor the pH of the soil. Soils tend to become more acidic as soluble alkalis are washed out of the soil. The use of ammonium sulphate can make the soil more acidic. **Lime** (calcium hydroxide) can be used to neutralize the soil if it is acidic. However, lime and ammonium sulphate should not be used together as ammonia gas is released.

$$(NH_4)_2SO_4(s) + Ca(OH)_2(s) \rightarrow CaSO_4(s) + 2NH_3(g) + 2H_2O(l)$$
ammonium sulphate + calcium hydroxide → calcium sulphate + ammonia + water

Summary

Ammonia is produced in the laboratory by heating together an ammonium compound and an alkali. Ammonia is a colourless gas which turns damp red litmus blue.

In industry ammonia is produced in the Haber process from nitrogen and hydrogen.

$$N_2(g) + 3H_2(g) \rightleftharpoons 2NH_3(g)$$

The process is carried out at high pressures and at as low a temperature as possible (about 500 °C) remembering that lowering the temperature slows down the process. An iron catalyst is used.

Ammonia reacts with acids to produce ammonium compounds.

Ammonia can be converted into nitric acid in industry in a three-stage process. The first stage is a very exothermic reaction where ammonia and air are passed over a heated platinum gauze. Nitrogen monoxide and steam are produced. Then the nitrogen monoxide is cooled and it reacts with oxygen forming nitrogen dioxide. Finally the nitrogen dioxide is dissolved in water in the presence of air to produce nitric acid.

For healthy plants the elements nitrogen, phosphorus and potassium are essential. Other elements are also required.

Nitrogen is required to build up healthy plants. Man-made nitrogen fertilizers include ammonium nitrate and urea. Apart from cost, the percentage of nitrogen and solubility in water must be considered.

Phosphorus is required to build up a good root system in a plant. Slag and bonemeal are widely used as phosphorus fertilizers.

Potassium is used to produce flowers and seeds in the plant.

Ready mixed fertilizers containing nitrogen, phosphorus and potassium are called NPK fertilizers.

Growing sufficient food to feed the population of the world is going to be an increasing problem. There are a number of ways of attempting to do it. One of these is to increase the use of fertilizers.

Chapter 23
Salt and chemicals from salt

23.1 Introduction

The chemical name for **salt** is **sodium chloride**. It is a very important raw material for the chemical industry. In this chapter we are going to consider where salt is available and how it can be used in the chemical industry to produce important products.

23.2 Occurrence of salt

Salt is dissolved in all the seas. In Mediterranean countries, for example, solid salt is obtained by the evaporation of sea water. Shallow lakes of salt water are allowed to evaporate using the heat of the sun.

In Great Britain there are vast underground salt deposits in Cheshire. These were formed by the evaporation of seas millions of years ago. These deposits can be exploited in two ways:

1. Underground caverns can be excavated and solid rock salt can be mined. This is used for 'salting' roads in winter.
2. A hole can be drilled down to the deposits and water pumped down. The water dissolves the salt and the salt water, or **brine** as it is called, can be pumped back to the surface.

The availability of these salt deposits in Cheshire was an important reason for the development of the chemical industries in North Cheshire and Lancashire.

Removing salt from underground can cause problems of subsidence.

23.3 Electrolysis processes using salt

In Unit 15.4 the extraction of sodium from molten sodium chloride was discussed. The by-product of this process is chlorine, which is very valuable.

Electrolysis of brine (sodium chloride solution) is an extremely important industry. There are two important alternative processes – the Diaphragm cell process and the Mercury cell process.

In both cases electrolysis of brine produces hydrogen and sodium hydroxide at the negative electrode and chlorine gas at the positive electrode. If the products are allowed to mix, the chlorine gas reacts with the alkaline solution to form sodium chlorate(I) (sodium hypochlorite).

$$Cl_2(g) + 2NaOH(aq) \rightarrow NaOCl(aq) + NaCl(aq) + H_2O(l)$$
chlorine + sodium hydroxide → sodium chlorate(I) + sodium chloride + water

Therefore the products must be kept separate from one another. The two cells – the Diaphragm and Mercury cells – are two ways of doing this.

In the **Mercury cell** (sometimes called the Kellner–Solvay cell) purified, saturated brine passes between a flowing film of mercury (the cathode) and titanium plates (the anodes) (Fig. 23.1). The cell is sloping so that the mercury runs through the cell. Direct current of about five volts is used. During this electrolysis, the brine loses about 20 per cent of its sodium chloride.

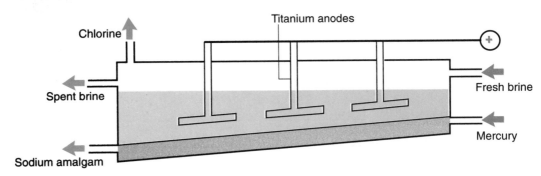

Fig. 23.1 Mercury cell

The electrode reactions are:

anode $\quad\quad\quad\quad\quad\quad\quad\quad\quad\quad 2Cl^-(aq) \rightarrow Cl_2(g) + 2e^-$
cathode $\quad\quad\quad\quad\quad\quad\quad Na^+(aq) + e^- \rightarrow Na(s)$

At the cathode the sodium ions are discharged in preference to hydrogen ions, forming an amalgam with mercury ($Na_{amalgam}$).

When the sodium amalgam leaves the cell it passes through a tank of cold water and sodium hydroxide and hydrogen are produced.

$$2Na_{amalgam}(l) + 2H_2O(l) \rightarrow 2NaOH(aq) + H_2(g)$$
sodium amalgam + water → sodium hydroxide + hydrogen

The mercury is then recycled.

In the **Diaphragm cell** the electrolysis of purified, saturated brine takes place with a titanium anode and a steel cathode. The anode and cathode are in separate compartments separated by an asbestos diaphragm, which allows the brine to pass through but prevents the products, chlorine and sodium hydroxide solution, from coming into contact.

Figure 23.2 shows a simple representation of the cell. The level of liquid in the anode compartment is kept higher than the level in the cathode compartment to ensure that the flow of solution is from anode compartment to cathode compartment.

The electrode reactions are the same as for the Mercury cell.

The solution leaving the cathode compartment contains approximately 12 per cent by mass of sodium hydroxide and 15 per cent sodium chloride. When this solution is evaporated to about one-fifth of its volume the solution contains 50 per cent sodium hydroxide and less than 1 per cent sodium chloride.

Table 23.1 compares some of the factors which would affect the choice of which cell would be most suitable for a particular purpose.

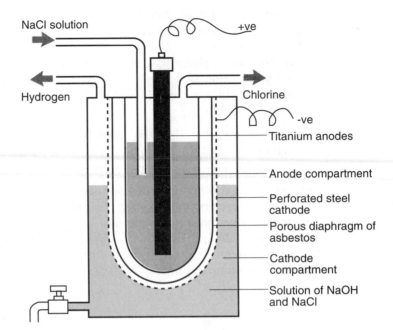

Fig. 23.2 Simple representation of a Diaphragm cell

Table 23.1

	Diaphragm cell	Mercury cell
Output (kilotonnes/year)		
chlorine	100	250
sodium hydroxide	113	282
Quantity of electricity required (kW/tonne Cl_2)	3000	3550
Cost of plant construction	Relatively simple and inexpensive	Expensive to build and provide mercury
Operating the cell	Frequent replacement of diaphragms necessary	Mercury potentially hazardous. Must all be recovered from effluent for economic and environmental reasons
Product quality	Product contains sodium chloride	High purity product

23.4 Uses of chlorine and sodium hydroxide

About 30 per cent of the chlorine produced is used to make the polymer PVC (see Table 21.1). This is used for electric wire insulation, floor coverings, clothing, etc. The chloroethene (vinyl chloride) produced during this process is extremely toxic and must be handled with the greatest of care.

About 20 per cent of the chlorine produced is used to make solvents. Tetrachloroethene and 1,1,1-trichloroethane are used as solvents in the dry cleaning of clothing.

Other uses include treatment of water and production of chemicals. Household bleach contains sodium chlorate(I) (sodium hypochlorite) and is produced by mixing chlorine and sodium hydroxide solution.

Sodium hydroxide has a wide range of uses. These include the manufacture of soap (see Unit 30.5), sodium compounds, rayon, paper pulp and organic chemicals, and purification of aluminium ores for aluminium extraction (see Unit 15.3).

Hydrogen is also produced in the electrolysis of brine.

23.5 Manufacture of sodium carbonate

Sodium carbonate can be manufactured by the **Solvay process**. Ammoniacal brine (made by saturating a concentrated solution of sodium chloride with ammonia) descends a large tower called the carbonator in which there is an upward flow of carbon dioxide under pressure. Sodium hydrogencarbonate precipitates in the lower part of the tower.

$$NH_3(g) + CO_2(g) + H_2O(l) \rightarrow NH_4HCO_3(aq)$$
ammonia + carbon dioxide + water → ammonium hydrogencarbonate

$$NH_4HCO_3(aq) + NaCl(aq) \rightarrow NaHCO_3(s) + NH_4Cl(aq)$$
ammonium hydrogencarbonate + sodium chloride → sodium hydrogencarbonate
+ ammonium chloride

After filtration and washing to remove ammonium compounds, the sodium hydrogencarbonate is heated to convert it to sodium carbonate.

$$2NaHCO_3(s) \rightarrow Na_2CO_3(s) + H_2O(g) + CO_2(g)$$
sodium hydrogencarbonate → sodium carbonate + water + carbon dioxide

This process is efficient in that the raw materials (salt and limestone) are inexpensive and certain by-products can be recycled.

Sodium carbonate is used in the manufacture of glass, and in the softening of water (see Unit 30.4).

Summary

Salt (sodium chloride) is an important raw material for the chemical industry. Cheshire is an important source of salt.

Electrolysis of molten sodium chloride produces sodium and chlorine.

Electrolysis of brine (sodium chloride solution) produces sodium hydroxide, hydrogen and chlorine. There are two alternative ways of doing this – the Diaphragm cell and the Mercury cell.

Sodium carbonate is produced by the Solvay process.

Chapter 24
Sulphuric acid

24.1 Introduction

Sulphuric acid, H_2SO_4, is probably the most important chemical in industry as it has so many important industrial uses. It is often said that the economic success of a country can be judged by the amount of sulphuric acid it uses.

24.2 Industrial manufacture of sulphuric acid (Contact process)

1 Production of sulphur dioxide

Sulphur dioxide is produced by burning sulphur or heating other sulphide minerals in air.

$$S(s) + O_2(g) \rightarrow SO_2(g)$$
sulphur + oxygen $\rightarrow$ sulphur dioxide

$$2ZnS(s) + 3O_2(g) \rightarrow 2ZnO(s) + 2SO_2(g)$$
zinc sulphide + oxygen $\rightarrow$ zinc oxide + sulphur dioxide

$$4FeS_2(s) + 11O_2(g) \rightarrow 2Fe_2O_3(s) + 8SO_2(g)$$
iron pyrites + oxygen $\rightarrow$ iron(III) oxide + sulphur dioxide

Sulphur dioxide is also produced by oxidation of hydrogen sulphide found in certain natural gas samples.

$$2H_2S(g) + 3O_2(g) \rightarrow 2H_2O(g) + 2SO_2(g)$$
hydrogen sulphide + oxygen $\rightarrow$ water + sulphur dioxide

2 Purification of the sulphur dioxide

The sulphur dioxide produced by these methods contains certain impurities, e.g. arsenic compounds, which if not removed would prevent the catalyst working ('poison the catalyst') in the next step.

The sulphur dioxide is passed through electrostatic dust precipitators, which remove charged particles, e.g. dust. The sulphur dioxide is then washed with water and dried.

3 Catalytic oxidation of sulphur dioxide

The important step in the manufacture of sulphuric acid is the reversible reaction:

$$2SO_2(g) + O_2(g) \rightleftharpoons 2SO_3(g) \qquad \Delta H = -385 \text{ kJ}$$
sulphur dioxide + oxygen $\rightleftharpoons$ sulphur trioxide

Effect of temperature

As the forward reaction is exothermic (ΔH is negative), lowering the temperature should cause the equilibrium to move to the right, producing more sulphur trioxide.

Effect of pressure

Two moles of sulphur dioxide molecules react with 1 mole of oxygen molecules to produce 2 moles of sulphur trioxide molecules. This means there will be a reduction in the number of molecules, and in the volume, as the forward reaction proceeds.

An increase in pressure will cause the equilibrium to move to the right.

Effect of concentration

Removal of the sulphur trioxide produced would cause the equilibrium to move to produce more sulphur trioxide.

An increase in the oxygen concentration will cause the equilibrium to move to reduce this, producing more sulphur trioxide.

Industrial conditions for the Contact process

1. Atmospheric pressure. Although an increased pressure should improve the yield, about 98 per cent of the gases can be converted without increasing the pressure.
2. Temperature of 450 °C.
3. Sulphur trioxide removed from the mixture.
4. Catalyst of vanadium(V) oxide (vanadium pentoxide) V_2O_5.

4 Absorption of sulphur trioxide

In theory, if sulphur trioxide is dissolved in water, sulphuric acid is produced. But this is not done in practice on a large scale because the reaction is too exothermic and boils the sulphuric acid produced.

The sulphur trioxide is dissolved first in concentrated sulphuric acid to form oleum (fuming sulphuric acid).

$$SO_3(g) + H_2SO_4(l) \rightarrow H_2S_2O_7(l)$$
Sulphur trioxide + sulphuric acid $\rightarrow$ oleum

The oleum is then diluted with the correct amount of water to produce concentrated sulphuric acid.

$$H_2S_2O_7(l) + H_2O(l) \rightarrow 2H_2SO_4(l)$$
oleum + water $\rightarrow$ sulphuric acid

3.10d be able to use scientific information from a range of sources to evaluate the social, economic, health and safety and environmental factors associated with a major manufacturing process.

The acid produced is very pure because all the impurities have been removed during the production.

24.3 Properties of sulphuric acid

Concentrated sulphuric acid is a colourless oily liquid which does not show any acidic properties unless water is present. A great deal of heat is produced when concentrated sulphuric acid is diluted with water. It is therefore sensible to add the acid to water (rather than water to the acid).

Concentrated sulphuric acid is hygroscopic. For this reason it is a good drying agent for most gases (e.g. SO_2).

The properties of sulphuric acid can be remembered under four headings.

1 As an acid – when dilute.

2 As a producer of other acids – when concentrated.

3 As a dehydrating agent – when concentrated.

4 As an oxidizing agent – when concentrated.

24.4 Sulphuric acid as an acid

Sulphuric acid is a dibasic mineral acid. It contains two replaceable hydrogens per molecule.

In the presence of water, sulphuric acid shows the usual acidic properties.

Dilute sulphuric acid turns blue litmus red.

Dilute sulphuric acid produces hydrogen gas with magnesium or zinc.

$$Mg(s) + H_2SO_4(aq) \rightarrow MgSO_4(aq) + H_2(g)$$
magnesium + sulphuric acid → magnesium sulphate + hydrogen

Dilute sulphuric acid produces carbon dioxide gas with a metal carbonate or hydrogencarbonate, e.g. sodium carbonate.

$$Na_2CO_3(s) + H_2SO_4(aq) \rightarrow Na_2SO_4(aq) + H_2O(l) + CO_2(g)$$
sodium carbonate + sulphuric acid → sodium sulphate + water + carbon dioxide

Dilute sulphuric acid produces salts (called sulphates) with metal oxides and hydroxides.

E.g.
$$CuO(s) + H_2SO_4(aq) \rightarrow CuSO_4(aq) + H_2O(l)$$
copper(II) oxide + sulphuric acid → copper(II) sulphate + water

Because there are two replaceable hydrogens, it is possible to form acid salts.

E.g.
$$2NaOH(aq) + H_2SO_4(aq) \rightarrow Na_2SO_4(aq) + 2H_2O(l)$$
sodium hydroxide + sulphuric acid → sodium sulphate + water

$$NaOH(aq) + H_2SO_4(aq) \rightarrow NaHSO_4(aq) + H_2O(l)$$
sodium hydroxide + sulphuric acid → sodium hydrogensulphate + water

Dilute sulphuric acid can be distinguished from other dilute acids because it is a sulphate and gives a positive sulphate test (see Unit 29.2).

24.5 Sulphuric acid as a producer of other acids

Concentrated sulphuric acid can be used to prepare nitric and hydrochloric acids.

If concentrated sulphuric acid is added to any metal nitrate (e.g. sodium nitrate) and the mixture is heated, nitric acid vapour is produced.

$$NaNO_3(s) + H_2SO_4(l) \rightarrow NaHSO_4(s) + HNO_3(g)$$
sodium nitrate + sulphuric acid → sodium hydrogensulphate + nitric acid

If concentrated sulphuric acid is added to any metal chloride (e.g. sodium chloride), hydrogen chloride gas is produced, which dissolves in water to form hydrochloric acid. Gentle heating may be necessary.

$$NaCl(s) + H_2SO_4(l) \rightarrow NaHSO_4(s) + HCl(g)$$
sodium chloride + sulphuric acid → sodium hydrogensulphate + hydrogen chloride

Both of these reactions take place because the nitric acid and hydrogen chloride have lower boiling points than sulphuric acid. (They are more volatile.) They escape from the reaction mixture in preference to sulphuric acid.

24.6 Sulphuric acid as a dehydrating agent

This is a consequence of the affinity of concentrated sulphuric acid for water.

1 Sugar $C_{12}H_{22}O_{11}$

Sugar (sucrose) is a carbohydrate and contains the constituent elements of water (hydrogen and oxygen).

If concentrated sulphuric acid is added to a sample of sugar, the sugar turns yellow, then brown, and finally black. The black solid residue is carbon, which is formed when the concentrated sulphuric acid has removed the hydrogen and oxygen. The reaction is very exothermic.

$$C_{12}H_{22}O_{11}(s) \rightarrow 12C(s) + 11H_2O(g)$$
$$\text{sugar} \rightarrow \text{carbon} + \text{water}$$

Similar reactions take place when other carbohydrates are used. For this reason concentrated sulphuric acid has to be used carefully with carbon compounds.

2 Copper(II) sulphate crystals $CuSO_4 \cdot 5H_2O$

Copper(II) sulphate crystals contain water of crystallization. When concentrated sulphuric acid is added to blue copper(II) sulphate crystals, the crystals turn white because the water of crystallization has been removed by the concentrated sulphuric acid.

$$CuSO_4 \cdot 5H_2O(s) \rightleftharpoons CuSO_4(s) + 5H_2O(l)$$
$$\text{copper(II) sulphate crystals} \rightleftharpoons \text{anhydrous copper(II) sulphate} + \text{water}$$

24.7 Sulphuric acid as an oxidizing agent

Concentrated sulphuric acid acts as an oxidizing agent in a wide range of reactions. Usually the sulphuric acid is hot and concentrated. In each case the sulphuric acid (H_2SO_4) is reduced to water and sulphur dioxide.

1 Copper

$$Cu(s) + 2H_2SO_4(l) \rightarrow CuSO_4(aq) + 2H_2O(l) + SO_2(g)$$
$$\text{copper} + \text{sulphuric acid} \rightarrow \text{copper(II) sulphate} + \text{water} + \text{sulphur dioxide}$$

2 Carbon and sulphur

Hot concentrated sulphuric acid oxidizes carbon and sulphur to carbon dioxide and sulphur dioxide, respectively.

$$C(s) + 2H_2SO_4(l) \rightarrow CO_2(g) + 2SO_2(g) + 2H_2O(g)$$
$$\text{carbon} + \text{sulphuric acid} \rightarrow \text{carbon dioxide} + \text{sulphur dioxide} + \text{water}$$

$$S(s) + 2H_2SO_4(l) \rightarrow 3SO_2(g) + 2H_2O(g)$$
$$\text{sulphur} + \text{sulphuric acid} \rightarrow \text{sulphur dioxide} + \text{water}$$

24.8 Uses of sulphuric acid

There are many uses of sulphuric acid. In the list that follows the major uses are given in order of importance.

1. One-third of the sulphuric acid manufactured is used to make ammonium sulphate fertilizer and superphosphates (see Chapter 22).

2. Sulphuric acid is used to make titanium dioxide, which is used in making paint pigments.

3. Sulphuric acid is used to make plastics and other chemicals.

4. Sulphuric acid is used to make soapless detergents from by-products of oil refining (see Chapter 30). Products include washing powders, washing-up liquids and shampoos.

5. Sulphuric acid is used to make man-made fibres such as rayon. It is also used for making dyes for textiles.

6. Sulphuric acid is used for removing the oxide coating from steel before giving the steel a coating to prevent rusting. This process is called **pickling**.

Summary

Sulphuric acid is manufactured by the Contact process. Sulphur dioxide and air are passed over a heated vanadium(V) oxide catalyst. Sulphur trioxide is produced which on dissolving produces sulphuric acid.

Apart from the usual acid properties, sulphuric acid is a maker of other acids, a dehydrating agent and a strong oxidizing agent.

Sulphuric acid is used in the production of fertilizers, paint pigments, plastics, soapless detergents and man-made fibres and in metallurgy for pickling steel.

Chapter 25

The mole and chemical calculations

This chapter is the basis of most chemical calculations that appear on examination papers. Questions based on this chapter appear frequently and provide a useful discrimination between candidates. In the Scottish Standard grade syllabus, the 'mole' concept is restricted to that of gram formula weight, and the definition of the mole as the Avogadro number of particles is deferred until the Higher grade.

25.1 Relative atomic mass

All atoms are too small to be weighed individually. It is possible, however, to compare the mass of one atom with the mass of another. This is done using a mass spectrometer. A magnesium atom has twice the mass of a carbon-12 atom and six times the mass of a helium atom.

The **relative atomic mass** of an atom is the number of times an atom is heavier than a hydrogen atom (or one-twelfth of a carbon-12 atom). Relative atomic masses are not all whole numbers because of the existence of isotopes.

$$\text{relative atomic mass} = \frac{\text{mass of 1 atom of element}}{\text{mass of 1 atom of hydrogen}}$$

The relative atomic mass is simply a number and has no units. You are not expected to remember relative atomic masses. They are given on examination papers in one of the following ways:

1. $A_r(\text{Ca}) = 40$ or   **2.** $(\text{Ca} = 40, \text{C} = 12)$

Throughout this book relative atomic masses will be shown as in **1**.

Relative atomic masses are sometimes just called atomic masses or atomic weights.

25.2 The mole

As an alternative to comparing masses of individual atoms of different elements, it is possible to consider large numbers of atoms. For example:

1 atom of magnesium weighs twice as much as 1 atom of carbon-12
2 atoms of magnesium weigh twice as much as 2 atoms of carbon-12
100 atoms of magnesium weigh twice as much as 100 atoms of carbon-12

The mass of magnesium atoms will always be twice the mass of the carbon-12 atoms, providing the numbers of magnesium and carbon-12 atoms are the same.

We are used to collective terms to describe a number of objects, e.g. a dozen eggs, a gross of test tubes, etc. In chemistry, the term **mole** (abbreviation mol) is used in the same way. We speak of a mole of magnesium atoms, a mole of carbon dioxide or a mole of electrons.

A mole provides a quantity of material that can be used in the laboratory. A mole of carbon atoms (12 grams) is just a small handful.

A mole contains approximately 6×10^{23} particles (600 000 000 000 000 000 000 000). This number is called **Avogadro's** constant (L). A very large number is consequently difficult for us to appreciate. If one were to stand on a sandy beach and look along the beach in both directions, you would not see enough particles of sand to make 1 mole of grains of sand.

It is conveniently arranged that 1 mole of atoms of any element has a mass equal to the relative atomic mass (but with units of grams).

E.g. $\quad\quad\quad\quad$ relative atomic mass of Na $\;=\;$ 23 (i.e. A_r(Na) = 23)
$\quad\quad\quad \therefore$ mass of 1 mole of sodium atoms $\;=\;$ 23 g

The mole may be defined as the amount of substance which contains as many elementary units as there are atoms in 12 grams of carbon-12. These elementary units can be considered as:

atoms	e.g. Mg, C, He
molecules	e.g. CH_4, H_2O
ions	e.g. Na^+, Cl^-
specified formula units	e.g. H_2SO_4

There are other terms that might be seen in books or examination papers:

E.g. $\quad\quad$ 1 gram-atom – mass of 1 mole of atoms
$\quad\quad\quad\quad$ 1 gram-molecule – mass of 1 mole of molecules
$\quad\quad\quad\quad$ 1 gram-ion – mass of 1 mole of ions
$\quad\quad\quad\quad$ 1 gram-formula – mass of 1 mole of formula unit
$\quad\quad\quad\quad$ 1 faraday – 1 mole of electrons

The term '1 mole of chlorine' can be ambiguous. It could mean 1 mole of chlorine atoms (6×10^{23} atoms) or 1 mole of chlorine molecules (12×10^{23} atoms).

25.3 Volume of one mole of molecules of a gas

There is no simple relationship that predicts the volume occupied by 1 mole of molecules in a solid or a liquid. However, 1 mole of molecules of any gas occupies 24 000 cm^3 (24 dm^3) at room temperature and pressure or 22 400 cm^3 (22.4 dm^3) at stp (standard temperature and pressure). This information is given on the examination paper if it is required.

25.4 Molar solutions

When 1 mole of a substance is dissolved in water and the volume of solution made up to 1000 cm^3 (1 dm^3), the resulting solution is called a **molar (or M) solution**. If 2 moles of a substance are made up to 1000 cm^3 (or 1 mole made up to 500 cm^3) the solution is said to be a 2 M solution. E.g. 8 g of sodium hydroxide NaOH is dissolved in water to make 100 cm^3 of solution. What is the molarity of the solution? (A_r(H) = 1, A_r(O) = 16, A_r(Na) = 23)

mass of 1 mole of sodium hydroxide NaOH = 23 + 16 + 1 = 40 g
8 g of sodium hydroxide is $\frac{8}{40}$ = 0.2 mole

0.2 moles of sodium hydroxide dissolved to make 100 cm^3 of solution
0.2 × 10 moles of sodium hydroxide dissolved to make 1000 cm^3 of solution

The solution produced is then 0.2 × 10 M, i.e. 2 M sodium hydroxide.

25.5 Conversion of mass (in grams) of substance to amount (in moles)

It is useful to convert, for example, 18 g of water to 1 mole of water molecules. This is because we know that there are 6 × 10^{23} water molecules in 1 mole of water but we have no idea how many particles there are in a given mass of water.

$$\text{number of moles} \quad = \quad \frac{\text{number of grams}}{\text{mass of 1 mole}}$$

E.g. How many moles of carbon dioxide molecules are present in 11 grams of carbon dioxide? (A_r(C) = 12, A_r(O) = 16)

mass of 1 mole of carbon dioxide CO$_2$ = 12 + (2 × 16) g
= 44 g
number of moles of carbon dioxide = $\frac{11}{44}$
= 0.25 moles

25.6 Conversion of amount (in moles) to mass (in grams) of substance

This is the reverse of the previous section.

number of grams = number of moles × mass of 1 mole

E.g. What is the mass of 2 moles of ethanol molecules (C$_2$H$_5$OH)? (A_r(H) = 1, A_r(C) = 12, A_r(O) = 16)

mass of 1 mole of ethanol molecules = (2 × 12) + (5 × 1) + 16 + 1 g
= 46 g

number of grams of ethanol = 2 × 46 g
= 92 g

25.7 Finding the formula of a compound

In Chapter 7 there is information to enable you to work out the formula of a compound. It should be remembered that each formula could be worked out following a suitable experiment involving weighing.

E.g. Magnesium oxide

A known mass of magnesium ribbon is burnt in a crucible in contact with air. The mass of magnesium oxide produced is found.

① mass of crucible and lid	=	20.12 g
② mass of crucible, lid and magnesium	=	20.36 g
mass of magnesium	=	0.24 g, i.e. ② − ①
③ mass of crucible, lid and magnesium oxide	=	20.52 g
mass of magnesium oxide	=	0.40 g, i.e. ③ − ①

0.24 g of magnesium combines with 0.16 g of oxygen (0.40 − 0.24) to form 0.40 g of magnesium oxide.

(This is the key statement that you must write down. It will help you and also will give you marks.)

Multiply this statement through by 100 to remove decimals and prevent arithmetical mistakes:

24 g of magnesium combines with 16 g of oxygen to form 40 g of magnesium oxide

Divide masses of magnesium and oxygen by the appropriate relative atomic masses to give the number of moles of atoms of magnesium and oxygen (see Unit 25.5) (A_r(O) = 16, A_r(Mg) = 24):

$$\frac{24}{24} \text{ moles of magnesium atoms combine with } \frac{16}{16} \text{ moles of oxygen atoms}$$

1 mole of magnesium atoms combines with 1 mole of oxygen atoms. Since 1 mole of magnesium atoms contains the same number of atoms as 1 mole of oxygen atoms (i.e. 6×10^{23}), the simplest formula of magnesium is MgO. Since these questions are very common, here are two further examples:

1 2.00 g of mercury combines with 0.71 g of chlorine to form 2.71 g of a mercury chloride. What is the simplest formula for the mercury chloride? (A_r(Cl) = 35.5, A_r(Hg) = 200)

Key statement:
2.00 g of mercury combines with 0.71 g of chlorine to form 2.71 g of mercury chloride.

Multiply throughout by 100 to remove decimals:

200 g of mercury combines with 71 g of chlorine

Divide by the appropriate relative atomic masses:

$$\frac{200}{200} \text{ moles of mercury atoms combine with } \frac{71}{35.5} \text{ moles of chlorine atoms}$$

1 mole of mercury atoms combines with 2 moles of chlorine atoms
∴ simplest formula is $HgCl_2$

2 11.2 g of iron combines with 4.8 g of oxygen to form an iron oxide. What is the simplest formula for the iron oxide? (A_r(O) = 16, A_r(Fe) = 56)

Key statement:
11.2 g of iron combines with 4.8 g of oxygen to form 16.0 g of iron oxide.

Multiply throughout by 10 to remove decimals:

112 g of iron combines with 48 g of oxygen

Divide by the appropriate relative atomic masses:

$$\frac{112}{56} \text{ moles of iron atoms combine with } \frac{48}{16} \text{ moles of oxygen atoms}$$

2 moles of iron atoms combine with 3 moles of oxygen atoms
∴ simplest formula is Fe_2O_3

25.8 Calculating the simplest formula from percentages

E.g. A hydrocarbon contains 75 per cent carbon and 25 per cent hydrogen. Calculate the simplest and the molecular formulae for this compound given that the mass of 1 mole of molecules is 16 g ($A_r(H) = 1$, $A_r(C) = 12$).

	C	H
percentage	75	25
relative atomic mass	12	1
divide percentage by relative atomic mass	6.25	25
divide by smallest, i.e. 6.25	1	4
Simplest formula (or empirical) formula = CH_4		

This may not be the molecular formula. It could be C_2H_8, C_3H_{12}, etc. – always four times as many hydrogens as carbons.

If the formula is CH_4, the mass of 1 mole of molecules is 16 g.

$$\therefore \text{molecular formula is } CH_4$$

25.9 Calculating the percentages of elements in a compound

E.g. Calculate the percentage of nitrogen in ammonium nitrate NH_4NO_3 ($A_r(H) = 1$, $A_r(N) = 14$, $A_r(O) = 16$).

$$\text{mass of 1 mole of ammonium nitrate } NH_4NO_3 = 14 + (4 \times 1) + 14 + (3 \times 16)$$
$$= 80 \text{ g}$$

Each 80 g of ammonium nitrate contains 28 g of nitrogen (it contains two nitrogen atoms, i.e. 2×14):

$$\text{percentage of nitrogen} = \frac{28}{80} \times 100$$
$$= 35 \text{ per cent}$$

This type of calculation is useful for calculating the percentage of nitrogen in a fertilizer (Unit 22.9).

25.10 Calculations from equations

This type of question appears frequently on GCSE examination papers. It is necessary to have a balanced equation. Usually this equation is supplied.

E.g. $$Na_2CO_3(s) + 2HCl(aq) \rightarrow 2NaCl(aq) + H_2O(l) + CO_2(g)$$
sodium carbonate + hydrochloric acid → sodium chloride + water + carbon dioxide

This equation gives the following information:

3.9c be able to interpret chemical equations quantitatively

1 mole of sodium carbonate (Na_2CO_3) reacts with 2 moles of hydrochloric acid (HCl) to produce 2 moles of sodium chloride (NaCl), 1 mole of water (H_2O) and 1 mole of carbon dioxide (CO_2).

Using the relative atomic masses ($A_r(H) = 1$, $A_r(C) = 12$, $A_r(O) = 16$, $A_r(Na) = 23$, $A_r(Cl) = 35.5$) we can find the masses of the substances that react together and the masses of the substances produced.

$$Na_2CO_3(aq) + 2HCl(aq) \rightarrow 2NaCl(aq) + H_2O(l) + CO_2(g)$$

$(2 \times 23) + 12 + (3 \times 16) \quad 2(1 + 35.5) \quad 2(23 + 35.5) \quad (2 \times 1) + 16 \quad 12 + (2 \times 16)$

106 g   73 g   117 g   18 g   44 g

At this stage it is worthwhile checking that the sum of the masses on the left-hand side (106 g + 73 g = 179 g) equals the sum on the right-hand side (117 g + 18 g + 44 g = 179 g). Silly arithmetical mistakes, frequently seen on examination papers, should be avoided if you do this.

The calculations now are just proportion sums.

1 Calculate the maximum mass of sodium chloride that could be produced from 5.3 g of sodium carbonate.

From the information following the equation:

106 g of sodium carbonate (1 mole) produces 117 g of sodium chloride (2 moles)

1 g of sodium carbonate produces $\dfrac{117}{106}$ g of sodium chloride

5.3 g of sodium carbonate produces $\dfrac{117}{106} \times 5.3$ g of sodium chloride $= \dfrac{11.7}{2} = 5.85$ g

2 Calculate the volume of 2 M hydrochloric acid which would exactly react with 5.3 g of sodium carbonate.

Using the information above again:

106 g of sodium carbonate (1 mole) reacts with 73 g of hydrochloric acid (2 moles)

Since hydrochloric acid is in a dilute solution it is worth remembering that:

1 mole of hydrochloric acid dissolved and made up to 1000 cm^3 (1 dm^3) produces a M solution (see Unit 25.4).
2 moles of hydrochloric acid dissolved and made up to 1000 cm^3 produces a 2 M solution.

$\therefore$ 106 g of sodium carbonate reacts with 1000 cm^3 of 2 M hydrochloric acid

1 g of sodium carbonate reacts with $\dfrac{1000}{106}$ cm^3 of 2 M hydrochloric acid

5.3 g of sodium carbonate reacts with $\dfrac{1000}{106} \times 5.3$ cm^3 of 2 M hydrochloric acid

$= 50$ cm^3 of 2 M hydrochloric acid

3 Calculate the volume of carbon dioxide (at room temperature and pressure) produced when 5.3 g of sodium carbonate reacts with excess hydrochloric acid.

Using the information above again:

106 g of sodium carbonate (1 mole) produces 44 g of carbon dioxide (1 mole).
However, 1 mole of any gas at room temperature and pressure occupies 24 000 cm^3 (24 dm^3) (see Unit 25.3).

$\therefore$ 106 g of sodium carbonate produces 24 000 cm^3 of carbon dioxide

1 g of sodium carbonate produces $\dfrac{24\,000}{106}$ cm^3 of carbon dioxide

5.3 g of sodium carbonate produces $\dfrac{24\,000}{106} \times 5.3$ cm^3 of carbon dioxide

$= 1200$ cm^3

(All measurements at room temperature and pressure.)

These chemical calculations using equations enable a chemist to calculate the quantities of materials required for a particular reaction and to calculate the quantities of products formed.

Summary

Chemical calculations appear regularly on all chemistry papers.

The relative atomic mass of an atom is the number of times an atom is heavier than a hydrogen atom (or one-twelfth of a carbon-12 atom). Relative atomic masses are given to you on examination papers.

A mole is an amount of substance which contains 6×10^{23} particles. You can calculate the number of moles of particles using the formula:

$$\text{number of moles} = \frac{\text{number of grams}}{\text{mass of 1 mole}}$$

A molar (or M) solution is a solution in which 1 mole of chemical is dissolved and made up to 1000 cm^3.

Calculations can be made using an equation. It is possible to calculate masses of reacting substances and products. It is also possible to calculate volumes of reacting solutions and volumes of gases required or produced.

Chapter 26
Rocks

26.1 Introduction

The Earth is composed of a wide variety of rocks. These rocks are themselves composed of a variety of **minerals**. In this chapter we are going to consider the three types of rock and then look at the processes producing new rocks and processes wearing away existing rocks. We will find out that there is a cycling of rocks but this cycling process is very slow.

26.2 Minerals

A **geologist** identifies the minerals present in a rock by a series of tests. These tests include:

1. Colour. There can be considerable variations in the colours of minerals. Many can have a range of colours and colour alone can be misleading.
2. Streak test. The colour of the mineral in a powdered form is helpful in identification. The simplest way of doing this is a streak test where the mineral is scratched across an unglazed ceramic tile. The tile may be called a streak plate. Different minerals produce different colours.
3. Lustre. Looking at the mineral – is it shiny, glassy, dull, etc.?
4. Hardness. Hardness is measured on Moh's scale. This is a scale of hardness from 1 to 10 using certain standard materials.

Moh's scale	Mineral	Moh's scale	Mineral
1	talc	6	feldspar
2	gypsum	7	quartz
3	calcite	8	topaz
4	fluorite	9	corundum
5	apatite	10	diamond

If a mineral can be scratched with a fingernail it has a hardness of about 2. A 2p coin has a hardness of about 3.5 and a steel penknife about 6. These tests will give the geologist a guide to the hardness of a mineral.

5. Density. The density can give some clues to the identification of minerals. Galena, for example, has a very high density.
6. Acid test. When dilute acid is added to a carbonate mineral such as calcite (a form of calcium carbonate), fizzing will be seen as carbon dioxide is produced.
7. Crystal shape. This again can be useful in identification of minerals.

Having identified the minerals present in a rock, the geologist will classify the rock according to its rock type.

26.3 Rock types

Rocks can be divided into three groups – **sedimentary rocks, igneous rocks** and **metamorphic rocks**.

A **sedimentary rock** is produced when fragments of rocks and minerals, derived from weathering existing rocks, are deposited, often in the sea or a river, and form layers. These sediments are then compressed to form a hard rock. When you look at a sedimentary rock you will often see grains which are rounded due to the effect of water wearing down the rock. This process occurs over millions of years. The layers of a sedimentary rock are often tilted, twisted, broken and even turned upside down. This shows the great forces present and the unstable nature of the Earth's crust.

An **igneous rock** is formed when the molten magma from inside the Earth crystallizes. These rocks are composed of randomly arranged interlocking crystals of a variety of different minerals. The size of the crystals is determined by the rate of cooling of the magma. If the crystallization is slow, large crystals are formed, while rapid cooling produces small crystals. There are two types of igneous rock – **intrusive** and **extrusive**. Intrusive rocks solidify within the Earth's crust and are found at the Earth's surface only when overlying rocks are worn away. Because they are formed on slow cooling, they usually contain larger crystals. Granite is an example of an intrusive igneous rock. Extrusive rocks solidify on the surface when the liquid magma reaches the Earth's surface. Because the rate of cooling is faster, smaller crystals are formed on crystallization. Basalt is an example of an extrusive igneous rock. Some igneous rocks contain tiny bubbles formed because the molten magma contained gases.

Metamorphic rocks are formed by the action of heat and/or pressure on igneous or sedimentary rocks without melting them. Metamorphic rocks are often found with present day and ancient mountain belts. This reflects the fact that heat and pressure accompany mountain-building processes. Marble is a metamorphic rock formed from limestone and slate is a metamorphic rock produced by the action of heat and pressure on clay.

Fossils, the remains of plants and animals from millions of years ago, are commonly found in sedimentary rocks and less commonly in metamorphic rocks. They are not found in igneous rocks. The types of fossil present in a rock sample can be used to date a rock.

3.6h understand the scientific processes involved in the formation of igneous, sedimentary and metamorphic rocks including the timescales over which these processes operate.

26.4 The rock cycle

Rocks are constantly being broken down and new rocks are being formed. The process is summarized in the rock cycle (Fig. 26.1). All rocks on the surface are broken down by **weathering** or **erosion**. The weathering of rocks includes the effects of repeated heating and cooling. If water is trapped in a rock when freezing occurs, the water expands forming ice. Repeated expansion and contraction, on thawing, will break even the hardest rock. Chemical action, especially with acid rain, breaks down rocks. Even the action of the wind can weather rocks, with particles of sand grinding down the surface of rocks.

The tiny fragments of rock, mixed with the remains of dead plants and animals (called humus), forms soil.

The rock cycle is driven by two energy processes. On the surface, processes are powered by the Sun's energy. Within the Earth, energy is provided by radioactive disintegrations.

3.4e know that weathering, erosion and transport lead to the formation of sediments and different types of soil.

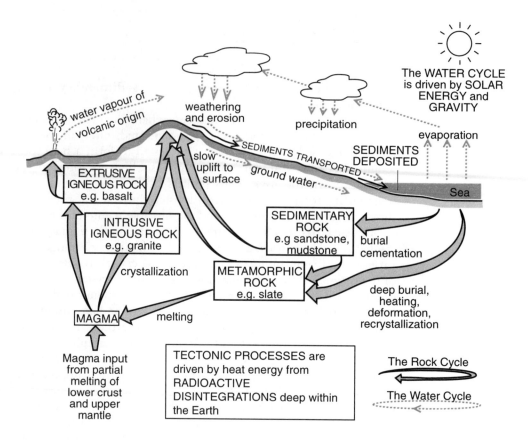

Fig. 26.1 The rock cycle

26.5 Rocks in use

Although many rocks are used in buildings and for other processes, many other materials are used which copy some of the properties of rocks. The move towards replacements for stone has largely been due to the high price of rocks. Concrete consists of crushed rock and sand mixed with cement. On setting, a hard structure results. Bricks and tiles are made from firing clay at a high temperature. They are, therefore, an artificial metamorphic material.

Summary

Rocks are made up from minerals. There are three types of rock – sedimentary, metamorphic and igneous. Sedimentary rocks (sandstone and limestone) are formed from the deposition of sediments produced from weathering and erosion of existing rocks. When these rocks are subjected to heat and pressure, metamorphic rocks are produced. Igneous rocks are produced when the molten magma crystallizes. Metamorphic and sedimentary rocks can be melted and returned to the magma.

The rock cycle explains the way that rocks can be cycled. The process is very slow, with only a couple of cycles having been completed.

Chapter 27

The structure of the Earth

27.1 Introduction

The Earth consists of three parts – the core, the mantle and the crust. These are shown in Fig. 27.1.

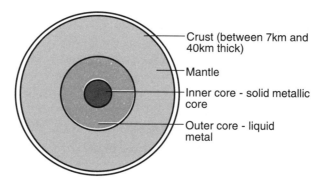

Fig. 27.1
Structure of the Earth

The outer 'skin' of the Earth is called the **crust**. This consists of large plates of rock which are floating on the mantle. Since the deepest hole drilled into the Earth is only about 13 km deep and has not penetrated the crust, information about the internal structure of the Earth must come from other studies.

The mantle is largely solid rock but from time to time this rock escapes at the surface as a liquid in volcanic eruptions. At the centre of the Earth there is believed to be a core. This is believed to be partly liquid and partly solid. Since the average density of the Earth is greater than the density of the rocks in the crust and the magma, it is reasonable to assume that the mantle has a high density.

27.2 Evidence from earthquakes

3.9f be able to describe and explain the supporting evidence, in simple terms, for the layered structure of the inner Earth.

The passage of sound waves through the Earth can give information about the inner structure of the Earth. The study of these sound waves is called seismography. There are three types of wave which can be detected: P-waves, S-waves and L-waves.

P-waves are compression waves that travel through the Earth. They are longitudinal waves. They travel quickly and are the first to be detected. They travel through solids and liquids.

S-waves are transverse waves. These can move through solids but cannot move through liquids.

L-waves are the slowest moving waves and are most important in the surface layers of the Earth. They cause much of the damage to buildings in an earthquake.

Figure 27.2 shows the traces produced by receiving P-, S- and L-waves.

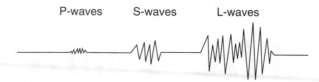

Fig. 27.2 Traces produced by P-, S- and L-waves

Figure 27.3 shows the traces produced at five detecting stations from one earthquake at A.

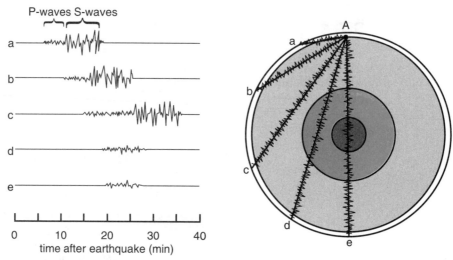

Fig. 27.3 Traces produced by five detecting stations

You will notice that the L-waves do not travel any distance and are not detected. P-waves are detected first at all stations. These are detected earlier at **a** than at **b** because the distance travelled is less. Because the traces received at **d** and **e** do not contain S-waves, we can conclude that the core must contain a liquid through which the S-waves will not pass. Finally, you may be surprised that the P-waves are detected at the same time at **d** and **e** despite the different distances travelled. The P-waves travel slower through a liquid. It is therefore reasonable to assume that the waves received at **e** arrive earlier than might be expected. This can be explained if the centre of the core is solid.

Summary

The Earth is made up of a core, the mantle and the outer crust. The structure of the Earth has largely been determined by study of the passage of sound waves through the Earth.

Chapter 28
Plate tectonics

28.1 Introduction

Until the beginning of the twentieth century it was believed that the Earth's crust had been unchanged for millions of years. Alfred Wegener, a German scientist, first proposed the theory of plate tectonics in 1912. He looked at various pieces of evidence. He looked at South America and Africa and noticed:

1. The eastern coast of South America and the western coast of Africa could be fitted together (Fig. 28.1).

2. There were common fossils in the two continents.

3. There were similar geological features in the two continents.

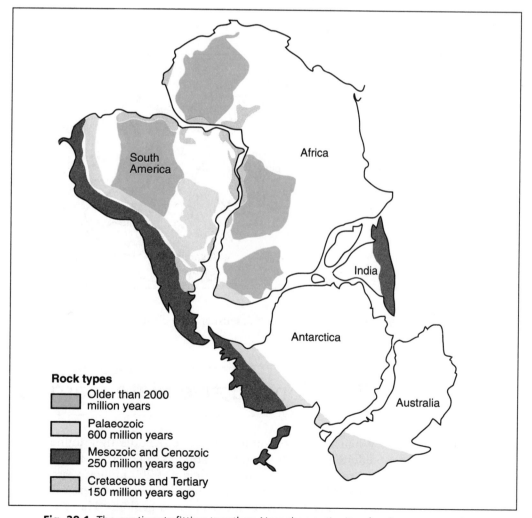

Fig. 28.1 The continents fitting together. Note the continuity of rocks across continents

3.10e understand the theory of plate tectonics and the contribution this process makes to the recycling of rocks.

It was reasonable to conclude that the two were once joined. Further investigations suggested that all of the continents were once joined together in a 'supercontinent' which he called the Pangaea (Fig. 28.2). He proposed that the continents have been moving apart because they are part of giant tectonic plates which float on the mantle. The plates move only 1–2 cm each year. Figure 28.3 shows the different plates and the directions in which they are moving and also the distribution of earthquakes. You will notice that most earthquake activity occurs on the edges of the plates.

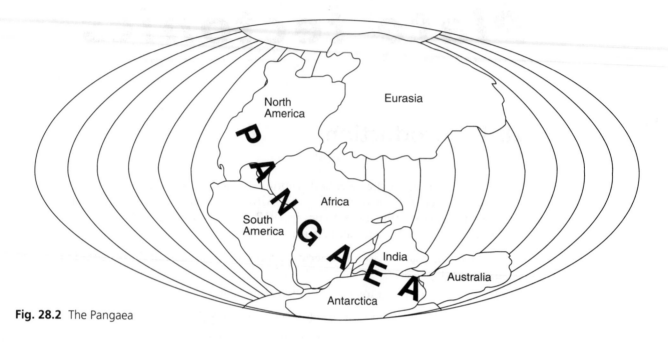

Fig. 28.2 The Pangaea

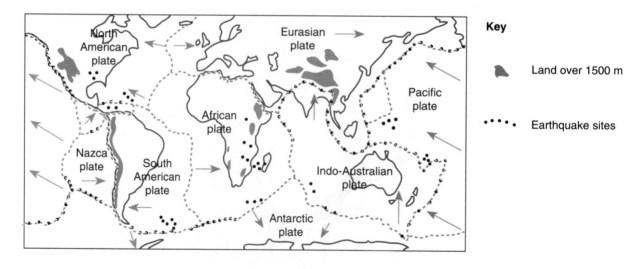

Fig. 28.3 The plates making up the Earth's crust and the distribution of earthquakes

28.2 Constructive plate margins

When scientists examined the ocean floors they found the geology to be profoundly different from that of the continents. The ocean floor is thin and much younger than the rocks making up the continents – 200 million years compared to over 3000 million years. The ocean floor is also not flat, but has a series of ridges and trenches. All of the data was considered by the American geologist Harry Hess in 1960 and he put forward the idea of the sea floor spreading. New rocks were being created as the convection currents brought magma to the surface. This caused the plates to move apart (Fig. 28.4). This is called a constructive plate margin as new rocks are being produced. A constructive plate margin exists in the Atlantic Ocean.

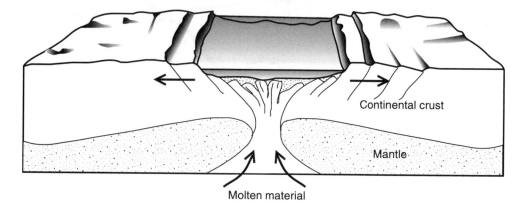

Fig. 28.4
Constructive plate margins

28.3 Collisions between plates

When plates collide the result depends upon the different densities of the plates. Typical densities are:

> continental crust 2.7 g/cm³
> oceanic crust 2.95 g/cm³
> upper mantle 3.3 g/cm³

If a continental plate and an oceanic plate collide (Fig. 28.5), the oceanic plate dips below the continental plate and rejoins the magma. An example of this occurs in South America where the Pacific Ocean bed dips beneath South America. This occurs because the oceanic crust is denser than the continental crust. This is called a destructive plate margin.

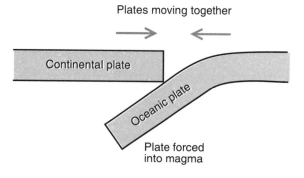

Fig. 28.5
Destructive plate margins

Where two continents collide, i.e. two plates with the same density, crumpling or folding occurs. A fold mountain chain is produced. The Himalayas mountain chain was produced when the Indian and Eurasian plates collided.

28.4 Earthquakes

Earthquakes often occur where two plates rub against each other (Fig. 28.6). An example of this is the San Andreas Fault in the U.S.A. where the Pacific and American Plates are rubbing together. Along this fault there are about 300 earthquakes each year, fortunately many are very slight.

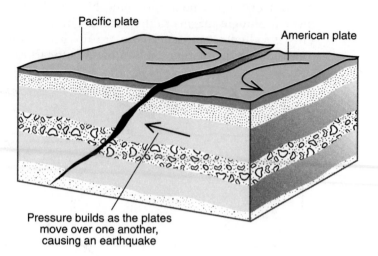

Fig. 28.6
Earthquakes caused
by plates rubbing
together

The strength of an earthquake is measured on the Richter scale. This is a logarithmic scale. This means that an earthquake measuring seven on the Richter scale is 10 times greater than one measuring six, 100 times greater than one measuring five, 1000 times greater than one measuring four, and so on.

Summary

Many observable geological features on the Earth can be explained by the theory of plate tectonics. This theory proposes that large plates float on the magma and are constantly moving. The shape of the planet is therefore constantly changing.

New rocks are produced below the oceans at constructive plate margins. At destructive plate margins, where continental and oceanic plates collide, the oceanic plate is pushed back into the magma. Mountain chains are produced where two continental plates collide. Earthquakes often occur where two plates rub together.

Chapter 29
Qualitative analysis

29.1 Introduction

Being able to identify simple inorganic substances by carrying out simple chemical reactions is an important skill that you should master in your GCSE Chemistry course. Often questions are set on this work on theory papers. This chapter will therefore be useful to you in preparing for both the theory and practical parts of your examination.

29.2 Tests for anions (negative ions)

Carbonate (CO_3^{2-})

When dilute hydrochloric acid is added to a carbonate, carbon dioxide gas is produced. No heat is required. The carbon dioxide turns limewater milky.

E.g. $Na_2CO_3(s) + 2HCl(aq) \rightarrow 2NaCl(aq) + H_2O(l) + CO_2(g)$
sodium carbonate + hydrochloric acid $\rightarrow$ sodium chloride + water + carbon dioxide

Hydrogencarbonate (HCO_3^-)

Hydrogencarbonates behave in a similar way to carbonates with dilute hydrochloric acid.

When a solution of a hydrogencarbonate is heated, carbon dioxide is produced.

E.g. $2NaHCO_3(aq) \rightarrow Na_2CO_3(aq) + H_2O(l) + CO_2(g)$
sodium hydrogencarbonate $\rightarrow$ sodium carbonate + water + carbon dioxide

Chloride (Cl^-)

When a chloride is treated with concentrated sulphuric acid, a colourless gas is produced. This gas (hydrogen chloride) forms steamy fumes in moist air and forms dense white fumes when mixed with ammonia gas.

$NH_3(g) + HCl(g) \rightleftharpoons NH_4Cl(s)$
ammonia + hydrogen chloride $\rightleftharpoons$ ammonium chloride

If a chloride is mixed with manganese(IV) oxide and concentrated sulphuric acid added, the chloride and acid react as above to give HCl. This reacts with the manganese(IV) oxide when the mixture is warmed and a greenish-yellow gas is produced. This gas is chlorine and it turns blue litmus red and then bleaches it.

$$MnO_2(s) + 4HCl(aq) \rightarrow MnCl_2(aq) + 2H_2O(l) + Cl_2(g)$$
manganese(IV) oxide + hydrochloric acid $\rightarrow$ manganese(II) chloride + water + chlorine

When a solution of a chloride is acidified with dilute nitric acid and silver nitrate solution added, a white precipitate of silver chloride is formed immediately. This precipitate turns purple in sunlight and dissolves completely in concentrated ammonia solution.

E.g $$NaCl(aq) + AgNO_3(aq) \rightarrow AgCl(s) + NaNO_3(aq)$$
sodium chloride + silver nitrate $\rightarrow$ silver chloride + sodium nitrate

Bromide (Br⁻)

When a solution of a bromide is acidified with dilute nitric acid and silver nitrate solution added, a creamish precipitate of silver bromide is formed immediately. This precipitate dissolves partially in concentrated ammonia solution.

E.g. $$NaBr(aq) + AgNO_3(aq) \rightarrow AgBr(s) + NaNO_3(aq)$$
sodium bromide + silver nitrate $\rightarrow$ silver bromide + sodium nitrate

Iodide (I⁻)

When a solution of an iodide is acidified with dilute nitric acid and silver nitrate solution added, a yellow precipitate of silver iodide is formed immediately. This precipitate is insoluble in ammonia solution.

E.g. $$NaI(aq) + AgNO_3(aq) \rightarrow AgI(s) + NaNO_3(aq)$$
sodium iodide + silver nitrate $\rightarrow$ silver iodide + sodium nitrate

Sulphate (SO₄²⁻)

When dilute hydrochloric acid and barium chloride solution are added to a solution of a sulphate, a white precipitate of barium sulphate is formed immediately.

E.g. $$Na_2SO_4(aq) + BaCl_2(aq) \rightarrow BaSO_4(s) + 2NaCl(aq)$$
sodium sulphate + barium chloride $\rightarrow$ barium sulphate + sodium chloride

Nitrate (NO₃⁻)

There are two tests that can be used to test for a nitrate in solution:

1 Sodium hydroxide solution is added to a suspected nitrate and aluminium powder is added. (Sometimes **Devarda's alloy** is used in place of aluminium. This is an alloy containing aluminium that reacts more slowly than pure aluminium.) The mixture is warmed and hydrogen is produced. If a suspected nitrate is added, it will be reduced to ammonia gas. This will turn red litmus paper blue.

$$3NO_3^-(aq) + 8Al(s) + 5OH^-(aq) + 2H_2O(l) \rightarrow 3NH_3(g) + 8AlO_2^-(aq)$$
nitrate ions + aluminium + hydroxide ions + water $\rightarrow$ ammonia + aluminate ions

2 An equal volume of iron(II) sulphate solution (acidified with dilute sulphuric acid) is added to a suspected nitrate in a test tube. Concentrated sulphuric acid is poured carefully down the inside of the test tube so that if forms a separate sulphuric acid layer below the aqueous layer. (This is because concentrated sulphuric acid is denser than water or aqueous solutions.) If a nitrate is present a brown ring forms at the junction of the two layers. The brown substance is $FeSO_4 \cdot NO$, produced by the reduction of nitrate to nitrogen monoxide by iron(II) ions.

$$NO_3^-(aq) + 4H^+(aq) + 3Fe^{2+} \rightarrow NO(g) + 3Fe^{3+}(aq) + 2H_2O(l)$$

nitrate ions + hydrogen ions + iron(II) ions → nitrogen monoxide + iron(III) ions
+ water

This is called the **brown ring test**. Nitrites and bromides can give similar results.

Nitrite (NO_2^-)

When dilute hydrochloric acid is added to a nitrite, brown nitrogen dioxide gas is produced and the solution turns pale blue. No heat is required. The nitrogen dioxide turns blue litmus paper red but does not bleach it.

Sulphide (S^{2-})

When dilute hydrochloric acid is added to a sulphide, colourless hydrogen sulphide gas is produced. The hydrogen sulphide smells of bad eggs and turns filter paper, soaked in lead nitrate solution, black.

$$Na_2S(s) + 2HCl(aq) \rightarrow 2NaCl(aq) + H_2S(g)$$

sodium sulphide + hydrochloric acid → sodium chloride + hydrogen sulphide

Sulphite (SO_3^{2-})

When dilute hydrochloric acid is added to a sulphite and the mixture is heated, colourless sulphur dioxide gas is produced. The sulphur dioxide has a pungent odour and turns potassium dichromate from orange to green. It does not change lead nitrate solution.

E.g.
$$Na_2SO_3(s) + 2HCl(aq) \rightarrow 2NaCl(aq) + SO_2(g) + H_2O(l)$$

sodium sulphite + hydrochloric acid → sodium chloride + sulphur dioxide + water

29.3 Tests for cations (positive ions)

There are three tests that can be used to identify cations.

1 Flame tests

A small quantity of the compound is taken and a couple of drops of concentrated hydrochloric acid are added. A clean piece of platinum wire is dipped into the mixture and put into a hot Bunsen burner flame. Certain cations colour the Bunsen flame. Common flame colours are shown in Table 29.1.

Table 29.1 Flame tests for identifying cations

Flame colour	Cation
Orange-yellow	Sodium Na$^+$
Lilac-pink	Potassium K$^+$
Brick red	Calcium Ca^{2+}
Pale green	Barium Ba^{2+}
Green	Copper(II) Cu^{2+}
Blue	Lead Pb^{2+}

2 With sodium hydroxide solution

If a small quantity of the compound in solution is treated with sodium hydroxide solution an insoluble hydroxide may be precipitated. If a precipitate is formed it may redissolve in excess sodium hydroxide solution. A summary of the precipitation of metal hydroxides with sodium hydroxide solution is shown in Table 29.2.

Table 29.2 Precipitation of metal hydroxides with sodium hydroxide

| Cation | Addition of sodium hydroxide solution | |
	A couple of drops	Excess
Potassium K^+	No precipitate	No precipitate
Sodium Na^+	No precipitate	No precipitate
Calcium Ca^{2+}	White precipitate	Precipitate insoluble
Magnesium Mg^{2+}	White precipitate	Precipitate insoluble
Aluminium Al^{3+}	White precipitate	Precipitate soluble – colourless solution
Zinc Zn^{2+}	White precipitate	Precipitate soluble – colourless solution
Iron(II) Fe^{2+}	Green precipitate	Precipitate insoluble
Iron(III) Fe^{3+}	Red-brown precipitate	Precipitate insoluble
Lead Pb^{2+}	White precipitate	Precipitate soluble – colourless solution
Copper(II) Cu^{2+}	Blue precipitate	Precipitate insoluble
Silver Ag^+	Grey-brown precipitate	Precipitate insoluble

If no precipitate is formed, the solution is warmed. If the ammonium ion (NH_4^+) is present ammonia gas is produced, which turns red litmus blue.

E.g.

$$NH_4Cl(aq) + NaOH(aq) \rightarrow NH_3(g) + NaCl(aq) + H_2O(g)$$
ammonium chloride + sodium hydroxide $\rightarrow$ ammonia + sodium chloride + water

3 With aqueous ammonia solution (ammonium hydroxide)

If a small quantity of the compound in solution is treated with ammonia solution an insoluble hydroxide may be precipitated. If a precipitate is formed it may redissolve in excess ammonia solution. A summary is shown in Table 29.3.

Table 29.3 Precipitation of metal hydroxides with ammonia solution

| Cation | Addition of ammonia solution | |
	A couple of drops	Excess
Potassium	No precipitate	No precipitate
Sodium	No precipitate	No precipitate
Calcium	No precipitate	No precipitate
Magnesium	White precipitate	Precipitate insoluble
Aluminium	White precipitate	Precipitate insoluble
Zinc	White precipitate	Precipitate soluble – colourless solution
Iron(II)	Green precipitate	Precipitate insoluble
Iron(III)	Red-brown precipitate	Precipitate insoluble
Lead	White precipitate	Precipitate insoluble
Copper(II)	Blue precipitate	Precipitate soluble – blue solution
Silver	Brown precipitate	Precipitate soluble

29.4 Testing for gases

Table 29.4 summarizes the tests for common gases.

Table 29.4 Summary of properties of common gases

Gas	Formula	Colour	Smell	Test with moist litmus	Test with lighted splint	Other tests
Hydrogen	H_2	✗	✗	✗	Squeaky pop splint extinguished	
Oxygen	O_2	✗	✗	✗	Relights glowing splint	
Nitrogen	N_2	✗	✗	✗	Extinguished	Forms compound with magnesium
Chlorine	Cl_2	Greenish-yellow	✓	Blue → red then bleaches	Extinguished	
Hydrogen chloride	HCl	✗	✓	Blue → red	Extinguished	White fumes with ammonia
Carbon dioxide	CO_2	✗	✗	Little change	Extinguished	Turns limewater milky
Carbon monoxide	CO	✗	✗	✗	Burns with blue flame	
Ammonia	NH_3	✗	✓	Red → blue	Extinguished	White fumes with hydrogen chloride
Sulphur dioxide	SO_2	✗	✓	Blue → Red	Extinguished	Turns potassium dichromate green. No effect on lead nitrate

Summary

There are certain tests for anions that you should be able to do. Tests for carbonate (with dilute hydrochloric acid), sulphate (with barium chloride), chloride (with silver nitrate) and nitrate (by one of the two tests given) are especially important.

Most of the common cations you will meet can be identified using a flame test. Sodium hydroxide and ammonia solutions can be used to identify certain cations.

Chapter 30
Water

30.1 Introduction

Water is a compound of hydrogen and oxygen (hydrogen oxide H_2O). It is a colourless, odourless liquid at room temperature and pressure.

The **water cycle** explains the regular supply of rain which provides the water essential for life. Evaporation of water from rivers, lakes and the sea provides water vapour which is held in the atmosphere in clouds. When the clouds cool, the water vapour condenses and falls as rain.

The water supply to our homes comes from unpolluted rivers, lakes or suitable underground sources. It is not pure but contains a range of dissolved substances depending on the rocks through which the water has passed. The water is filtered and treated with a small quantity of chlorine to kill bacteria.

30.2 Water as a solvent

Water dissolves a wide range of different substances. Water is said to be a good **solvent** and the substances dissolved are called **solutes**. Water is a **polar solvent**, i.e. it contains small positive and negative charges caused by the slight movement of electrons in the covalent bonds. Polar solvents dissolve compounds containing ionic bonds, e.g. sodium chloride. **Nonpolar solvents** (e.g. tetrachloromethane CCl_4) are poor at dissolving ionic compounds but are good solvents for molecular compounds.

A solution which contains as much solute as can be dissolved at a particular temperature is called a **saturated solution**. If any more solute is added to a saturated solution, the extra solute remains undissolved. The **solubility** of a solute is the mass of solute (in grams) which dissolves in 100 g of solvent at a particular temperature to form a saturated solution.

Generally the solubility of ionic compounds in water (e.g. potassium nitrate) increases as the temperature rises but the solubility of gases in water decreases as the temperature rises. A graph of solubility versus temperature for a solute is called a **solubility curve**. Figure 30.1 shows the solubility curves for some common solutes.

30.3 Hard and soft water

Distilled water (pure water) contains no dissolved solid impurities. It lathers well with soap. Rain water quite closely resembles distilled water.

Some water samples do not lather well with soap but form scum. These water samples are said to be hard. **Hard water** is caused by certain dissolved substances in

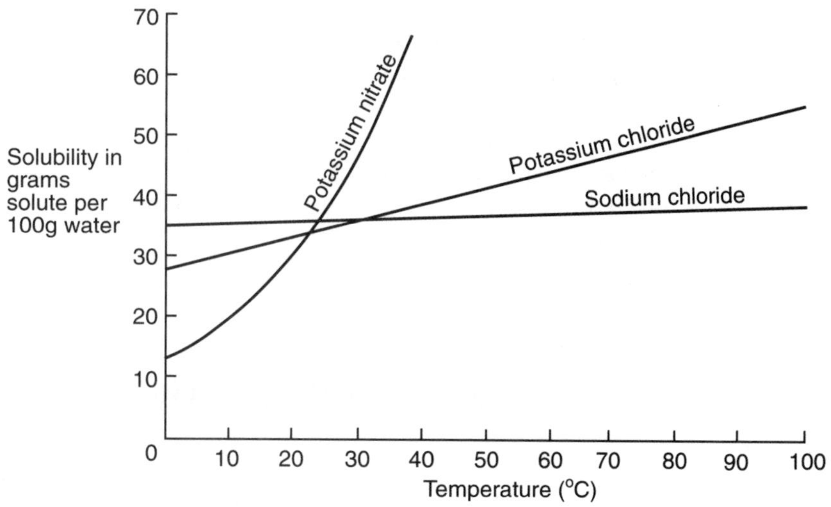

Fig. 30.1 Solubility curves

water. These substances become dissolved as the water trickles through the ground. Water (containing dissolved carbon dioxide from the air) trickling through chalk (calcium carbonate) dissolves some of the chalk, forming calcium hydrogencarbonate.

$$CaCO_3(s) + H_2O(l) + CO_2(g) \rightleftharpoons Ca(HCO_3)_2(aq)$$
calcium carbonate + water + carbon dioxide $\rightleftharpoons$ calcium hydrogencarbonate

Hard water is caused by dissolved calcium and magnesium compounds in water.

There are two types of hardness in water – permanent hardness and temporary hardness. **Permanent hardness** is caused by dissolved **calcium sulphate** and **magnesium sulphate**. This type of hardness is not removed by boiling. It has to be softened (i.e. the hardness removed) by chemical reaction. **Temporary hardness** is caused by dissolved **calcium hydrogencarbonate**.

Apart from using more soap than would otherwise be required, using hard water has other effects. It causes deposits in kettles, boilers and hot water pipes. Hard water is, however, better for brewing beer and supplies calcium to the human body.

30.4 Removal of hardness

Temporary hardness is removed by boiling because of the decomposition of calcium hydrogencarbonate forms calcium carbonate, which is insoluble.

$$Ca(HCO_3)_2(aq) \rightleftharpoons CaCO_3(s) + H_2O(l) + CO_2(g)$$
calcium hydrogencarbonate $\rightleftharpoons$ calcium carbonate + water + carbon dioxide

It is this deposit of calcium carbonate which forms the scale or 'fur' in a kettle.

Permanent and temporary hardness can be removed by adding washing soda crystals (sodium carbonate crystals).

$$Ca(HCO_3)_2(aq) + Na_2CO_3(aq) \rightarrow CaCO_3(s) + 2NaHCO_3(aq)$$
calcium + sodium carbonate $\rightarrow$ calcium carbonate + sodium
hydrogencarbonate   hydrogencarbonate

$$CaSO_4(aq) + Na_2CO_3(aq) \rightarrow CaCO_3(s) + Na_2SO_4(aq)$$
calcium sulphate + sodium carbonate $\rightarrow$ calcium carbonate + sodium sulphate

$$MgSO_4(aq) + Na_2CO_3(aq) \rightarrow MgCO_3(s) + Na_2SO_4(aq)$$
magnesium sulphate + sodium carbonate $\rightarrow$ magnesium carbonate + sodium sulphate

In each case the calcium or magnesium ions in solution are precipitated and no longer cause problems. Other substances, e.g. calcium hydroxide, 'Calgon' (sodium metaphosphate) and sodium sesquicarbonate, work in a similar way by precipitating the substances which cause hardness. Sodium sesquicarbonate is better than sodium carbonate for household use because it is less alkaline.

Hardness can be removed by using an **ion exchange column**. A column is filled with a suitable resin in small granules. The resin contains an excess of sodium ions. When the hard water passes through the column, the calcium and magnesium ions in the water (causing hardness) are exchanged for sodium ions. When the sodium ions on the column have all been removed, the column is recharged.

30.5 Soaps and soapless detergents

Soap is produced by treating vegetable or animal fats with concentrated sodium hydroxide solution, and precipitating the soap with salt solution. This reaction is an example of **saponification**.

Soapless detergents are produced from residues from crude oil distillation (see Unit 20.8). These hydrocarbons are treated with concentrated sulphuric acid.

Soap and soapless detergent molecules are very similar in structure despite the different methods of production. Both have a long hydrocarbon chain (e.g. $C_{17}H_{35}$—) attached to an ionic group (—CO_2^- in soap or —SO_3^- in soapless detergents). The hydrocarbon 'tail' will dissolve in fats and grease while the ionic 'head' will dissolve readily in water. The cleansing actions of soap or soapless detergents are summarized in Fig. 30.2. The soap or soapless detergent molecules are represented as 'tadpoles'. When the detergent (soap or soapless) is added to water the molecules are in clusters in the solution. The tails of the detergent molecules stick into the greasy dirt and attraction between the water molecules and the detergent molecules lifts the dirt from the fibre. Agitation of the solution helps to lift the dirt. The grease is then suspended in the solution, with repulsive forces between detergent molecules preventing grease from returning to the material.

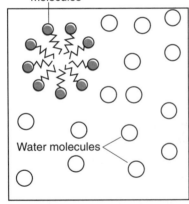 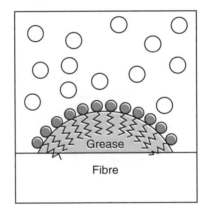 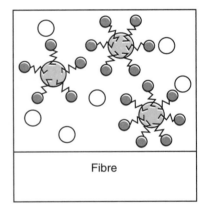

Fig. 30.2 Cleansing action of soap

Whereas soap forms scum with calcium and magnesium compounds in hard water, soapless detergents do not. This is an advantage of soapless detergents.

$$2C_{17}H_{35}CO_2^-Na^+(aq) + Ca^{2+}(aq) \rightarrow (C_{17}H_{35}CO_2)_2Ca(s) + 2Na^+(aq)$$
sodium stearate (soap) + calcium ions → calcium stearate (scum) + sodium ions

N.B. Sodium stearate is sometimes called sodium octadecanoate.

30.6 Water of crystallization

Certain substances crystallize (form crystals) with a fixed number of molecules of water contained within the crystal. This water is called **water of crystallization**. For example, copper(II) sulphate crystallizes into copper(II) sulphate crystals $CuSO_4 \cdot 5H_2O$. They are blue in colour and are said to be **hydrated**. On heating, the water of crystallization is given off and white anhydrous copper(II) sulphate is formed. Other examples of substances containing water of crystallization are:

hydrated sodium sulphate	$Na_2SO_4 \cdot 10H_2O$
hydrated sodium carbonate	$Na_2CO_3 \cdot 10H_2O$
hydrated magnesium sulphate	$MgSO_4 \cdot 7H_2O$

There is no way of predicting the number of molecules of water of crystallization in a particular substance.

30.7 Changes taking place when chemicals are exposed to the air

Some substances absorb water vapour from the air and are not appreciably changed. They are said to be **hygroscopic**. For example, copper(II) oxide absorbs small amounts of water vapour and should always be thoroughly dried before use in experiments involving weighing.

Other substances absorb water vapour to a much greater extent and the substance dissolves in the water absorbed. These substances are said to be **deliquescent**. An example of deliquescence is anhydrous calcium chloride. When left exposed to the atmosphere, the anhydrous calcium chloride absorbs water vapour from the air and after a couple of days a pool of calcium chloride solution results.

Hygroscopic substances increase in mass by a small amount but deliquescent substances increase in mass considerably when left exposed to the atmosphere.

Some compounds containing water of crystallization can lose some of this water on standing exposed to the air. This is called **efflorescence** (not to be confused with effervescence). Efflorescent compounds include hydrated sodium carbonate $Na_2CO_3 \cdot 10H_2O$ and hydrated sodium sulphate $Na_2SO_4 \cdot 10H_2O$. Hydrated sodium carbonate crystals are colourless, transparent crystals which on standing in the air turn to a white, opaque powder $Na_2CO_3 \cdot H_2O$. The mass of efflorescent compounds decreases on standing in air.

30.8 Testing for water

Water is frequently produced during chemical reactions. However, you cannot assume that any colourless, odourless liquid that you come across is water. Either anhydrous copper(II) sulphate or cobalt(II) chloride paper can be used to show that water is present in a liquid.

Anhydrous copper(II) sulphate is a white powder produced when blue copper(II) sulphate crystals are heated. When a liquid containing water is added to anhydrous copper(II) sulphate the mixture goes blue and becomes very hot.

Cobalt(II) chloride paper is produced by dipping a piece of filter paper into an aqueous solution of cobalt(II) chloride and then drying the paper thoroughly. During the drying process the paper turns from pink to blue. If a piece of cobalt(II) chloride paper is dipped into liquid containing water the paper turns from blue to pink.

Neither of these tests show that pure water is present. The presence of pure water is proved by doing melting and boiling point tests. If the liquid freezes at 0 °C and boils at 100 °C it is pure water.

30.9 Importance of water to industry

Many industries use large quantities of water. For this reason many factories are built alongside rivers or on the coast.

The water used by industry can be used for various reasons. These include:

1 As an essential ingredient in the product, e.g. beer making, whisky production.

2 For water to cool parts of the process, e.g. making electricity in a oil- or coal-fired power station.

3 As a source of energy, e.g. making electricity in a hydroelectric power station.

4 As a raw material which is removed during the process, e.g. paper making.

30.10 Water pollution

The quality of water in rivers, lakes, estuaries and the sea has become a cause for concern in recent years and now water authorities regularly check farms, factories and sewage works to ensure that no harmful effluents enter waterways. As a result we have seen considerable improvements in community health and river life. A salmon has been caught in the River Thames for the first time for centuries.

Many different kinds of effluents find their way into rivers. The following are the most important of these.

- AMMONIA is a very common pollutant. It can enter rivers in the form of excretion from farm animals, untreated sewage and fertilizers washed off farmland. When ammonia gets into a river it is oxidized by bacteria which produce first nitrites and then nitrates, and in doing so use up the very limited amounts of oxygen dissolved in water. As a result the river is unable to support fish life. The nitrates do, however, encourage the growth of plants and when the plants eventually decay the river becomes smelly and stagnant.

  A fast-flowing river will quickly dissolve oxygen from the air to overcome the loss of oxygen owing to ammonia but a slower river will be unable to recover the loss.

  Even with careful control of the amount of ammonia entering rivers there is evidence that levels of nitrites and nitrates in rivers are close to maximum permitted levels set by the World Health Organization.

- HEAVY METALS such as lead and cadmium are extremely poisonous and even small amounts can cause serious problems. Factories producing wastes containing heavy metals require complicated plants to remove them before water is pumped into rivers. The River Tame in the West Midlands had considerable pollution from the many metal-working factories on its banks, but owing to recent efforts the quality of water in the river has been considerably improved.

- DETERGENTS in rivers are also powerful pollutants. In the early days of detergents, frothing was a frequent sight on rivers as the detergents from homes and industry remained in the water for a long time. However, modern detergents are *biodegradable* – they can be broken down by the bacteria which inhabit rivers.

  Discharges from factories into the sea can be just as harmful as discharges into rivers but are considerably more difficult to monitor. In theory, because the sea is so vast it should be safe to discharge waste into it – especially if the waste is dissolved. However, this does not mean that we can discharge anything and everything into the sea. Some substances are highly dangerous even in small quantities, e.g. nuclear waste. The dumping of low-level radioactive waste from the nuclear plant at Sellafield has damaged local fishing and tourism industries, and traces of the waste have been found on the Irish coast.

30.11 Producing a safe water supply

We all use vast amounts of water at home – about 120 litres per day per person – for washing, flushing toilets, cooking, etc. Industry too uses a great deal of water: it takes 26 000 litres of water to make a tonne of newsprint, 45 500 litres to make a tonne of steel and up to 7 litres to make a pint of beer. How is all this water produced? We shall now look at the provision of safe water to homes and factories.

Production of tap water

The water supplied to our houses is not pure but it is safe to use. It is said to be **potable** (i.e. drinkable).

Water is taken from underground sources, unpolluted rivers and reservoirs and is treated before being released into the domestic system. Exposure to sunlight bleaches out any undesirable colour. Unwanted mineral salts and other solid material may be precipitated and removed by filtering. The last stage in the treatment is **disinfection**. Chlorine, a highly poisonous gas, is bubbled through the water to kill any germs present. This process is sometimes known as **chlorination**.

Recycling of waste water

After water has been used by a home or factory, it must be cleaned up before being returned to rivers or reintroduced into the water supply. This is done in a sewage works, where waste water from drains, toilets and industry is recycled. The treatment of waste water involves:

- filtering it to remove solids;
- using bacteria to break down the waste.

The water leaving the sewage works is pure enough to be used again for drinking water. In fact, water in the River Thames is used several times before it reaches the sea.

30.12 Sea water

Sea water contains a wide range of soluble substances. These have been washed out of rocks and into the sea. Salt (sodium chloride) is the most commonly extracted substance. It is obtained by evaporation of sea water, usually using solar energy.

Many other elements are present in sea water in very small concentrations. Magnesium and bromine can be extracted commercially. It is not economic to extract other elements. It has been estimated that one cubic mile of sea water contains £100 000 000 worth of gold. The cost of trying to extract this gold, mixed with 150 000 000 tonnes of other dissolved material, from such a large volume of water is greater than the value of the gold.

30.13 Extraction of magnesium and bromine

Sea water contains about 0.13% of magnesium by mass and much smaller amounts of bromine.

The extraction of bromine from sea water involves processing large volumes of water: about 20 000 tonnes of sea water are required to produce 1 tonne of bromine. Sea water normally has a pH of about 8.1 due to dissolved hydrogencarbonates,

carbonates and borates. It is acidified to pH 3.5 with sulphuric acid and chlorine is added. A displacement reaction (Unit 5.3) takes place and bromine is liberated.

$$2Br^- + Cl_2 \rightarrow Br_2 + 2Cl^-$$

Air is blown through the sea water to force out the bromine and the bromine-rich air is mixed with sulphur dioxide. The resultant hydrobromic acid and sulphuric acid, together with hydrochloric acid produced in a similar manner by traces of chlorine, are absorbed in water.

$$Br_2 + SO_2 + 2H_2O \rightarrow 2HBr + H_2SO_4$$

The mixture is then treated again with chlorine to displace the bromine which is then obtained by distillation. Finally pure bromine is obtained by fractional distillation.

To extract magnesium, sea water is run into settling tanks and mixed with an alkali, calcium hydroxide. This precipitates magnesium hydroxide.

$$Mg^{2+} + 2OH^- \rightarrow Mg(OH)_2$$

Magnesium chloride is then produced by reaction with chlorine. The solution is then evaporated to produce solid magnesium chloride. Electrolysis of molten magnesium chloride is used to produce magnesium. The melt contains sodium chloride and calcium chloride in addition to magnesium chloride and the temperature is about 700 °C.

$$Mg^{2+} + 2e^- \rightarrow Mg \qquad 2Cl^- \rightarrow Cl_2 + 2e^-$$

Summary

Water is a very important compound of hydrogen and oxygen. It is a very good solvent dissolving a wide range of substances. For this reason it is very difficult to get pure water.

The solubility of most solutes increases with rise in temperature.

Water that does not lather well with soap but forms scum is called hard water. Hard water is caused by dissolved calcium and magnesium compounds. There are two types of hardness. Temporary hardness is caused by calcium hydrogencarbonate. Permanent hardness is caused by dissolved calcium and magnesium sulphates.

When hardness is removed by a softening process, soft water is produced. Softening can be done by adding chemicals such as sodium carbonate crystals or by using an ion exchange column.

Soapless detergents produce a lather with hard water without forming scum. They are easier to use, therefore, in hard water areas.

Some chemicals absorb water vapour from the atmosphere and dissolve in this water. These substances are said to be deliquescent. Other hydrated chemicals lose water vapour to the atmosphere. They are said to be efflorescent.

The presence of water in a substance can be shown with anhydrous copper(II) sulphate (turns from white to blue) or cobalt(II) chloride paper (turns from blue to pink). Pure water boils at 100 °C and freezes at 0 °C.

Water pollution can cause considerable problems. These problems often involve a reduction in the small volume of dissolved oxygen in the water.

Producing a potable source of drinking water and disposing safely of waste water are extremely important for health reasons. Drinking water is treated with chlorine to kill bacteria.

Sea water is a source of chemicals. As well as sodium chloride, magnesium and bromine are extracted from sea water.

Chapter 31
Chalk, limestone and marble

31.1 Introduction

Chalk, limestone and marble are three forms of the same chemical compound – calcium carbonate. It has been estimated that there are about 60 000 000 000 000 000 tonnes of these minerals in the rocks of the Earth's crust. Large amounts of these minerals are used in industry. They are used in construction as building stone and for making cement and concrete. They are used in iron and steel making, glass making and have many other uses.

31.2 The carbon cycle

3.8g understand how the atmosphere has evolved and how its composition remains broadly constant.

Figure 31.1 shows the carbon cycle. Photosynthesis by plants produces oxygen. The processes of respiration, decay and combustion produce carbon dioxide. There is a balance which keeps the composition of the atmosphere constant.

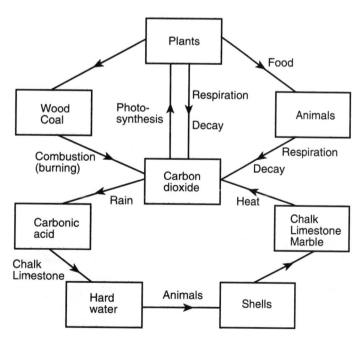

Fig. 31.1 The carbon cycle

31.3 Reactions of calcium carbonate

All forms of calcium carbonate – chalk, limestone and marble – react in similar ways.

Calcium carbonate does not dissolve in pure distilled water. However, it does dissolve slightly in water in the presence of carbon dioxide. Calcium hydrogencarbonate is formed in solution and this causes temporary hardness in water (see Unit 30.3).

calcium carbonate + water + carbon dioxide $\rightleftharpoons$ calcium hydrogencarbonate
$$CaCO_3(s) + H_2O(l) + CO_2(g) \rightleftharpoons Ca(HCO_3)_2(aq)$$

Dissolving of calcium carbonate leads to the formation of underground caverns. Stalagmites and stalactites are formed when calcium hydrogencarbonate decomposes into insoluble calcium carbonate, carbon dioxide and water.

Calcium carbonate does not easily decompose on heating. A temperature of about 900 °C is needed to decompose it. When calcium carbonate is strongly heated it decomposes, forming calcium oxide and carbon dioxide gas.

calcium carbonate $\rightarrow$ calcium oxide + carbon dioxide
$$CaCO_3(s) \rightarrow CaO(s) + CO_2(g)$$

This reaction is accompanied by a dim white light. Calcium oxide is sometimes called **quicklime**.

In industry calcium carbonate is converted into calcium oxide in a lime kiln.

When cold water is added to cold calcium oxide, a violent reaction takes places. A great deal of steam is produced and the mixture becomes very hot. The white solid remaining is calcium hydroxide, sometimes called **slaked lime**.

calcium oxide + water $\rightarrow$ calcium hydroxide
$$CaO(s) + H_2O(l) \rightarrow Ca(OH)_2(s)$$

This reaction is exothermic and the heat produced causes some of the water to boil.

When solid calcium hydroxide is added to water it forms a creamy-coloured suspension called 'milk-of-lime'. If this suspension is filtered a clear solution of calcium hydroxide is produced. This is called **limewater**.

When carbon dioxide is bubbled through a solution of limewater the solution first goes milky white and then goes clear again. The milkiness is caused by the formation of insoluble calcium carbonate. Calcium hydrogencarbonate, which is soluble in water, is formed in the final clear solution.

calcium hydroxide + carbon dioxide $\rightarrow$ calcium carbonate + water
$$Ca(OH)_2(aq) + CO_2(g) \rightarrow CaCO_3(s) + H_2O(l)$$

calcium carbonate + water + carbon dioxide $\rightarrow$ calcium hydrogencarbonate
$$CaCO_3(s) + H_2O(l) + CO_2(g) \rightarrow Ca(HCO_3)_2(aq)$$

Some of the relationships between calcium compounds are shown in Fig. 31.2.

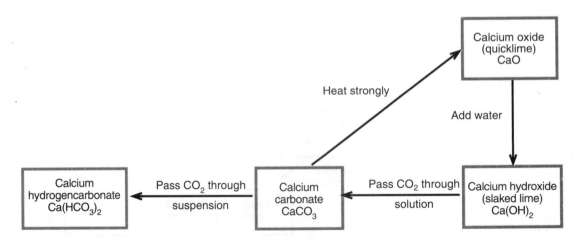

Fig. 31.2 Relationships between common calcium compounds

31.4 Laboratory preparation of carbon dioxide

Chalk, limestone and marble are attacked by acids. Carbon dioxide is a product of all reactions between calcium carbonate and an acid.

E.g.

calcium carbonate + hydrochloric acid → calcium chloride + water + carbon dioxide
$$CaCO_3(s) + 2HCl(aq) \rightarrow CaCl_2(aq) + H_2O(l) + CO_2(g)$$

Carbon dioxide can be prepared by the reaction between marble chips (calcium carbonate) and dilute hydrochloric acid using the apparatus in Fig. 31.3.

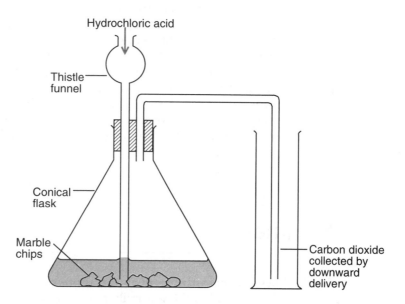

Fig. 31.3
Preparation of carbon dioxide

The carbon dioxide can be collected by downward delivery (because carbon dioxide is much denser than air) or over water (although it is quite soluble in water). A solution of calcium chloride remains in the flask.

If a pure, dry sample of carbon dioxide is required it may be passed through a solution of potassium hydrogencarbonate (to remove hydrochloric acid spray which may become suspended in the gas), dried by passing it through concentrated sulphuric acid and collected by downward delivery.

The reaction between calcium carbonate and sulphuric acid is much slower because the product, calcium sulphate, is not very soluble.

31.5 Uses of chalk, limestone and marble

Chalk, limestone and marble are very widely used raw materials in industry. Marble is used for statues. It is hard to shape but, being very hard, it is very long lasting.

Limestone is used as a building material. Blocks of limestone can be used to construct buildings. It is not, however, as resistant as brick to conditions such as atmospheric pollution.

Mortar is a mixture of calcium hydroxide (slaked lime), sand and water. It is mixed to a thick paste and used to fix bricks together when building. It sets by losing water and by absorbing carbon dioxide from the air. Long crystals of calcium carbonate form and give strength to the mortar.

Cement is a more advanced material used in building. It is made by heating limestone with clay (containing aluminium and silicates). A complex mixture of calcium and aluminium silicates is formed and this is called cement. On adding water complex reactions occur producing calcium hydroxide. The setting of cement is similar to the setting of mortar.

Cement is used with sand, small stones and water to make **concrete**. The properties of concrete depend upon the proportions of the different ingredients. Concrete is not very strong but it can be strengthened by rods of steel or steel meshing (reinforced concrete).

Ordinary **glass** is made by mixing calcium carbonate, silicon dioxide (sand) and sodium carbonate together and melting them. The resulting mixture of sodium and calcium silicates produces glass on cooling. This type of glass is used for windows. Hardened glass, such as 'Pyrex', contains boron and is called 'borosilicate' glass. This can be cooled quickly without cracking. Lead added to glass makes it very hard and suitable for making 'cut glass'.

Glass is often coloured and this is due to the presence of impurities such as metal oxides. When glass is collected in 'bottle banks' for recycling it is necessary to collect glass of different colours in different containers.

Calcium carbonate is used as a raw material in the manufacture of a number of important industrial chemicals. Sodium hydrogencarbonate and sodium carbonate are produced in the Solvay process (Unit 23.5). Calcium carbide CaC_2 is also produced from calcium carbonate. Large quantities of calcium carbonate are used in iron extraction (Unit 15.6) to remove unwanted materials from the furnace.

Calcium carbonate and calcium hydroxide are used widely in agriculture. They neutralize excess acidity in the soil.

Summary

Chalk, limestone and marble are all forms of calcium carbonate. They are the remains of sea shells deposited in the seas millions of years ago.

Calcium carbonate is decomposed on strong heating to form calcium oxide and carbon dioxide.

When water is added to calcium oxide, calcium hydroxide is formed.

When carbon dioxide is bubbled through a solution of calcium hydroxide (limewater) the solution first turns cloudy (due to the formation of calcium carbonate) and then clear again (due to the formation of calcium hydrogencarbonate). This reaction is used as a test for carbon dioxide.

When dilute hydrochloric acid is added to calcium carbonate, effervescence is seen and colourless carbon dioxide gas is produced. This reaction is used for the laboratory preparation of carbon dioxide.

Large amounts of chalk, limestone and marble are used in industry. Mortar, cement, concrete, iron and glass all require limestone in their making.

Chapter 32
Salt formation

32.1 Introduction

In Chapter 2, you will have been introduced to acids and alkalis. You will also know something of the process of neutralization which occurs when acids and alkalis react. The product of the reaction of an acid and an alkali is a **salt**. In this chapter we are going to consider the ways of making salts. When we do this it is important to know whether the salt we are trying to produce is soluble in water or insoluble, as there are different methods for producing soluble and insoluble salts. Also in this chapter we are going to consider some quantitative aspects of salt formation. Before you attempt this part of the chapter, ensure you understand Chapter 25.

32.2 Preparation of salts

Before we can decide on the method of preparation of a salt, we need to know whether or not it is soluble in water.
   The rules are as follows:

1 All nitrates are soluble in water.

2 All sulphates are soluble in water except lead sulphate and barium sulphate. (Calcium sulphate is only slightly soluble in water.)

3 All chlorides are soluble in water except silver chloride, lead chloride and mercury(I) chloride.

4 All carbonates are insoluble in water except sodium carbonate, potassium carbonate and ammonium carbonate.

5 All sulphides are insoluble except sodium sulphide, potassium sulphide and ammonium sulphide.

6 All salts of sodium, potassium and ammonium are soluble in water.

Both soluble and insoluble salts can be prepared by direct combination, e.g. iron(III) chloride, sodium chloride.

32.3 Preparation of soluble salts

For soluble salts, there are four general methods of preparation. These are the same reactions as the general reactions of an acid (see Unit 2.2).

1 Acid + metal

This method is only suitable for fairly reactive metals, e.g. magnesium, zinc and iron. The reaction is too vigorous for the more reactive metals. For metals below hydrogen in the reactivity series this method is not suitable.

E.g. $$Mg(s) + H_2SO_4(aq) \rightarrow MgSO_4(aq) + H_2(g)$$
magnesium + sulphuric acid $\rightarrow$ magnesium sulphate + hydrogen

Magnesium powder is added to warm, dilute sulphuric acid in small amounts until excess magnesium powder remains in the solution. Excess magnesium powder is removed by filtering. Magnesium sulphate crystals are obtained by evaporating the solution until crystals form on the end of a glass rod, which was previously dipped into the hot solution. The solution is then left to cool.

2 Acid + metal oxide

This reaction needs warming to speed up the reaction. The method is the same as in 1.

E.g. $$H_2SO_4(aq) + CuO(s) \rightarrow CuSO_4(aq) + H_2O(l)$$
sulphuric acid + copper(II) oxide $\rightarrow$ copper(II) sulphate + water

3 Acid + metal carbonate

This reaction takes place at room temperature. The method is again the same as in 1.

E.g. $$2HNO_3(aq) + CaCO_3(s) \rightarrow Ca(NO_3)_2(aq) + CO_2(g) + H_2O(l)$$
nitric acid + calcium carbonate $\rightarrow$ calcium nitrate + carbon dioxide + water

4 Acid + alkali

This reaction requires a special technique as both reactants are solutions and so an indicator has to be used to show when reacting quantities of acid and alkali have been used.

Acid is added to a measured volume of alkali until the indicator changes colour. The process is then repeated using the same volumes of acid and alkali but without the indicator. The solution is then evaporated to obtain the salt.

E.g. $$HCl(aq) + NaOH(aq) \rightarrow NaCl(aq) + H_2O(l)$$
hydrochloric acid + sodium hydroxide $\rightarrow$ sodium chloride + water

32.4 Preparation of acid salts

To prepare an acid salt the exact amount of acid must be added to the alkali. If 25 cm^3 of sulphuric acid is required to produce the normal salt, sodium sulphate, then 50 cm^3 of sulphuric acid is required to produce the acid salt, sodium hydrogensulphate.

$$2NaOH(aq) + H_2SO_4(aq) \rightarrow Na_2SO_4(aq) + 2H_2O(l)$$
sodium hydroxide + sulphuric acid $\rightarrow$ sodium sulphate + water
$$NaOH(aq) + H_2SO_4(aq) \rightarrow NaHSO_4(aq) + H_2O(l)$$
sodium hydroxide + sulphuric acid $\rightarrow$ sodium hydrogensulphate + water

32.5 Preparation of insoluble salts

There is only one method for preparing insoluble salts. This involves mixing together solutions of two soluble salts each containing half of the required salt. The required insoluble salt is then **precipitated**.

For example the insoluble salt lead carbonate can be prepared by mixing together solutions of a soluble lead salt (lead nitrate) and a soluble carbonate (sodium carbonate).

$$Pb(NO_3)_2(aq) + Na_2CO_3(aq) \rightarrow PbCO_3(s) + 2NaNO_3(aq)$$
$$\text{lead nitrate} + \text{sodium carbonate} \rightarrow \text{lead carbonate} + \text{sodium nitrate}$$

Ionic equation:

$$Pb^{2+}(aq) + CO_3^{2-}(aq) \rightarrow PbCO_3(s)$$

This type of reaction is sometimes called **double decomposition** and is represented by the equation:

$$AX + BY \rightarrow AY + BX$$

In order to obtain a pure sample of the insoluble salt it is necessary to filter off the precipitate and then wash it with distilled water and finally dry the precipitate thoroughly.

32.6 Quantitative salt making

In this section we are concerned with the volumes of standard solutions that react exactly together; with this information various calculations can be done.

In Chapter 25, it was explained that the concentration of a solution can be expressed in terms of molarity. Alternatively the concentration of a solution may be written in terms of moles per cubic decimetre. A 0.1 M solution has a concentration of 0.1 moles/dm^3.

E.g. What is the concentration of a solution of hydrochloric acid containing 7.3 g of hydrogen chloride in 100 cm^3 of solution? ($A_r(H) = 1$, $A_r(Cl) = 35.5$)

$$\text{mass of 1 mole of hydrogen chloride HCl} = 1 + 35.5 \text{ g}$$
$$= 36.5 \text{ g}$$

7.3 g of hydrogen chloride in 100 cm^3 of solution has the same molarity as 73 g of hydrogen chloride in 1000 cm^3 of solution.

$$\text{the solution contains } \frac{73}{36.5} \text{ moles of hydrogen chloride}$$
$$\therefore \text{ the solution is 2 M (i.e. 2 mol/dm}^3)$$

Remember: 1 mole of a substance dissolved to make 1000 cm^3 of solution produces a molar (M) solution.

A solution of known concentration or known molarity is called a **standard solution**. In volumetric chemistry, a series of **titrations** are carried out. In each titration, a solution A is added in small measured quantities, from a burette, to a fixed volume of a solution B, measured with a pipette, in the presence of an indicator. At least one of the solutions must be a standard solution. The addition of solution A is continued until the indicator just changes colour. At this stage, called the **end point**, the two substances in solution are present in quantities that exactly react.

In any titration, accuracy of measurement is very important.

32.7 Titration of sodium hydroxide with standard sulphuric acid

A solution of sodium hydroxide (of unknown concentration) is going to be standardized (i.e. its concentration found) by titration with 0.1 M sulphuric acid.

Exactly 25 cm^3 of sodium hydroxide solution is added to a conical flask using a pipette. A couple of drops of screened methyl orange (indicator) are added and the solution turns green. (Litmus is not sufficiently sensitive.) 0.1 M sulphuric acid is put into the burette and the reading on the burette recorded. The sulphuric acid is added to the flask in small volumes. After each addition, the flask is swirled. The process is continued until the solution turns colourless. The final reading on the burette is recorded.

The procedure is repeated until consistent results are obtained. Sample results:

$$\text{volume of sodium hydroxide solution} = 25.00 \text{ cm}^3$$
$$\text{volume of sulphuric acid} = 24.00 \text{ cm}^3$$

(This result would be the average of the results obtained.)
Molarity of sulphuric acid = 0.1 M.

The reaction is represented by the equation:

$$2NaOH(aq) + H_2SO_4(aq) \rightarrow Na_2SO_4(aq) + 2H_2O(l)$$
sodium hydroxide + sulphuric acid → sodium sulphate + water

If 1000 cm³ of M sulphuric acid were used, this would contain 1 mole of sulphuric acid.

$$\therefore 24.00 \text{ cm}^3 \text{ of } 0.1 \text{ M sulphuric acid contains } 0.1 \times \frac{24}{1000} \text{ moles of sulphuric acid}$$
$$= 0.0024 \text{ moles sulphuric acid}$$

From the equation:
  1 mole of sulphuric acid exactly reacts with 2 moles of sodium hydroxide
  ∴ 0.0024 moles of sulphuric acid exactly react with 0.0048 moles of sodium hydroxide

Now, 0.0048 moles of sodium hydroxide are contained in 25.00 cm³ of solution.

$$\therefore 1000 \text{ cm}^3 \text{ of sodium hydroxide solution would contain}$$
$$\frac{0.0048 \times 1000}{25} = 0.192 \text{ moles}$$
$$\text{molarity of sodium hydroxide} = 0.192 \text{ M}$$

32.8 Titration of standard sodium carbonate with hydrochloric acid

A solution of hydrochloric acid (of unknown concentration) is going to be standardized by titration with 0.1 M sodium carbonate solution.

Exactly 25 cm³ of sodium carbonate solution is added to a conical flask from a pipette. A couple of drops of screened methyl orange is added. Hydrochloric acid is added to the flask in small volumes and the volume of acid required to change the colour of the indicator is found. Again further titrations are carried out until consistent results are obtained.

Sample results:

$$\text{volume of sodium carbonate solution} = 25.00 \text{ cm}^3$$
$$\text{volume of hydrochloric acid} = 23.50 \text{ cm}^3 \text{ (average)}$$
$$\text{molarity of sodium carbonate solution} = 0.1 \text{ M}$$

The equation for the reaction is:

$$Na_2CO_3(aq) + 2HCl(aq) \rightarrow 2NaCl(aq) + CO_2(g) + H_2O(l)$$
sodium carbonate + hydrochloric acid → sodium chloride + carbon dioxide + water

1000 cm³ of M sodium carbonate contains 1 mole of sodium carbonate.

$$\therefore 25 \text{ cm}^3 \text{ of } 0.1 \text{ M sodium carbonate contain}$$
$$\frac{0.1 \times 25}{1000} \text{ moles sodium carbonate} = 0.0025 \text{ moles sodium carbonate}$$

From the equation:

1 mole of sodium carbonate reacts with 2 moles of hydrochloric acid

∴ 0.0025 moles of sodium carbonate react with 0.005 moles of hydrochloric acid

Now, 0.005 moles of hydrochloric acid are contained in 23.50 cm³ of solution.

$$\therefore 1000 \text{ cm}^3 \text{ of solution would contain } \frac{0.005 \times 1000}{23.5} \text{ moles} = 0.213 \text{ moles}$$

molarity of hydrochloric acid = 0.213 M

N.B. If phenolphthalein had been used as indicator, the volume of acid required would have been 11.75 cm³ (exactly half the volume required when screened methyl orange was used). This is because phenolphthalein is detecting the end point in the reaction

$$Na_2CO_3(aq) + HCl(aq) \rightarrow NaHCO_3(aq) + NaCl(aq)$$

sodium carbonate + hydrochloric acid → sodium hydrogencarbonate + sodium chloride

32.9 Points to remember when doing volumetric experiments

Simple volumetric experiments are frequently used in practical assessments. When doing this type of experiment accuracy is very important and the following points should be remembered:

1. Shake up all solutions thoroughly before use to make sure the solution is the same throughout.
2. Rinse out the conical flask with distilled water only.
3. The burette and pipette should be rinsed out with the solution that is to go into them. These rinsing solutions should then be discarded.
4. The last drop of solution in the pipette should not be blown or shaken out of the pipette.
5. Distilled water can be added to the conical flask during the titration.

32.10 Volumetric analysis used to determine an equation

Suppose an exactly 0.1 M solution of a metal hydroxide $M(OH)_x$ is provided together with 0.2 M hydrochloric acid. It is possible to find the value of x and then the equation from a volumetric experiment.

E.g. 25.00 cm³ of 0.1 M metal hydroxide exactly reacts with 25.00 cm³ of 0.2 M hydrochloric acid.

25.00 cm³ of 0.1 M metal hydroxide contains:

$$\frac{0.1 \times 25}{1000} \text{ moles of metal hydroxide} = \frac{1}{400} \text{ moles} = 0.0025 \text{ moles}$$

25.00 cm³ of 0.2 M hydrochloric acid contains:

$$\frac{0.2 \times 25}{1000} \text{ moles of hydrochloric acid} = \frac{1}{200} \text{ moles} = 0.005 \text{ moles}$$

∴ 1 mole of $M(OH)_x$ would exactly react with 2 moles of hydrochloric acid

So the formula of the metal hydroxide is $M(OH)_2$ and the equation is:

$$M(OH)_2(aq) + 2HCl(aq) \rightarrow MCl_2(aq) + 2H_2O(l)$$

32.11 Titration without an indicator

The end point in a titration can be found by following the pH or electrical conductivity during the reaction. For example, the titration of barium hydroxide solution with dilute sulphuric acid can be carried out using electrical conductivity to detect the end point. At the end point, the electrical conductivity is zero.

$$Ba(OH)_2(aq) + H_2SO_4(aq) \rightarrow BaSO_4(s) + 2H_2O(l)$$
barium hydroxide + sulphuric acid → barium sulphate + water

Figure 32.1 shows the apparatus required and the graph obtained. The end point is the minimum point on the graph.

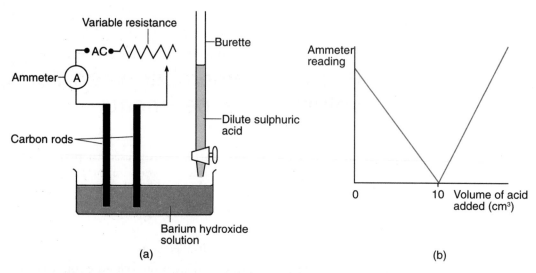

Fig. 32.1 Neutralization of barium hydroxide solution with dilute sulphuric acid: (a) apparatus to follow the reaction by measuring conductivity changes; (b) graph of sample results

32.12 To find the number of molecules of water of crystallization in a sample of sodium carbonate

Hydrated sodium carbonate has the formula $Na_2CO_3 \cdot yH_2O$. In this experiment the value of y is going to be calculated.

7.15 g of hydrated sodium carbonate was dissolved to make 250 cm³ of solution. A 25 cm³ sample of this solution was taken and screened methyl orange indicator added. 50.00 cm³ of 0.1 M hydrochloric acid was added to change the colour of the indicator.

$$Na_2CO_3(aq) + 2HCl(aq) \rightarrow 2NaCl(aq) + H_2O(l) + CO_2(g)$$
sodium carbonate + hydrochloric acid → sodium chloride + water + carbon dioxide

50.00 cm³ of 0.1 M hydrochloric acid contain:

$$\frac{0.1 \times 50}{1000} \text{ moles of hydrogen chloride} = 0.005 \text{ moles}$$

0.005 moles of hydrochloric acid react with 0.0025 moles of sodium carbonate.

Let the molarity of the sodium carbonate solution be z M.

1000 cm³ of M sodium carbonate contain 1 mole of sodium carbonate.

25 cm³ of M sodium carbonate contain $\frac{1 \times 25}{1000}$ moles of sodium carbonate

$$25 \text{ cm}^3 \text{ of } z \text{ M sodium carbonate contain } \frac{1 \times 25 \times z}{1000} \text{ moles of sodium carbonate}$$

Now,

$$\frac{1 \times 25 \times z}{1000} = 0.0025$$

$$z = 0.1$$

sodium carbonate solution is 0.1 M

$$\text{Concentration of } Na_2CO_3 \text{ in sodium carbonate solution} = 0.1 \times 106$$
$$= 10.6 \text{ g/dm}^3$$

$$\text{Concentration of } Na_2CO_3 \cdot yH_2O = 7.15 \times 4 = 28.6 \text{ g/dm}^3$$

$\therefore$ 28.6 g of sodium carbonate crystals contain 10.6 g of sodium carbonate Na_2CO_3 and 18.0 g of water ($Na_2CO_3 = 106$, $H_2O = 18$)

0.1 moles of sodium carbonate combine with 1 mole of water.

$$\therefore \text{ 1 mole of sodium carbonate combines with 10 moles of water}$$
$$\therefore y = 10$$

Sodium carbonate crystals are $Na_2CO_3 \cdot 10H_2O$.

Summary

A salt is formed when all or part of the replaceable hydrogen is replaced by a metal.

Soluble salts are formed by reacting the metal, metal oxide, metal hydroxide or metal carbonate with the correct acid.

Insoluble salts are prepared by mixing suitable aqueous solutions. The insoluble salt is formed by precipitation and can be removed by filtration.

Accurate experiments to find the volumes of solutions of known concentration which react together are called titrations. Many titrations involve reactions between an acid and an alkali and an indicator is used to find the end point, i.e. where the acid and alkali exactly react together.

This type of question always contains the use of an equation as a central feature.

Chapter 33
Transition elements

33.1 Introduction

In Chapter 5 we saw that the elements can be arranged in order of atomic number in the Periodic Table. Elements with similar properties, and similar electronic arrangements, are in the same vertical column or group. In this chapter we are going to look a little more closely at the elements between groups II and III. We call them the transition elements. There are three complete rows:

> Scandium – Zinc
> Yttrium – Cadmium
> Lanthanum – Mercury

These elements have many similarities.

33.2 Properties of transition elements

The transition elements are generally shiny, unreactive metals which have higher densities than alkali and alkaline earth metals (groups I and II). They have higher melting and boiling points.

One property which transition elements possess is the ability to form more than one positively charged ion. For example, iron can form iron(II) ions, Fe^{2+}, and iron(III) ions, Fe^{3+}. The conversion of iron(II) into iron(III) is oxidation.

$$Fe^{2+} \rightarrow Fe^{3+} + e^-$$

Manganese commonly forms manganese(II), manganese(IV), manganese(VI) and manganese(VII). Each of these different oxidation states has a characteristic colour. For example, iron(II) compounds are usually green and iron(III) are red or brown.

The existence of different oxidation states is important in catalysis. If you look through this book for examples of catalysts you will find they are usually transition elements or compounds of transition elements. For example:

> Contact process for sulphuric acid – catalyst is vanadium(V) oxide
> Haber process for ammonia – catalyst is finely divided iron.

There are two theories of how catalysts work. One theory, which certainly explains some catalysts, is a surface theory. The reaction takes place at the surface of the catalyst. The other theory, called the intermediate compound theory, uses the idea of variable oxidation state.

Let us take the decomposition of hydrogen peroxide using manganese(IV) oxide as our example. This is the most common example quoted. The overall reaction is:

$$2H_2O_2 \rightarrow 2H_2O + O_2$$

Let us consider it in two steps. In the first step the manganese(IV) oxide is oxidized to manganese(VII) oxide and the hydrogen peroxide is reduced:

$$2H_2O_2 + 2MnO_2 + [O] \rightarrow 2Mn_2O_7 + 2H_2O$$

The second step is the decomposition of the manganese(VII) oxide to recover the manganese(IV) oxide and produce oxygen. This catalyst reaction works because manganese can exist in different oxidation states.

33.3 Why are transition elements similar?

Table 33.1 gives the electron arrangements of some of the transition elements in the first row.

Table 33.1 The electron arrangements of some transition elements

Element	Symbol	Electron arrangement
Scandium	Sc	2,8,9,2
Titanium	Ti	2,8,10,2
Iron	Fe	2,8,14,2
Nickel	Ni	2,8,16,2

You will notice that all of these transition elements have two electrons in the outer shell, the fourth shell. The differences occur in the number of electrons in the third shell, which is being expanded. The chemical properties of an element depend upon electron arrangement, but especially the outer electrons because these are the ones which are most likely to be lost and gained in chemical reactions. These elements, because they have similar outer electron arrangements, are going to have similar properties.

Summary

The transition elements are a block of unreactive, but fairly typical, metals placed between groups II and III of the Periodic Table. They form ions with different oxidation states. As a result of this their compounds are coloured and they, and their compounds, are able to act as catalysts. Their similar properties are due to similar outer electron arrangements.

Chapter 34
Natural products

34.1 Introduction

In this chapter we will consider organic compounds which are present naturally or can be made readily from natural products. We will consider carbohydrates, fats, proteins, ethanol and other alcohols, and ethanoic acid. Many of these natural products are found in the food we eat.

34.2 Carbohydrates

Carbohydrates are compounds containing carbon, hydrogen and oxygen. The last two elements are present in the same proportion as in water. All carbohydrates have a general formula $C_x(H_2O)_y$.

Carbohydrates may be divided into **monosaccharides** (e.g. glucose and fructose, both $C_6H_{12}O_6$), **disaccharides** (e.g. sucrose and maltose, both $C_{12}H_{22}O_{11}$) and **polysaccharides** (e.g. starch and cellulose). Monosaccharides and disaccharides are often referred to as sugars.

34.3 Tests for starch and reducing sugars

Starch produces a dark blue coloration with iodine solution. This is used as a test for starch.

Certain sugars will reduce hot **Fehling's** (or **Benedict's**) **solution** to a brick red precipitate of copper(I) oxide. These sugars are called **reducing sugars**. Examples of reducing sugars are glucose, fructose and maltose.

34.4 Hydrolysis of starch

Starch is a natural condensation polymer (Unit 21.4) with glucose as the monomer. It is stored in plants as a reserve supply of energy. It is found in the stems of plants, as in the sago palm, in the tubers of potatoes, and in the roots, as in cassava from which tapioca is made. It is also found in seeds, such as the cereal grains – wheat, barley and oats.

Starch may be broken down into simpler carbohydrates by **hydrolysis** in aqueous solution. The breakdown involves the reaction of the starch with water but unless a catalyst is present the reaction is extremely slow. The reaction can be catalysed in two ways:

1 Acid-catalysed hydrolysis

This is carried out by heating starch solution with dilute acid. The product is **glucose**.

2 Enzyme-catalysed hydrolysis

The hydrolysis reaction may also be catalysed by the enzyme α-amylase which is present in saliva. This reaction proceeds at room temperature to produce **maltose**.

Starch can be spilt up by hydrolysis. Depending upon the conditions, the polymer can be split up into single glucose molecules or pairs of glucose molecules (maltose). This is summarized in Fig. 34.1.

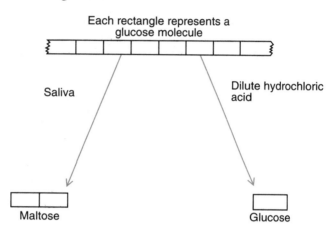

Fig. 34.1 Hydrolysis of starch

34.5 Fats and oils

Fats and oils, such as cooking oil, are chemically very similar. Fats are solid and oils are liquid. They both contain the same three elements as carbohydrates – carbon, hydrogen and oxygen. They are smaller molecules than polysaccharides and the molecules are always built from four linked units. All food fats are built up from a substance called glycerol which is an alcohol with three —OH groups. It is a colourless syrupy liquid. The glycerol molecules are able to link up with three acid molecules to form a triester. Water molecules are split out. These are condensation reactions but a condensation polymer is not possible. The process is summarized in Fig. 34.2.

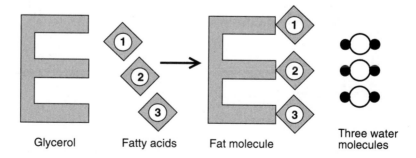

Fig. 34.2 Fat molecule made from four units

The big difference between oils and fats, apart from state, is the degree of unsaturation. An oil contains carbon–carbon double bonds. The process of making margarine from natural oils involves passing the natural oil and hydrogen over a heated nickel catalyst. The double bond between carbon atoms then becomes a single bond and the oil becomes a solid fat.

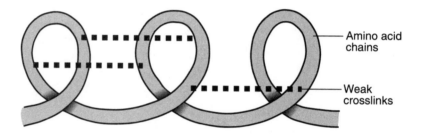

Hydrolysis of fats and oils, i.e. splitting up by boiling with alkali, produces soap.

fat or oil + alkali → soap (sodium or potassium salt of acid) + glycerol

The process is called saponification.

34.6 Proteins

Proteins differ from carbohydrates and fats and oils because they contain other elements. In addition to carbon, hydrogen and oxygen they contain nitrogen and often sulphur and phosphorus as well. They are very complicated polymers, built up from large numbers of simple units called **amino acids**. A single protein can contain as many as 500 amino acid units combined together. The sequence of amino acid units is complicated, as is the structure. A protein can be pictured as in Fig. 34.3 as coils, with the loops of the coils held in position by weak crosslinks.

Fig. 34.3 Part of a protein chain

About 20 different amino acids are found in protein foods but the different combinations of these is endless.

Egg white contains a protein called ovalbumin. When it is heated the weak links which hold the protein chains in place break and the coiled chains unfold. This is what happens when the egg white turns to a white solid. This change is called **coagulation**.

All proteins are very delicate substances and many are affected by heat in a similar way to egg white. Many are affected by acids and alkalis and also by beating them. For instance, if you beat up egg white it becomes foamy, and if you beat it up long enough, the foam becomes quite stiff. This is because the protein has partly coagulated. If the foam is now heated, more coagulation occurs. The foam becomes rigid. This is what happens when meringues are made.

34.7 Ethanol

Ethanol C_2H_5OH is an organic chemical of great importance. It belongs to the homologous series of alcohols. **Alcohols** have a general formula $C_nH_{2n+1}OH$. They may be regarded as being derived from an alkane by replacing a hydrogen atom by a hydroxy (—OH) group.

Ethanoic acid CH_3COOH (which used to be called acetic acid) is a weak acid that is closely related to ethanol. Both compounds contain two carbon atoms.

Both ethanol and ethanoic acid are widely used in industry.

34.8 Laboratory preparation of ethanol

Ethanol can be prepared by the fermentation of glucose (or any other sugar solution) using enzymes in yeast. The apparatus (Fig. 34.4) is kept at about 30 °C for several days. The fermentation lock allows the escape of carbon dioxide gas without the entry of oxygen, which could oxidize the ethanol produced.

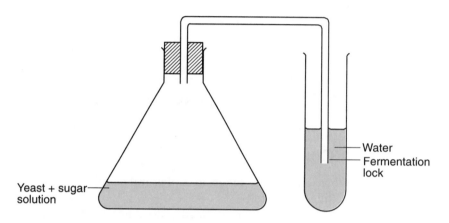

Fig. 34.4
Fermentation

During the fermentation the glucose is converted to ethanol by the enzyme zymase in the yeast.

$$C_6H_{12}O_6(aq) \rightarrow 2C_2H_5OH(aq) + 2CO_2(g)$$
glucose → ethanol + carbon dioxide

The final solution will be a dilute solution of ethanol. This process is used in wine and beer making.

A more concentrated ethanol solution can be produced by fractional distillation of the resulting solution (see Unit 1.3). This is the basis of industries producing whisky, gin and other spirits.

The production of large quantities of ethanol for industry by fermentation is possible with surplus wine production in the EEC. In Brazil factories exist for the production of ethanol on a large scale by fermentation of sugar cane for use as a petrol substitute.

34.9 Industrial production of ethanol

Ethanol is produced in large quantities from ethene; ethene is produced by cracking (see Chapter 20).

Ethene is mixed with steam and passed over a phosphoric acid catalyst at 300 °C.

$$C_2H_4(g) + H_2O(g) \rightarrow C_2H_5OH(g)$$
ethene + water(steam) → ethanol

34.10 Uses of ethanol

Ethanol is a widely used solvent. It is, however, very flammable. It is used in the manufacture of varnishes, inks, glues and paints. It evaporates quickly and its evaporation explains the cooling effect on the skin when deodorants, perfumes, etc. are used.

Ethanol is the alcohol present in alcoholic drinks. There is more and more evidence for the harmful effects of ethanol, especially on the liver. The adverse effects of ethanol on the nervous system – impaired coordination and slower responses – are responsible for many road accidents. Alcoholic drinks are very heavily taxed.

Pure ethanol cannot be purchased in shops or people would drink it and avoid taxes. We usually buy 'methylated spirits'. This is ethanol but with added methanol. Methanol is highly poisonous. Other substances are added to make it undrinkable and a purple dye is added as a warning.

34.11 Reactions of ethanol

1 Combustion

When ethanol is ignited in a plentiful supply of air or oxygen the products are carbon dioxide and water.

The ethanol burns with an almost invisible blue flame.

2 Dehydration of ethanol

This is the reverse of the reaction used to produce ethanol from ethene. It can be carried out using concentrated sulphuric acid or by passing ethanol vapour over heated aluminium oxide.

$$C_2H_5OH(g) \rightarrow C_2H_4(g) + H_2O(g)$$
$$\text{ethanol} \rightarrow \text{ethene} + \text{water}$$

3 Reaction with sodium

Ethanol reacts with sodium metal to produce hydrogen gas. This reaction is similar to the reaction of sodium with water, but slower.

$$2C_2H_5OH(l) + 2Na(s) \rightarrow 2C_2H_5O^-\cdot Na^+(\text{ethanol}) + H_2(g)$$

4 Oxidation

If ethanol is allowed to come into contact with air it can be oxidized by the oxygen in the air. The result of this atmospheric oxidation is ethanoic acid. This souring of ethanol was the original method of making vinegar.

If oxidation is carried out in the laboratory using an acidified solution of potassium dichromate(VI), it is possible to produce ethanal (an aldehyde) and then ethanoic acid.

$$C_2H_5OH + [O] \rightarrow CH_3CHO + H_2O$$
$$\text{ethanol} + [\text{oxygen}] \rightarrow \text{ethanal} + \text{water}$$

$$CH_3CHO + [O] \rightarrow CH_3COOH$$
$$\text{ethanal} + [\text{oxygen}] \rightarrow \text{ethanoic acid}$$

34.12 Ethanoic acid

Ethanoic acid is a weak acid produced by the oxidation of ethanol. In aqueous solution it ionizes slightly.

$$CH_3COOH(aq) \rightleftharpoons CH_3COO^-(aq) + H^+(aq)$$

Summary

Carbohydrates, fats and proteins all contain carbon, hydrogen and oxygen combined together. Proteins also contain nitrogen and other elements.

Cellulose and starch are carbohydrate polymers using glucose as the monomer unit. Splitting up starch by hydrolysis can produce monosaccharides and disaccharides.

Fats and oils are esters of fatty acids and glycerol. Oils tend to be more unsaturated. Addition of hydrogen to produce a fat using a catalyst produces margarine.

Proteins are condensation polymers with amino acids as the monomers.

Ethanol is produced by the fermentation of carbohydrate solutions using enzymes in yeast. Carbon dioxide is the other product of the process.

Oxidation of ethanol produces ethanoic acid. This occurs when wine sours.

Chapter 35
The atmosphere and air pollution

35.1 The atmosphere

The composition of the atmosphere remains approximately constant because of the balance caused by processes such as photosynthesis, combustion, respiration, etc. (Chapter 31).

The composition of air varies from place to place because air is a mixture of gases. The composition, by volume, of a typical sample of air is as follows:

nitrogen	78%
oxygen	21%
carbon dioxide	0.03%
argon	0.09%
helium	0.0005%
neon	0.002%
krypton	0.00001%
xenon	0.000001%

Air also contains varying amounts of water vapour. Air does not usually contain hydrogen.

35.2 Separating air into its constituent gases

Separating air into its constituent gases is a very difficult process. It cannot be done satisfactorily in the laboratory.

However, it is an important process in industry because all of the gases are valuable as pure gases. The separation involves the fractional distillation (Unit 1.3) of liquid air.

The air is first cooled in a refrigeration plant to separate carbon dioxide and water vapour. Both of these gases solidify in the cooler and the solid can be removed. If these gases were not removed at this stage, they would later solidify in the pipes and block them.

The compressed air is then allowed to expand through a small hole. This expansion causes the gas to cool rapidly. The compressing and expanding cycles are repeated until the temperature is about −200 °C. At this temperature most of the air has liquified.

When liquid air warms up, the different compounds boil off at different temperatures. Nitrogen boils at −196 °C and oxygen later, at −183 °C.

35.3 Percentage of oxygen in air by volume

An approximate value of the percentage of oxygen in air can be obtained by burning a piece of phosphorus in a fixed volume of air trapped over water.

Figure 35.1 shows the apparatus that can be used to find the percentage of oxygen accurately.

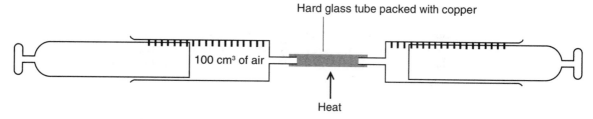

Fig. 35.1 Percentage of oxygen in air

One hundred cubic centimetres of air is trapped in one of the syringes. This air is passed backwards and forwards over heated copper turnings in a hard glass tube. The copper reacts with oxygen in the sample of air, producing solid copper(II) oxide. The heating is continued until there is no further reduction in the volume of air. The apparatus is left to cool to room temperature and the volume of gas remaining (i.e. air minus the oxygen) is measured.

E.g.

$$\text{volume of gas before} = 100 \text{ cm}^3$$
$$\text{volume of gas after} = 80 \text{ cm}^3$$
$$\therefore 100 \text{ cm}^3 \text{ of air contains } 20 \text{ cm}^3 \text{ of oxygen}$$
$$\text{percentage of oxygen} = 20 \text{ per cent}$$

35.4 Processes involving gases in the air

Table 35.1 Processes that involve the gases in the air

Gas	Combustion	Rusting	Respiration	Photosynthesis
Nitrogen	Usually not involved	Not involved	Not involved	Not involved
Oxygen	Usually necessary	Necessary	Necessary	Produced
Carbon dioxide	Formed when carbon and carbon compounds burn	Speeds up rusting but it is not essential	Produced	Necessary
Noble (inert) gases	Not involved	Not involved	Not involved	Not involved
Water vapour	Formed when hydrogen and hydrogen compounds burn	Necessary	Produced	Necessary

35.5 Air pollution

Apart from the gases normally found in air, other gases such as sulphur dioxide, oxides of nitrogen and carbon monoxide can be present. These gases can cause air pollution and are called **pollutants**.

Pollutants can cause a variety of problems to the environment.

35.6 Sulphur dioxide as a pollutant

Sulphur dioxide is a major cause of air pollution. Coal and fuel oil contain about 2 per cent sulphur. When they are burnt this sulphur is turned into sulphur dioxide. Sulphur dioxide is a colourless gas with a strong smell. It dissolves in water to form sulphurous acid.

$$\text{sulphur dioxide} + \text{water} \rightarrow \text{sulphurous acid}$$
$$SO_2(g) + H_2O(l) \rightarrow H_2SO_3(aq)$$

In the early 1950s sulphur dioxide and the smoke which is always with it caused great problems. Apart from blackening buildings and producing long term fogs, they caused serious health problems. In 1952, for example, over 4000 people died because of air pollution in London alone. Most of these deaths were due to lung illnesses, including bronchitis.

The Clean Air Act 1956 set up 'smokeless zones' in large towns and cities. Within these areas coal could not be burned and smokeless fuels had to be used. The result of this Act, and other measures taken, has been to improve greatly the conditions in towns and cities.

The burning of coal in household fires was regarded as the major problem. Even today considerable quantities of sulphur dioxide are lost from factories and power stations. The chimneys of factories and power stations are much higher than household chimneys and this gives more chance for the sulphur dioxide to disperse. Even today there are links between the emission of sulphur dioxide and **acid rain**.

35.7 Oxides of nitrogen as pollutants

About 30–40 per cent of the oxides of nitrogen in the air come from car exhausts. In the car engine nitrogen and oxygen combine together to form oxides of nitrogen. Other sources of nitrogen oxide pollution are factories and fires.

Even small concentrations of oxides of nitrogen can cause serious environmental problems. Like sulphur dioxide, oxides of nitrogen dissolve in water to form acids.

35.8 Carbon monoxide as a pollutant

Carbon monoxide is a poisonous gas produced by the partial combustion of fuels. Much of the carbon monoxide comes from the incomplete combustion of petrol in the car engine.

Around heavy traffic the concentration of carbon monoxide in the air can reach 10–20 parts per million (p.p.m.). Levels as high as 200 p.p.m. have been recorded. Levels above 50 p.p.m. can be harmful to adults. Carbon monoxide is poisonous because it forms a stable compound with the haemoglobin in the blood called carboxyhaemoglobin, which prevents the binding of haemoglobin to oxygen and so stops the transport of oxygen around the body. Low concentrations are still harmful as they affect the proper working of the brain.

35.9 Lead compounds as pollutants

A lead compound called tetraethyllead is added in small quantities to petrol. This increases the octane number of petrol (the number of stars on the petrol pump), lubricates the valves in the engine and enables more litres of petrol to be made from a given amount of petroleum.

A car covering 9000 miles per year consumes about 200 g of lead; most of this escapes into the air through the exhaust system. Recent studies have emphasized how serious the emission of lead into the air can be. Lead is an intoxicant in much the same way as alcohol is, and some studies have linked it with antisocial behaviour. A study in a London school has shown that children with high lead levels in their blood were less intelligent and found it more difficult to concentrate. There is also considerable evidence that vegetables such as lettuces and cabbages grown near busy roads contain high levels of lead.

35.10 Catalytic convertors

Many cars are now fitted with catalytic convertors to reduce atmospheric pollution from car exhausts. The car must use unleaded petrol as any lead in the exhaust gases will poison the catalyst and prevent it working.

Figure 35.2 shows a catalytic convertor fitted to a car exhaust. The convertor contains a platinum catalyst. The convertor reduces the amounts of carbon monoxide and oxides of nitrogen in the exhaust gases.

$$2CO + 2NO \rightarrow 2CO_2 + N_2$$

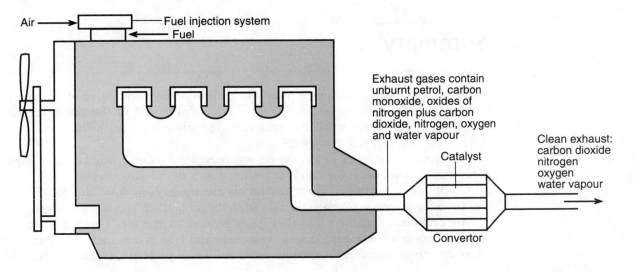

Fig. 35.2 Catalytic convertor

35.11 Problems caused by air pollution

Exhaust gases from cars are causing problems throughout the world. Strong sunlight acting on a mixture of oxides of nitrogen, carbon monoxide and hydrocarbon vapour (unburnt petrol) produces a new and more unpleasant mixture which includes ozone. Its acrid fumes collect in valleys and cause many problems. These fumes are sometimes called 'photochemical smog'. Apart from health problems these fumes:

1. Cause the breaking down of rubber and plastics.
2. Fade dyes.

Much of the problem of air pollution could be minimized by cleaning up car exhausts. A converter containing a platinum catalyst fitted to the exhaust system would convert all of the harmful gases into carbon dioxide, nitrogen, oxygen and water vapour. These gases are all normally present in air and therefore do not cause pollution.

Pure rainwater has a pH of approximately 5. Oxides of nitrogen and sulphur dioxide dissolve in water to form acids. The presence of these pollutants reduces the pH, making the rainwater more acidic and causing certain problems. The effects of **'acid rain'** include:

1. Stonework on buildings is damaged. St Paul's Cathedral and Westminster Abbey are just two of the buildings that show the damage caused by acid rain. First a black skin appears on the surface. This then blisters and cracks, causing the stonework to be seriously disfigured.

2. Rivers and lakes over a wide area become more acid. This is said to be affecting wildlife, e.g. otters. There are many lakes in Sweden and Norway that now have no life.

3. Forests are seriously damaged. Forests in Scandinavia and Germany especially are being damaged by acid rain. Trees are stunted, needles and leaves drop off and the trees die. It has been estimated that acid rain is costing the German forestry industry about £150 million each year.

4. Human life can be affected. Acid conditions can alter levels of copper, lead and aluminium in the body. These changes have been linked with diarrhoea in small babies, breathing disorders and mental deterioration in old age (senile dementia).

5. Metalwork is damaged. Acid rain can speed up corrosion of metals. Wrought iron railings in city areas can show considerable damage.

Summary

Air is a mixture of gases. Approximately four-fifths of air is composed of the inactive gas nitrogen. Approximately one-fifth of the air is composed of the active gas oxygen. Other gases present in small amounts include carbon dioxide, helium, neon, argon, krypton, xenon and water vapour.

The constituent gases in air can be separated by fractional distillation of liquid air. This process relies upon the different boiling points of the gases present.

Combustion, rusting and respiration all use up oxygen from the air. Fortunately photosynthesis removes carbon dioxide from the air and replaces it with oxygen.

Air pollution is caused by other gases present in the air. These include sulphur dioxide, oxides of nitrogen, carbon monoxide and lead compounds. Pollutants such as these can cause considerable environmental and social problems, including acid rain.

Self test questions

Chapter 1 Separation techniques in chemistry

1 When a mixture of sand and salt is added to water, the salt _____ and the sand sinks to the bottom because it is _____ in water.

2 When a mixture is filtered, the substance that is left in the filter paper is called the _____ .

3 A pure solvent can be obtained from a solution by _____ .

4 _____ _____ is a method of separating a mixture of liquids. This method depends on the liquids having different _____ _____ .

5 Liquids that do not mix are called _____ .

For questions 6–10 choose the best method of separation.

6 Oil and water.

7 Alcohol and water.

8 Nitrogen from liquid air.

9 Sodium chloride and ammonium chloride.

10 The dyes in ink.

Chapter 2 Acids and bases

1 An acid is a substance which turns litmus paper _____ .

2 Before anything can act as an acid, _____ must be present. This allows the acid to _____ and so form a solution which contains a high concentration of _____ _____ .

3 The strength of an acid is measured on the _____ scale. A strong acid has a _____ number of _____ . A weak acid has a _____ number between _____ and _____ .

4 A substance that is neither acid nor alkali is said to be _____ . An example of a _____ substance is water.

5 Explain why when hydrogen chloride gas is dissolved in water the temperature of the water increases and the resulting solution has acidic properties.

6 Explain why sulphuric acid is a strong acid whereas ethanoic acid is a weak acid.

7 Dilute acids have four general reactions. They are:

dilute acid + a fairly reactive metal → _____ + _____
dilute acid + a metal oxide → _____ + _____
dilute acid + a metal carbonate → _____ + _____ + _____ _____
dilute acid + an alkali → _____ + _____

Chapter 3 Metals and nonmetals

1 Give three physical properties that are common to most metals.

2 Name one metal that is a liquid at room temperature.

3 Name a nonmetal that conducts electricity.

4 What do all metals have in common when they react?

5 In order for a metal to displace _____ from a dilute acid the metal must be above _____ in the _____ _____ .

6 What is an alloy?

7 Name two alloys.

8 Metals can be distinguished from nonmetals by considering their oxides. Metal oxides are usually _____ at room temperature, whereas nonmetal oxides are usually _____ or _____ . If a metal oxide dissolves in water an _____ solution is formed. If an oxide of a nonmetal dissolves in water an _____ solution is formed. Most metal oxides are _____ in water.

9 Silicon and germanium have some properties of both metals and nonmetals. What is this type of element called?

10 Give two uses of the element copper and say on which properties of copper these uses depend.

Chapter 4 Atomic structure

1 Atoms are made up from three main particles: _____, _____ and _____ . The small centre of the atom is called the _____ and contains _____ and _____ . The _____ go round the centre in distinct energy levels or orbits.

2 The atomic number of an element is the number of _____ in an atom of the element.

3 An atom is electrically neutral because it has an equal number of _____ and _____ .

4 What is an isotope?

5 Carbon has two stable isotopes, $^{12}_{6}C$ and $^{13}_{6}C$. In terms of protons, neutrons and electrons, describe atoms of these two isotopes.

Use the following information to answer questions 6–9:

	Atomic number	Mass number
magnesium	12	24
calcium	20	40
fluorine	9	19
chlorine	17	35

6 What is the electron arrangement (configuration) of a calcium atom?

7 How many electrons will a magnesium *ion* have and how will they be arranged?

8 How many neutrons does an atom of fluorine have?

9 What do the electron arrangements of chlorine and fluorine have in common?

Chapter 5 Chemical families and the Periodic Table

1 Elements are grouped together because of their similar properties. Give three properties that lithium, sodium and potassium have in common.

2 Which is the most reactive of sodium, lithium and potassium?

3 Explain in terms of electron arrangement why fluorine is more reactive than chlorine.

4 Describe what you would see if a piece of potassium were put into a trough of water.

5 Why are the noble gases so unreactive?

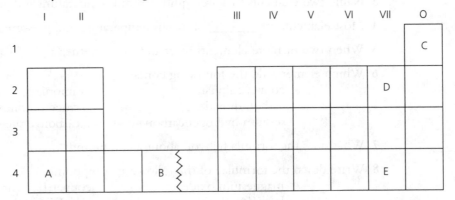

Use the skeleton Periodic Table to answer the following questions. Write down the letters for:

6 Two elements in the same group.

7 An alkali metal.

8 A noble gas.

9 A transition metal.

10 What type of bonding would you expect in a compound of A and D?

Chapter 6 States of matter

1 When a substance changes from a solid to a liquid it is said to change its _____ .

2 When a liquid changes to a gas it _____ . This process is fastest at the _____ _____ of the liquid.

3 Sublimation is when a solid changes directly to a _____ without changing to a _____ first.

4 In a solid the particles are very close together and can only _____ about a fixed position.

5 The particles in a liquid are free to _____ .

6 The ease with which a gas can be compressed is an indication that the particles are _____ _____ .

7 The automatic mixing of two gases or two liquids is called _____ . This is caused by the _____ _____ of the particles.

8 When smoke is viewed under a microscope, the particles of smoke appear to be jostled around in all directions. This movement is called _____ _____ .

9 Pure substances have definite _____ and _____ _____ .

10 The molecules in a dense gas move _____ than the molecules in a less dense gas.

Chapter 7 Elements, mixtures and compounds

1 A pure substance that cannot be split up into anything simpler is called an _____ .

2 There are about a _____ different elements.

3 Name two elements that are liquid at room temperature and pressure.

4 Most elements are _____ at room temperature and pressure.

5 When two or more elements react and join together a _____ is formed.

6 Which elements do the following contain:
copper sulphate   ammonia
carbon dioxide   nitrogen monoxide
sodium hydrogencarbonate   a carbohydrate

7 What does the formula tell you about a compound?

8 Write down the formulae of the following compounds:
magnesium oxide   copper(II) hydroxide
lead(II) chloride   iron(III) sulphate
ammonium sulphate

9 The properties of a compound are _____ from the properties of the elements that it is made from.

10 When a compound is made directly from the elements in it, the process is called _____ .

Chapter 8 Bonding

1 What is the charge on a chloride ion and how does this come about?

2 When an atom reacts it tries to obtain a _____ outer shell of _____ . If the shell is nearly empty the atom _____ _____ and so becomes a positive ion. If the shell is nearly full the atom _____ _____ and becomes a negative ion.

3 Some atoms complete their shells by sharing electrons. This is called _____ bonding.

4 Draw a diagram to show how the electrons are arranged in a molecule of water.

5 What are the main properties of an ionic compound?

6 Give an example of:
(a) a giant structure of atoms;
(b) a giant structure of ions;
(c) a giant structure of molecules.

7 Why are metals good conductors of electricity?

8 What is meant by the term 'allotropy'?

9 Name two allotropes of carbon.

Chapter 9 Radioactivity

1 Radioactivity originates in the _____ of an atom.

2 What are the three types of radiation?

3 Which form of radiation is the most penetrating?

4 What is meant by the half-life of an isotope?

5 Give two uses of radioactivity.

6 Why is the disposal of radioactive waste such a problem?

7 An isotope has a half-life of 24 hours. How long would it take for seven-eighths of the isotope to decay?

Chapter 10 Gas laws

1 Which law is used to calculate the volume of a fixed mass of gas when its pressure has changed at constant temperature?

2 Write down the general gas equation.

3 How would the pressure of a fixed mass of gas change if its volume remained unchanged but the temperature was increased?

Questions 4–7

A fixed mass of gas has a volume of 200 cm^3 at 77 °C and 100 kPa.

4 Calculate the pressure if the volume is halved but the temperature and pressure remain constant.

5 Calculate the pressure of the gas if the volume is constant but the temperature is increased to 127 °C.

6 Calculate the volume of the gas if the temperature is unchanged but the pressure is doubled.

7 Calculate the volume of the gas if the temperature is changed to 400 K and the pressure is increased to 150 kPa.

Chapter 11 Oxidation and reduction

1 Oxidation can be defined as the gaining of _____ or the loss of _____ .

2 Oxidation and _____ always go together.

3 A substance that brings about oxidation is called the _____ _____ and it is always _____ in the reaction.

4 In each of the following reactions say which substance is oxidized:

magnesium + oxygen → magnesium oxide
copper oxide + hydrogen → copper + water
methane + chlorine → carbon + hydrogen chloride

5 Define oxidation in terms of electron transfer.

6 Why is chlorine a good oxidizing agent?

7 Name three reducing agents.

8 Indicate in each of the following reactions which substance is reduced and which substance is oxidized.

$$\text{magnesium} + \text{copper oxide} \rightarrow \text{magnesium oxide} + \text{copper}$$
$$Cl_2 + 2I^- \rightarrow 2Cl^- + I_2$$
$$CO_2 + C \rightarrow 2CO$$

9 Which process always happens at the cathode in electrolysis?

10 Under what conditions does copper react with sulphuric acid and why is this an oxidation reaction?

Chapter 12 The reactivity series of metals

1 Name three metals that react with cold water.

2 Name a metal that reacts with dilute acid but does not react with cold water.

3 How is the stability of a metal compound related to the position of the metal in the reactivity series?

4 Which metal carbonates are *not* decomposed by heating?

5 Write a balanced symbol equation for the effect of heat on copper carbonate.

6 Which gas is **always** given off when a metal nitrate is heated?

7 If a piece of magnesium ribbon is dropped into a test tube containing copper(II) sulphate solution, the blue colour fades, the test tube becomes warm and a brown solid sinks to the bottom:
(a) Complete the equation for the reaction
$$Mg + CuSO_4 \rightarrow \underline{\hspace{2cm}}$$
(b) Explain why the above reaction takes place.
(c) What does the fact that the test tube becomes warm tell you about the reaction?

8 Write a balanced equation for the action of heat on silver nitrate.

9 Why do you think that gold has been known and used for many thousands of years whereas sodium has been known for only about two hundred years?

10 Sodium, zinc, lead, iron, aluminium, calcium, magnesium, silver. Choose a metal from this list which:
(a) reacts very slowly with cold water but burns in steam;
(b) reacts violently with cold water to form a hydroxide of the type MOH;
(c) is used as a protective shield from radiation;
(d) forms an oxide whose formula is of the type M_2O_3;
(e) cannot reduce lead(II) nitrate to lead.

Chapter 13 Chemical equations

1 Write a word and symbol equation for the reaction of magnesium ribbon with dilute sulphuric acid.

2 What 'state symbol' is used to indicate a solution in water?

3 Balance the following equations:

$$Na + H_2O \rightarrow NaOH + H_2$$
$$CuCO_3 + HCl \rightarrow CuCl_2 + CO_2 + H_2O$$
$$AgNO_3 + ZnCl_2 \rightarrow AgCl + Zn(NO_3)_2$$

4 What advantage does a balanced symbol equation have over a word equation?

5 Write the simplest ionic equations for the following:
   (a) the reaction between an acid and an alkali;
   (b) the precipitation of silver chloride;
   (c) the oxidation of iron(II) ions to iron(III) ions by chlorine.

Chapter 14 Rusting of iron and steel

1 What substances cause the rusting of iron and steel?

2 Write the ionic equation for the rusting of iron.

3 Which of these metals in contact with iron or steel will slow down the rusting?

$$\text{copper, lead, magnesium, zinc.}$$

4 Write down the formula for rust.

5 Why does a car exhaust made of steel rust more quickly than other parts of the car?

Chapter 15 Extraction of metals

1 A rock that contains a metal is called an _____ .

2 In the extraction of any metal from one of its compounds, the compound has to be _____ .

3 Metals at the top of the reactivity series are more _____ to obtain from their compounds.

4 Aluminium is extracted from _____ , which is a form of aluminium oxide. Aluminium oxide has a very high _____ _____ and so for this electrolysis it is dissolved in molten _____ . The anode is made of large blocks of _____ which have to be frequently replaced because the oxygen produced at the anode reacts with it to form _____ _____ .

5 The main chemicals added to the blast furnace are _____ , _____ and _____ . The reducing agent in the blast furnace is _____ _____ . The molten iron produced runs to the bottom of the furnace and is then covered with a layer of _____ . This contains several impurities but is mainly _____ _____ .

6 Most of the iron produced by the blast furnace is converted into _____ .

7 Which metal is used to reduce titanium chloride in order to obtain the titanium?

8 From which compound is sodium extracted?

9 Give the common name for an ore of iron.

10 Why is the recycling of copper so important?

Chapter 16 The effect of electricity on chemicals

1 What is an electrolyte?

2 Name three classes of substances that are electrolytes.

3 Solid sodium chloride will not conduct electricity. This is because the ions are not
_____ _____ _____ . When sodium chloride is in aqueous solution or
when it is _____ it will conduct because the ions can now _____ .

4 In any electrolysis the positive ions are attracted to the negative electrode, which is
called the _____ , and the negative ions are attracted to the positive electrode,
which is called the _____ .

5 In the electrolysis of molten lead(II) bromide, _____ is produced at the negative
electrode and _____ is produced at the positive electrode.

6 In the electrolysis of an aqueous solution, there will always be a few _____ ions
and _____ ions from the water.

7 Write down the equations for the electrode reactions in the electrolysis of aqueous
sulphuric acid.

8 Metals _____ _____ in the reactivity series are *not* usually produced in the
electrolysis of an aqueous solution; _____ is produced instead.

9 Give three industrial uses of electrolysis.

10 If a current of 5 A is passed through molten calcium bromide $CaBr_2$ for 3 minutes
13 seconds, calculate:
(a) the number of coulombs of electricity passed;
(b) the number of faradays passed (1 F = 96 500 coulombs);
(c) the mass of calcium deposited at the negative electrode;
(d) the mass of bromine given off at the positive electrode.

$$(A_r(Ca) = 40, A_r(Br) = 80)$$

Chapter 17 Rates of reaction

1 Explain what has to happen in order that two substances might react together.

2 What is meant by the term 'activation energy'?

3 Name three observable changes that you could use to follow the rate of a reaction.

4 What is a catalyst? Give two examples of industrial processes that use a catalyst. Say
what is reacting, what is produced and what the catalyst is.

5 An experiment was carried out to investigate the rate of reaction between
magnesium and dilute sulphuric acid. 0.07 g of magnesium ribbon were reacted with
excess dilute sulphuric acid.

The volume of gas produced was noted every 5 seconds. The following results were
obtained.

Time (s)	Volume (cm^3)	Time (s)	Volume (cm^3)
0	0	25	63
5	18	30	67
10	34	35	69
15	47	40	70
20	57	45	70

(a) On a piece of graph paper, plot these results with the volume as the vertical axis
and time as the horizontal axis. Draw a smooth curve through the points.
(b) When is the reaction fastest?
(c) How long does it take for the 0.07 g of magnesium to react completely?
(d) At what time was 0.02 g of magnesium *left unreacted*?
(e) On your graph, sketch a curve that might have been obtained if 0.07 g of
magnesium powder had been used instead of the magnesium ribbon.
(f) Give two other changes that would alter the rate of this reaction.

(g) Copy and complete the equation for the reaction.

$$Mg + H_2SO_4 \rightarrow \text{_____}$$

(h) How may the gas produced be identified?

Chapter 18 Reversible reactions and equilibrium

1 What is meant by a 'reversible reaction'?

2 For a reversible reaction in a closed vessel and under fixed conditions, a chemical _____ will be set up. When this happens the reaction will appear to _____ . In fact this is not the case; the rate of the forward reaction is _____ _____ the rate of the reverse reaction.

3 What happens to reversible reactions if the conditions are altered?

4 What effect does a catalyst have on an equilibrium reaction?

5 Explain why a high pressure favours the formation of ammonia in the following reversible reaction.

$$N_2 + 3H_2 \rightleftharpoons 2NH_3$$

Chapter 19 Energy changes in chemistry

1 What is meant by the term 'exothermic reaction'?

2 Give an example of an exothermic reaction.

3 Draw an energy level diagram for the combustion of methane. The heat of combustion of methane $CH_4 = -890$ kJ/mol.

4 Two grams of a liquid fuel were burnt using the apparatus shown in Fig. 19.4. The temperature of 100 g of water in the can rose by 50 °C. Assuming that all the heat from the burning fuel was transferred to the water, calculate (specific heat capacity of water = 4.2 J/g/°C):
(a) the heat produced by the 2 g of fuel;
(b) the heat produced by 1 g of fuel;
(c) the heat produced by 1 mol of the fuel (relative molecular mass of the fuel = 50).

5 If simple cells are set up between the following pairs of metals:
(a) copper and zinc;   (b) copper and copper;   (c) copper and magnesium;
which one would produce the greatest potential difference and which one would not produce any potential difference?

6 Calculate the energy change for the reaction

$$CH_4 + Cl_2 \rightarrow CH_3Cl + HCl$$

7 Calculate the energy change for the reaction

$$H_2 + I_2 \rightarrow 2HI$$

(Use the information in Table 19.1, page 105, for questions 6 and 7)

8 Suggest reasons why the following reaction will be endothermic

$$N_2 + O_2 \rightarrow 2NO$$

Chapter 20 Chemicals from petroleum

1 Petroleum is a complex mixture of _____ . These are compounds of _____ and _____ .

2 Petroleum is a fossil fuel and was formed _____ of years ago from dead _____ and _____ .

3 What are the main characteristics of a homologous series?

4 Write down the names, formulae and structural formulae of the first three alkanes.

5 What is the difference between a saturated and an unsaturated hydrocarbon?

6 What is an isomer? Write down and name three isomers which have the molecular formula C_5H_{12}.

7 Give an example of an addition reaction with an alkene.

8 What is meant by 'cracking' and why is it so important?

Chapter 21 Polymerization

Chloroethene

$$\overset{Cl}{\underset{H}{\diagdown}} C = C \overset{H}{\underset{H}{\diagup}}$$

1 How would you show that chloroethene contains a carbon–carbon double bond?

2 Name the polymer formed using chloroethene as the monomer.

3 Draw the structure of this polymer.

4 Draw the structure of the polymer formed using $HOOC- \# - NH_2$ as the monomer.

5 What type of polymer is formed in question 4?

6 Why is it easier to recycle thermoplastic polymers than thermosetting polymers?

Chapter 22 Ammonia, nitric acid and fertilizers

1 Ammonia is a compound of _____ and _____ .

2 The industrial manufacture of ammonia is a synthesis reaction, i.e. the compound is made from _____ _____ .

3 The industrial process is called the _____ process.

4 The catalyst in this reaction is _____ .

5 Two uses of ammonia are in the manufacture of _____ and of _____ _____ .

6 The normal laboratory preparation of ammonia is to heat an _____ _____ with an _____ .

   Two suitable chemicals are _____ _____ and _____ _____ .

7 Ammonia is collected by _____ _____ because it is _____ than air. It cannot be collected over water because it is _____ _____ .

8 Ammonia can be identified by its strong smell and by its effect on Universal Indicator. It is the only common _____ gas. A good test for ammonia is using the stopper from the concentrated hydrochloric acid bottle. In the presence of ammonia, dense _____ fumes of _____ _____ are formed.

9 In what form do most plants take in nitrogen?

10 Iron, boron and copper are required by plants in very small quantities. These are called _____ elements.

11 Name a natural fertilizer that contains nitrogen.

12 Which group of plants have bacteria living in their roots which enable them to make use of atmospheric nitrogen?

13 Calculate the percentage of nitrogen in ammonium sulphate $(NH_4)_2SO_4$.
$A_r(H) = 1$, $A_r(N) = 14$, $A_r(O) = 16$, $A_r(S) = 32$

14 Give an example of a fertilizer that contains phosphorus.

15 Why do plants need potassium?

16 What is meant by a NPK fertilizer?

17 Why must lime and an ammonium salt not be added to the soil at the same time?

18 Farmers use large amounts of nitrogen-containing fertilizers. Some of these fertilizers are washed off the farm land by rain into streams and lakes. Also present in streams and lakes are phosphates from domestic detergents. The dissolved fertilizers and phosphates increase the amount of chemicals needed by plants in the water. The surface of the water then becomes covered with algae. Because of this the plants below the surface die. When the algae decay, the amount of dissolved oxygen in the water is lowered.

(a) Give the chemical name of a fertilizer which contains nitrogen.
(b) Why are fertilizers used on farms?
(c) Name an element other than nitrogen which is needed for plant growth.
(d) How do phosphates get into the water system?
(e) What would be the effect of lowering the amount of dissolved oxygen in streams and lakes?

Chapter 23 Salt and chemicals from salt

1 A strong solution of salt is called _____ . This solution can be electrolysed using a Diaphragm cell or a Mercury cathode cell. In both cases the final three products are _____ gas, _____ gas and _____ _____ solution.

2 Write the equation for the reaction at the anode in the electrolysis of salt solution.

3 Give three uses of chlorine.

4 What is the main chemical in 'household bleach'?

5 Give two uses of sodium hydroxide.

6 What is manufactured by the 'Solvay process'?

Chapter 24 Sulphuric acid

1 Sulphuric acid is manufactured by the _____ process. The main stage is the _____ of sulphur dioxide to form _____ _____ . A catalyst of _____ _____ is used. The product of the reaction is not dissolved directly in water

because the reaction is too _____ . Instead it is dissolved in _____ _____
_____ to form _____ . This can then be carefully diluted with water to form
concentrated sulphuric acid.

2 When concentrated sulphuric acid is added to copper(II) sulphate crystals, the
crystals lose their _____ colour and turn _____ . This is because the sulphuric
acid is removing the _____ from the copper(II) sulphate crystals. The sulphuric
acid is acting as a _____ agent.

Chapter 25 The mole and chemical calculations

1 Write down the numbers of moles of atoms in the following (see Fig. 5.2 on page
43 for relative atomic masses):
(a) 60 g of carbon;
(b) 64 g of oxygen;
(c) 100 g of calcium;
(d) 64 g of sulphur;
(e) 39 g of potassium;
(f) 12 g of magnesium;
(g) 3 g of aluminium;
(h) 4 g of iron;
(i) 1 g of mercury;
(j) 0.1 g of hydrogen.

2 What is the mass of the following:
(a) 6 moles of nitrogen atoms;
(b) 5 moles of lead atoms;
(c) 3 moles of aluminium atoms;
(d) 0.5 moles of magnesium atoms;
(e) 0.01 moles of iron atoms?

3 Calculate the formula of an oxide of sulphur where 2 g of sulphur join with 3 g of
oxygen.

4 Calculate the formula of a compound containing 28 per cent iron, 24 per cent
sulphur and 48 per cent oxygen by mass.

5 What is the percentage of water of crystallization in copper sulphate $CuSO_4 \cdot 5H_2O$?

6 The formula of potassium hydrogencarbonate is $KHCO_3$.
(a) What is the mass of 1 mole of potassium hydrogencarbonate?
(b) What is the percentage of oxygen in potassium hydrogencarbonate?

7 How many times heavier is one atom of magnesium than one atom of carbon?

8 What are the masses of the following:
(a) 10 moles of water H_2O;
(b) 0.5 moles of ammonium nitrate NH_4NO_3;
(c) 2 moles of ethanol C_2H_5OH;
(d) 0.01 moles of lead nitrate $Pb(NO_3)_2$.

9
$$CaCO_3 + 2HCl \rightarrow CaCl_2 + CO_2 + H_2O$$

(a) What mass of calcium chloride would be produced if 10 g of calcium carbonate
were reacted with excess acid?
(b) What volume of carbon dioxide would be produced if 5 g of calcium carbonate
were reacted with excess acid? (1 mole of a gas has a volume of about 24 dm^3)

10
$$2C_2H_6 + 7O_2 \rightarrow 4CO_2 + 6H_2O$$

(a) What volume of oxygen is needed to react with 20 cm^3 of ethane?
(b) What volume of carbon dioxide would be produced by the complete
combustion of 20 cm^3 of ethane?

Chapter 26 Rocks

igneous   metamorphic   sedimentary

Which type of rock

1 is formed by the action of heat and pressure on other rocks?

2 is formed when fragments of other rocks are compacted?

3 is formed when molten rock crystallizes?

Basalt and granite are both igneous rocks.

4 Why are the crystals in granite larger than those in basalt?

5 What does this suggest about the way they were formed?

6 What sources of energy drive the rock cycle?

Chapter 27 The structure of the Earth

Complete the following:

The outer skin of the Earth is called its _____ . Below this skin is the _____ .
From time to time molten rock escapes to the surface through v_____ . At the centre
of the Earth is the _____ . Measurements taken after e_____ tell scientists that the
core is partly liquid and partly _____ .

P-waves are c_____ waves and they travel through _____ and liquids. S-waves are
t_____ waves which cannot travel through liquids.

Chapter 28 Plate tectonics

The continents are moving apart because they are on enormous _____ which float
on the mantle. At one time it is believed the continents were closely linked together in
the P_____ . The plates are moving apart very slowly.

   In the oceans, new rocks are being produced at _____ plate margins. When a
continental plate and an oceanic plate collide at a _____ plate margin, the denser
plate dips below the less dense plate and the rocks return to the _____ .

   _____ occur often at places where two plates rub against each other. The strength
of earthquakes can be measured on the _____ scale.

Chapter 29 Qualitative analysis

1 What are the flame test colours for:
   (a) sodium compounds;   (b) potassium compounds;   (c) calcium compounds?

2 What are the colours of:
   (a) copper(II) hydroxide;   (b) iron(II) hydroxide;   (c) iron(III) hydroxide?

3 Name two metal hydroxides that are insoluble in water, but that will dissolve in
   excess sodium hydroxide solution.

4 Name a substance that gives off carbon dioxide when it is reacted with a dilute acid.

5 What sort of substances produce a white precipitate if solutions of silver nitrate and nitric acid are added?

6 A white solid gives a lilac flame test and is soluble in water. When barium chloride and hydrochloric acid are added to the solution, a white precipitate is formed. What is the original white solid?

7 What is the usual test for chlorine gas?

8 Which gas relights a glowing splint?

9 Which is the lightest of all gases?

10 Is carbon dioxide 'heavier' or 'lighter' than air?

Chapter 30 Water

1 What is meant by saying that 'water is a good solvent'?

2 In general the solubility of a solid _____ with temperature but gases are _____ soluble in hot water.

3 The solubility of a substance is the _____ of the solute that will dissolve in _____ of water at a given _____ .

4 What is a saturated solution and how would you recognize one?

5 What is meant by hard water?

6 What is the difference between 'temporary hard water' and 'permanent hard water'?

7 Give two ways that 'permanent hard water' can be softened.

8 What is a detergent?

9 Give one advantage of a soapless detergent compared with soap.

Refer to Fig. 30.1

10 Which substance is least soluble at
(a) at 10 °C;
(b) at 50 °C?

11 Which substance has almost the same solubility at all temperatures?

12 At about which temperature are the solubilities of sodium chloride and potassium chloride the same?

13 Explain why crystals of potassium nitrate form when a hot saturated solution of potassium nitrate is cooled.

Chapter 31 Chalk, limestone and marble

1 Chalk, limestone and marble are all forms of _____ _____ .

2 When a piece of marble was heated strongly, _____ _____ was given off. The shiny surface of the marble disappeared and the hard marble turned _____ .
     After the solid had cooled down, a few drops of water were added to it. The solid seemed to expand and steam was given off showing that the reaction produced _____ . When the solid was tested with Universal Indicator paper, the paper turned _____ showing that the substance was an _____ .

3 What is the chemical name for limewater?

4 Describe what you would see when carbon dioxide is bubbled through limewater until there is no further change. Write down equations for any reactions taking place.

5 Which substance causes 'temporary hard water'?

6 How are stalactites and stalagmites formed?

7 Which substances are normally used to prepare carbon dioxide in the laboratory? Why is sulphuric acid not used?

8 Give two uses of carbon dioxide.

9 For what purpose is limestone used in the extraction of iron?

10 Name two other large scale uses of limestone.

Chapter 32 Salt formation

1
$$\text{metal} + \text{acid} \rightarrow \text{salt} + \text{water}$$
$$\text{metal oxide} + \text{acid} \rightarrow \text{salt} + \text{water}$$
These two reactions only work if the salt that is formed is _____ in water.

2 What is meant by the terms 'basicity' and 'acid salt'?

3 Magnesium sulphate crystals ($MgSO_4 \cdot 7H_2O$) can be made by adding excess magnesium oxide (MgO), which is insoluble in water, to dilute sulphuric acid.

(a) Why was the magnesium oxide in excess?
(b) The following apparatus could be used to separate the excess magnesium oxide from the solution. Say what each of the letters on the diagram refers to.

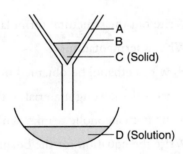

(c) Given the relative atomic masses $A_r(\text{H}) = 1$, $A_r(\text{Mg}) = 24$, $A_r(\text{O}) = 16$, $A_r(\text{S}) = 32$, calculate the relative formula mass of:
magnesium oxide MgO;
magnesium sulphate crystals $MgSO_4 \cdot 7H_2O$.
(d) Use your answer from (c) to calculate the maximum mass of magnesium sulphate crystals that could be obtained from 2.0 g of magnesium oxide.
(e) Describe how you could obtain pure dry crystals of magnesium sulphate from magnesium sulphate solution.

4 Name three insoluble salts.

5 How would you prepare an insoluble salt? Choose an example and write a word and symbol equation for the reaction.

6 Which piece of apparatus is usually used to measure exactly 25 cm³ of liquid into a flask?

7 Which piece of apparatus is usually used to add the acid in a titration?

8 What is a molar solution?

9 What mass of sulphuric acid (H_2SO_4) is needed to make 25 cm³ of 2 M acid?

10 $HCl + NaOH \rightarrow NaCl + H_2O$

25 cm³ of 0.1 M sodium hydroxide were titrated with 0.5 M hydrochloric acid.

(a) What mass of sodium hydroxide is needed to make 1 dm³ of 0.1 M sodium hydroxide solution?

(b) How many moles of sodium hydroxide are present in 25 cm³ of 0.1 M solution?

(c) How many moles of hydrochloric acid will react with this amount of sodium hydroxide?

(d) What volume of 0.5 M acid would this be?

Chapter 33 Transition elements

boron   chromium   silicon   vanadium

1 Which of the elements in the list above are transition elements?

2 Why do transition elements and their compounds frequently act as catalysts.

3 In the row of transition elements Sc–Zn as you move from left to right extra protons, electrons and neutrons are added. Why do the atoms get smaller?

4 What is the electron arrangement in
(i) a calcium atom?
(ii) a manganese atom?

Chapter 34 Natural products

1 Write out the structural formula for ethanol.

2 What is fermentation?

3 How can ethanol be obtained from a mixture of ethanol and water?

4 What is the starting material in the industrial production of ethanol?

5 Apart from alcoholic drinks, what is ethanol used for?

6 Write the equation for the burning of ethanol.

7 Ethanol can be oxidized by the air or by a good oxidizing agent such as _____ to form _____ _____. This is a weak monobasic acid.

8 An ester is the compound formed when an organic _____ reacts with an _____. An example of an ester is _____ _____ .

Chapter 35 The atmosphere and air pollution

1 What is the approximate percentage, by volume, of oxygen in normal air?

2 Oxygen is obtained industrially by the _____ _____ of liquid air. The air can be separated in this way because it is a _____ and the different components have different _____ _____ .

3 Although respiration and combustion use up oxygen, the approximate percentage of oxygen remains constant. Why is this?

4 Name three gases that pollute the atmosphere.

5 What are the main effects of acid rain?

Answers to self test questions

Chapter 1 Separation techniques in chemistry

1 Dissolves; insoluble.

2 Residue.

3 Distillation.

4 Fractional distillation; boiling points.

5 Immiscible.

6 Separating funnel.

7 Fractional distillation.

8 Fractional distillation.

9 Sublimation.

10 Chromatography.

Chapter 2 Acids and bases

1 Red.

2 Water; ionize; hydrogen ions.

3 pH; pH; 1; pH; 3; 6.

4 Neutral; neutral.

5 The hydrogen chloride changes from a covalent compound to hydrogen ions and chloride ions; energy is given out as the ions are formed; the hydrogen ions give the solution its acidic properties.

6 Sulphuric acid completely ionizes in water but ethanoic acid only partly ionizes.

7 Acid + metal → salt + hydrogen
Acid + metal oxide → salt + water
Acid + metal carbonate → salt + water + carbon dioxide
Acid + alkali → salt + water

Chapter 3 Metals and nonmetals

1 Shiny, high density, high melting point, bend, good conductors of heat and electricity, strong.

2 Mercury.

3 Carbon.

4 They lose electrons and so form positive ions.

5 Hydrogen; hydrogen; reactivity series.

6 It is a metal made by mixing two or more metals together.

7 Solder, steel, duralumin, brass or bronze.

8 Solids; gases; liquids; alkaline; acidic; insoluble.

9 Metalloid.

10 Coins – hard wearing; wires – very good electrical conductor; pipes – easily shaped; saucepans – good conductor of heat.

Chapter 4 Atomic structure

1 Protons; neutrons; electrons; nucleus; protons; neutrons; electrons.

2 Protons.

3 Protons; electrons.

4 Isotopes are atoms of the same element with different numbers of neutrons.

5 Carbon-12 has 6 protons, 6 neutrons and 6 electrons.

Carbon-13 has 6 protons, 7 neutrons and 6 electrons.

6 2,8,8,2.

7 10; 2,8.

8 10.

9 Seven electrons in outer shell.

Chapter 5 Chemical families and the Periodic Table

1 React with water, soft, metals, stored in oil, float in water, low melting point for metals.

2 Potassium.

3 Both want to gain one electron; in the case of fluorine this extra electron is in the second shell and so is closer to the positive attraction of the nucleus (electron arrangements are fluorine 2,7; chlorine 2,8,7).

4 A small piece of potassium would float on the surface of the water; it would melt into a ball and skim across the water; it would hiss and usually the hydrogen given off would burn with a lilac flame; the potassium would disappear into the water.

5 Noble gases are unreactive because they already have full shells of electrons, i.e. a stable electron arrangement.

6 D and E.

7 A.

8 C.

9 B.

10 Ionic.

Chapter 6 States of matter

1 State.

2 Evaporates; boiling point.

3 Gas; liquid.

4 Vibrate.

5 Move.

6 Widely spaced.

7 Diffusion; random motion.

8 Brownian motion.

9 Melting; boiling points.

10 Slower.

Chapter 7   Elements, mixtures and compounds

1 Element.

2 100.

3 Mercury, bromine.

4 Solid.

5 Compound.

6 Copper, sulphur and oxygen   nitrogen and hydrogen
carbon and oxygen   nitrogen and oxygen
sodium, hydrogen, carbon and oxygen   carbon, hydrogen and oxygen

7 It tells you which elements it contains and how much of each element.

8 MgO, $PbCl_2$, $(NH_4)_2SO_4$, $Cu(OH)_2$, $Fe_2(SO_4)_3$.

9 Different.

10 Synthesis.

Chapter 8   Bonding

1 When a chlorine atom forms an ion it gains one electron. It will then have a 1– charge.

2 Full; electrons; loses electrons; gains electrons.

3 Covalent.

4

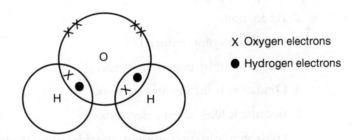

A molecule of water

5 High melting point crystalline solid, usually soluble in water, conducts electricity when molten or in aqueous solution.

6 (a) A metal, diamond or graphite.
(b) Sodium chloride, magnesium oxide or any other ionic compound.
(c) Sulphur crystals, iodine crystals or a polymer.

7 A metal has the metal ions in a 'sea' of electrons; electrons can easily move through the structure.

8 Allotropy is when an element can exist in two or more forms in the same state.

9 Diamond and graphite (or fullerine).

Chapter 9   Radioactivity

1 Nucleus.

2 Alpha, beta and gamma.

3 Gamma.

4 The time taken for half of the radioactive nuclei to decay or the level of radioactivity fall to half.

5 Treating cancer, sterilizing instruments, controlling the thickness of paper and metals, following the course of a process, atomic energy, preserving food.

6 Because of its dangerous nature and long life.

7 3 half-lives – 72 hours.

Chapter 10   Gas laws

1 Boyle's Law.

2 $\dfrac{p_1 V_1}{T_1} = \dfrac{p_2 V_2}{T_2}$

3 The pressure would increase.

4 200 kPa.

5 114.3 kPa.

6 100 cm^3.

7 152.4 cm^3.

Chapter 11   Oxidation and reduction

1 Oxygen; hydrogen.

2 Reduction.

3 Oxidizing agent; reduced.

4 Magnesium; hydrogen; methane.

5 Oxidation is the loss of electrons.

6 Because it likes to gain electrons.

7 Hydrogen, carbon, carbon monoxide, sulphur dioxide, hydrogen sulphide, metals.

8 Magnesium is oxidized; copper oxide is reduced. Iodide ions are oxidized; chlorine is reduced. Carbon is oxidized; carbon dioxide is reduced.

9 Reduction.

10 The acid must be hot and concentrated; the copper loses electrons.

Chapter 12   The reactivity series of metals

1 Potassium, sodium, lithium, calcium.

2 Magnesium, zinc, iron.

3 The higher up the reactivity series the metal is, the more stable its compounds are.

4 Potassium and sodium.

5 $CuCO_3 \rightarrow CuO + CO_2$

6 Oxygen.

7 (a) $Mg + CuSO_4 \rightarrow MgSO_4 + Cu$
  (b) The reaction takes place because magnesium is higher up the reactivity series than copper.
  (c) The reaction produces heat energy, i.e. it is exothermic.

8 $2AgNO_3 \rightarrow 2Ag + 2NO_2 + O_2$

9 Gold is very unreactive and can be found uncombined in the ground. Also gold is easy to obtain from its compounds. Sodium is very reactive. It is never found uncombined in the ground and it is very difficult to extract from its compounds.

10 (a) Magnesium; (b) sodium; (c) lead; (d) aluminium or iron; (e) lead or silver.

Chapter 13 Chemical equations

1 Magnesium + dilute sulphuric acid $\rightarrow$ magnesium sulphate + hydrogen
$$Mg + H_2SO_4 \rightarrow MgSO_4 + H_2$$

2 (aq).

3 $2Na + 2H_2O \rightarrow 2NaOH + H_2$
  $CuCO_3 + 2HCl \rightarrow CuCl_2 + CO_2 + H_2O$
  $2AgNO_3 + ZnCl_2 \rightarrow 2AgCl + Zn(NO_3)_2$

4 It tells you how much of each substance is reacting.

5 (a) $H^+ + OH^- \rightarrow H_2O$ (b) $Ag^+ + Cl^- \rightarrow AgCl$
  (c) $2Fe^{2+} + Cl_2 \rightarrow 2Fe^{3+} + 2Cl^-$

Chapter 14 Rusting of iron and steel

1 Oxygen (or air) and water (or moisture).

2 $Fe \rightarrow Fe^{3+} + 3e^-$

3 Magnesium and zinc – above iron in the reactivity series.

4 $Fe_2O_3 \cdot xH_2O$.

5 Steel not well protected by paint etc.; close to road so in contact with salt etc.; hot gases in the exhaust, so rusting speeded up; exhaust gases contain acidic gases.

Chapter 15 Extraction of metals

1 Ore.

2 Reduced.

3 Difficult.

4 Bauxite; melting point; cryolite; carbon; carbon dioxide.

5 Coke; limestone; iron ore; carbon monoxide; slag; calcium silicate.

6 Steel.

7 Sodium.

8 Sodium chloride.

9 Haematite, magnetite (limonite, pyrite).

10 Because there is a limited amount of copper in the ground and if it is not recycled it will soon run out.

Chapter 16 The effect of electricity on chemicals

1 An electrolyte is a compound that conducts electricity when it is molten or in aqueous solution and is decomposed by the electricity.

2 Acids, bases and salts.

3 Free to move; molten; move.

4 Cathode; anode.

5 Lead; bromine.

6 Hydrogen; hydroxide.

7 Cathode equation: $H^+ + e^- \rightarrow H$ Anode equation $2OH^- - 2e^- \rightarrow H_2O + O$
$$2H \rightarrow H_2 \qquad\qquad\qquad 2O \rightarrow O_2$$

8 Above hydrogen; hydrogen.

9 Extraction of aluminium, purifying copper, anodizing aluminium, manufacture of chlorine and sodium hydroxide, electroplating.

10 (a) 965 C;   (b) 0.01 F;   (c) 0.2 g calcium;   (d) 0.8 g bromine.

Chapter 17 Rates of reaction

1 The particles of the reactants must collide with enough energy.

2 The 'activation energy' is the energy needed to be reached by a collision for a reaction to take place.

3 Colour, mass, volume of gas evolved, pH, cloudiness.

4 A catalyst is a chemical that can alter the rate of reaction. The catalyst is not used up in the reaction and the reaction is not changed in any other way; e.g. iron in the Haber process (ammonia from nitrogen and hydrogen), vanadium(V) oxide in the Contact process (sulphuric acid from sulphur dioxide), platinum in the conversion of ammonia into nitric acid.

5 (a)

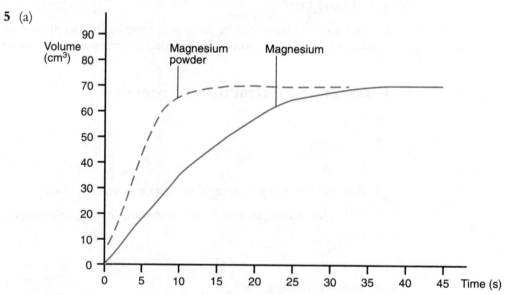

(b) At the start.
(c) 40 s
(d) When 0.05 g had reacted, 50 cm³ of gas had been given off; from the graph this is after 18 s.
(e) Your graph for the powder should be steeper but reach the same final level.
(f) The concentration of the acid, the temperature, a catalyst.
(g) $Mg + H_2SO_4 \rightarrow MgSO_4 + H_2$
(h) 'Pops' with a lighted splint.

Chapter 18 Reversible reactions and equilibrium

1 A reversible reaction is a reaction that can go in either direction depending on the conditions.

2 Equilibrium; stop; equal to.

3 The reaction moves in a direction to oppose any change.

4 A catalyst speeds up the establishment of the equilibrium; it does not alter the position of the equilibrium.

5 As the reaction proceeds to the right there is a decrease in volume (4 moles to 2 moles) and so an increase in pressure moves equilibrium to the right.

Chapter 19 Energy changes in chemistry

1 An exothermic reaction is one that gives out energy.

2 Burning (combustion) is one of many examples of an exothermic reaction.

3
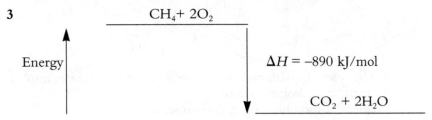

4 (a) 21 kJ;   (b) 10.5 kJ;   (c) 525 kJ.

5 Copper and magnesium; copper and copper.

6 Bonds broken   Cl–Cl   242 kJ/mol   C–H   412 kJ/mol
One bond of each type broken.   Energy required = + 654 kJ/mol
Bonds made   C–Cl   –338 kJ/mol   H–Cl   –431 kJ/mol
One bond of each type is made. Energy evolved = –769 kJ/mol
Exothermic reaction   Energy change = –115 kJ/mol

7 Energy required to break bonds = +436 + 151 = +587 kJ/mol
Energy liberated = 2 × 299 = –598 kJ/mol
Exothermic reaction   –11 kJ mol

8 Both triple bonds between nitrogen atoms and double bonds between oxygen atoms require a lot of energy to break.

Chapter 20 Chemicals from petroleum

1 Hydrocarbons; carbon; hydrogen.

2 Millions; plants; animals.

3 It can be represented by a general formula; its members have similar name endings, have similar reactions and show a gradation of physical properties.

4 Methane: CH_4 ethane: C_2H_6 propane: C_3H_8

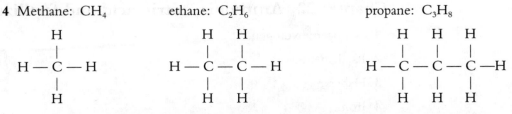

5 Unsaturated compounds contain a multiple bond between two carbon atoms (alkenes contain a double bond); saturated compounds contain only single bonds.

6 Isomers are compounds that have the same molecular formula but different structural formulae.

Pentane
C_5H_{12}

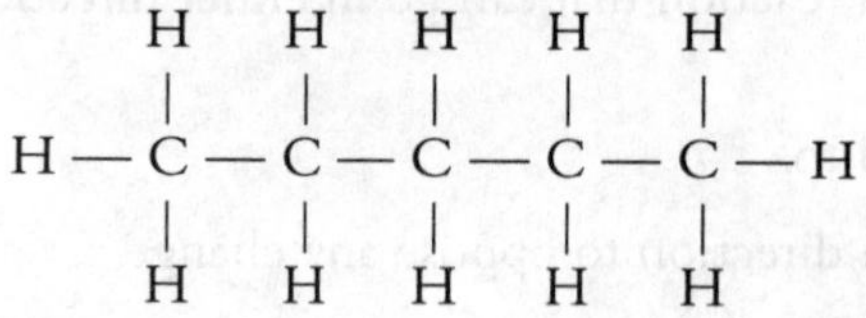

2-methylbutane
C_5H_{12}

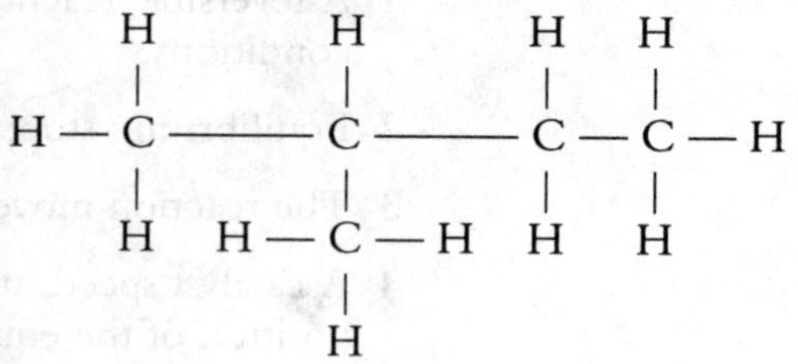

2,2-dimethylpropane
C_5H_{12}

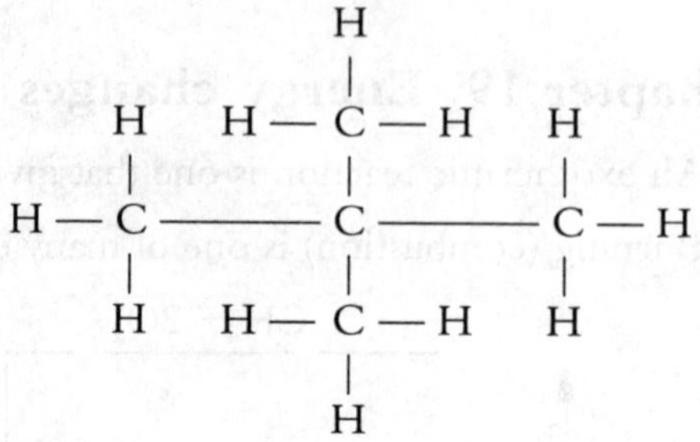

7 The reactions with hydrogen or bromine are the best examples:
ethene + hydrogen → ethane
ethene + bromine → 1,2-dibromoethane.

8 Cracking is the breaking down of large hydrocarbon molecules into smaller more useful ones.

Chapter 21   Polymerization

1 Add a solution of bromine which should turn from red/brown to colourless.

2 Poly(chloroethene).

3

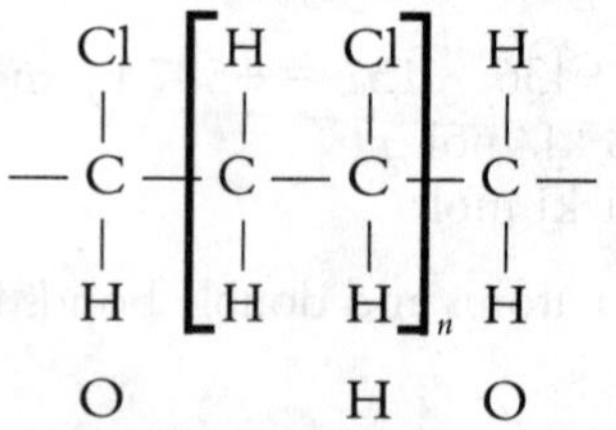

4

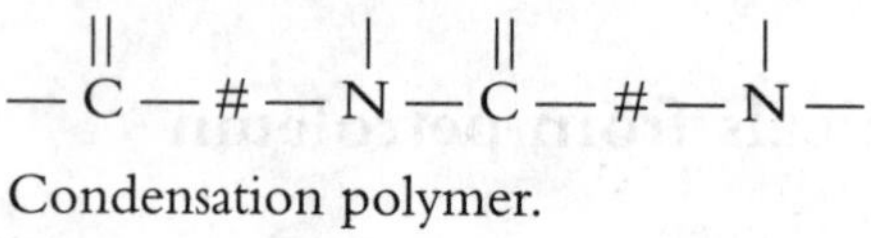

5 Condensation polymer.

6 Thermosetting polymers cannot be melted, thermoplastics can.

Chapter 22   Ammonia, nitric acid and fertilizers

1 Nitrogen; hydrogen.

2 Its elements.

3 Haber.

4 Iron.

5 Fertilizers; nitric acid.

6 Ammonium salt; alkali; ammonium chloride; calcium hydroxide.

7 Upward delivery; 'lighter'; very soluble.

8 Alkaline; white; ammonium chloride.

9 Nitrates in solution from the soil.

10 Trace.

11 Urea, manure.

12 Leguminous plants.

13 21%.

14 Calcium superphosphate.

15 To help form flowers and seeds.

16 A fertilizer that contains nitrogen, phosphorus and potassium.

17 The ammonium salt would react with the lime and give off ammonia to the air, so losing its nitrogen content.

18 (a) Any ammonium compound, sodium nitrate, nitrochalk.
 (b) To replace food taken out of the soil by other plants, so allowing more and better plants to be grown.
 (c) Carbon, oxygen, hydrogen.
 (d) From domestic detergents.
 (e) Fish, plants and other aquatic animals die.

Chapter 23   Salt and chemicals from salt

1 Brine; hydrogen; chlorine; sodium hydroxide.

2 $Cl^- - e^- \rightarrow Cl$ $2Cl \rightarrow Cl_2$

3 Bleach; disinfectant; making plastics, drugs, insecticides.

4 Sodium chlorate(I) (sodium hypochlorite).

5 Making soap, paper, rayon, purification of aluminium ore, fat solvent.

6 Sodium carbonate and sodium hydrogencarbonate.

Chapter 24   Sulphuric acid

1 Contact; oxidation; sulphur trioxide; vanadium(V) oxide; exothermic; concentrated sulphuric acid; oleum.

2 Blue; white; water; dehydrating.

Chapter 25   The mole and chemical calculations

1 (a) 5; (b) 4; (c) 2.5; (d) 2; (e) 1; (f) 0.5; (g) 0.11; (h) 0.0714; (i) 0.005; (j) 0.1.

2 (a) 84 g; (b) 1035 g; (c) 81 g; (d) 12 g; (e) 0.56 g.

3 SO_3.

4 $Fe_2(SO_4)_3$ is the simplest.

5 36%.

6 (a) 100 g; (b) 48%.

7 Twice as heavy.

8 (a) 180 g; (b) 40 g; (c) 92 g; (d) 3.31 g.

9 (a) 11.1 g; (b) 1.2 dm^3.

10 (a) 70 cm^3; (b) 40 cm^3.

Chapter 26 Rocks

1 Metamorphic.

2 Sedimentary.

3 Igneous.

4 Granite crystallizes more slowly, so forms larger crystals.

5 Granite is intrusive and crystallizes within the Earth's crust. Basalt is extrusive and crystallizes on the surface of the Earth.

6 Surface cycles are driven by the Sun's energy. Inside the Earth, the cycle is driven by radioactive processes.

Chapter 27 The structure of the Earth

Crust; mantle; volcanos; core; earthquakes; solid; compression; solids; transverse.

Chapter 28 Plate tectonics

Plates; Pangaea; constructive; destructive; mantle; earthquakes; Richter.

Chapter 29 Qualitative analysis

1 (a) Yellow/orange;   (b) lilac;   (c) brick-red.

2 (a) Light blue;   (b) pale green;   (c) orange.

3 Zinc hydroxide, aluminium hydroxide and lead hydroxide.

4 A metal carbonate or hydrogencarbonate.

5 A solution containing chloride ions.

6 Potassium sulphate.

7 It bleaches moist indicator paper.

8 Oxygen.

9 Hydrogen.

10 'Heavier'.

Chapter 30 Water

1 Water is very good at dissolving things.

2 Increases; less.

3 Mass; 100 g; temperature.

4 A saturated solution will not dissolve any more solute at that temperature; it is recognized by excess solid remaining undissolved even after prolonged stirring.

5 Water that will not lather easily with soap but forms scum.

6 Temporary hard water does not lather with soap but does after the water has been boiled. Boiling decomposes the temporary hardness.

7 Ion exchange column, adding sodium carbonate, distillation.

8 A soapless cleaning agent.

9 They lather well even in hard water.

10 (a) Potassium nitrate;   (b) sodium chloride.

11 Sodium chloride.

12 About 32 °C.

13 Potassium nitrate is much more soluble in hot water. The excess crystallizes out on cooling.

Chapter 31   Chalk, limestone and marble

1 Calcium carbonate.

2 Carbon dioxide; powdery; heat; blue; alkali.

3 Calcium hydroxide solution.

4 The clear solution of limewater soon turns cloudy; more carbon dioxide causes the cloudiness to disappear.

$$Ca(OH)_2(aq) + CO_2(g) \rightarrow CaCO_3(s) + H_2O(l)$$

$$CaCO_3(s) + H_2O(l) + CO_2(g) \rightleftharpoons Ca(HCO_3)_2(aq)$$

5 Calcium hydrogencarbonate.

6 A weak solution of calcium hydrogencarbonate, formed by the action of rain water on limestone, falls from the roof of caves and the reverse reaction takes place reforming the calcium carbonate.

7 Calcium carbonate (marble chips) and dilute hydrochloric acid. Sulphuric acid is not used because the calcium sulphate that would be formed is only slightly soluble in water.

8 Fizzy drinks, fire extinguishers, dry ice.

9 To produce carbon dioxide and to react with impurities to form slag.

10 Making cement, making sodium carbonate.

Chapter 32   Salt formation

1 Soluble.

2 Basicity is the number of replaceable hydrogen atoms in one molecule of the acid. An acid salt is a salt where only part of the replaceable hydrogen of the acid has been replaced.

3 (a) To make sure that all the acid was used up.
   (b) A, filter paper; B, filter funnel; C, residue (magnesium oxide); D, filtrate (magnesium sulphate solution).
   (c) $MgO = 40$; $MgSO_4 \cdot 7H_2O = 246$.
   (d) 12.3 g.
   (e) Evaporate about half of the solution, leave it to cool and to evaporate further at room temperature, filter the crystals, rinse with a little water and leave to dry.

4 Any carbonates except sodium, potassium and ammonium; lead, silver and mercury(I) chlorides; lead and barium sulphates.

5 An insoluble salt is prepared by mixing together two soluble salts each containing 'half' the required insoluble salt, e.g.

silver nitrate + sodium chloride → silver chloride + sodium nitrate

$$AgNO_3 + NaCl \rightarrow AgCl + NaNO_3$$

6 A pipette.

7 A burette.

8 A solution where 1 dm^3 of solution contains 1 mole of solute.

9 4.9 g.

10 (a) 4.0 g;   (b) 0.0025 moles;   (c) 0.0025 moles;   (d) 5 cm^3.

Chapter 33 Transition elements

1 Vanadium and chromium.

2 Elements have variable oxidation states – able to be oxidized and reduced from one state to another; enables the reaction to go in steps.

3 Electrons are going into inner energy shells. Extra protons in the nucleus increase the force of attraction between the nucleus and the outer electrons.

4 (a) 2,8,8,2;   (b) 2,8,13,2.

Chapter 34 Natural products

1

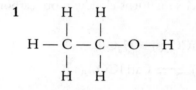

2 The process whereby enzymes in yeast convert sugar into ethanol and carbon dioxide.

3 Fractional distillation.

4 Ethene obtained from petroleum.

5 It is a good solvent.

6 Ethanol + oxygen → carbon dioxide + water

$$C_2H_5OH + 3O_2 \rightarrow 2CO_2 + 3H_2O$$

7 Potassium dichromate(VI); ethanoic acid.

8 Acid; alcohol; ethyl ethanoate.

Chapter 35 The atmosphere and air pollution

1 20–21%.

2 Fractional distillation; mixture; boiling points.

3 Plants produce oxygen by photosynthesis.

4 Nitrogen oxide, carbon monoxide, sulphur dioxide.

5 Corrosion of metals, erosion of rocks, making lakes acidic, killing trees, killing organisms in lakes.

Types of exam questions

Objective questions

These are sometimes called **multiple choice questions**. They are used by some examination groups for testing candidates of all abilities. At first sight these questions may seem comparatively easy because it is simply a matter of choosing the correct answer from the possible answers given. In practice candidates do not always do as well as they expect, because the questions are specially designed to test your knowledge and understanding of the whole syllabus and because the amount of time available is limited.

There are two types of multiple choice questions used for GCSE examinations.

1 Simple multiple choice

In this type of question you are given an incomplete statement or a question (called the stem) together with four or five possible answers (or responses) and you have to choose the only one that correctly fits the stem. The wrong answers are called distractors.

E.g. What colour is hydrated copper(II) sulphate?

    A Blue
    B Green
    C White
    D Yellow
    E Black

A is the correct answer (or key). B, C, D and E are distractors. This question is entirely a recall of information that a candidate should have learnt. If he or she confuses hydrated copper(II) sulphate with anhydrous copper(II) sulphate, the answer C might be given.

Many questions like the one above appear on GCSE papers. They test factual learning. Providing you have mastered the units in this book these questions should not be too difficult.

Other questions of this type require, in addition to factual learning, understanding and/or the application of principles.

E.g. Which one of the italicized substances is an element?

A A *green substance* which is separated into two substances by chromatography.
B A *black liquid* which boils over a range of temperature.
C A *black solid* which burns in oxygen completely to form a single colourless gas.
D A *white substance* which turns yellow on heating but white again on cooling.
E A *colourless liquid* which turns to a colourless solid on cooling.

Any candidate who has just learnt the definition of the term 'element' but does not understand it is unable to answer this question. The correct response is C because the black solid burns completely to form only one product. There is no need to try to identify these substances.

Sometimes a number of these items may be linked to the same experimental situation.

2 Classification

This type of question is used when a number of similar type 1 multiple choice questions are being set with identical responses. The five lettered responses are given first, followed by a series of questions.

E.g. For each of the questions 1–4 choose the one process labelled A, B, C, D or E with which it is chiefly associated.

A Cracking
B Polymerization
C Oxidation
D Hydrogenation
E Neutralization

1 Decane vapour is changed to ethene when passed over heated china.

2 Margarine is produced by passing hydrogen through a heated oil in the presence of a catalyst.

3 Sodium carbonate is added to ethanoic acid (acetic acid) until no further carbon dioxide is evolved.

4 Ethene is completely burnt in excess oxygen.

The correct responses to these questions are:

1 A   2 D   3 E   4 C

In this type of question each response may be used once, more than once or not at all.

Points to be remembered for multiple choice tests

1. Read through each question carefully. Often a candidate gives a wrong answer because the question has not been read and understood. Often some of the distractors are designed to appeal to the candidate who has not completely read and understood the question.

2. Do not spend too much time on the early items or on any single item. Invariably the questions get longer and more involved as the test progresses, and you will need more time to tackle the questions at the end of the test.

3. Because there are a large number of questions in each test, perhaps 50, and the test is designed to cover the whole syllabus, it is unwise to study only parts of the syllabus. You should attempt to study as much of the syllabus as possible.

4. Do not be afraid to guess. Guessing sensibly can help you and you do not lose marks for a wrong answer. If there are five possible responses and you know that three are wrong but you cannot decide between the other two, then guess. You have increased you chances of success by ruling out incorrect responses. Never leave any question unattempted at the end of the test.

5. Make sure you use all of the information given in the questions. It would not be given unless it was required.

6. Research has shown that in multiple choice tests repeated checking of your answers does not improve the final mark obtained. You are at least as likely to change a correct answer to an incorrect one. The amount of time allowed is not intended to give you 'checking time'.

   On pages 218–224 you will find a sample multiple choice test of the type used for GCSE. There are 40 questions and the test should take no longer than three-quarters of an hour.

Short answer questions

Short answer questions are very common on GCSE papers. They have the same advantage to the examiner as multiple choice questions because with a large number of questions virtually the whole syllabus can be covered.

Short answer questions can be used for candidates of all abilities but are especially suitable for candidates achieving grades C–G.

There are many different types of short answer question. Sometimes the answer required is a single word, several words or a sentence. Sometimes, however, the candidate may be required to complete a table or a diagram.

On pages 225–228 there is a selection of short answers questions.

Structured questions

Structured questions are perhaps the most common questions on GCSE papers. A structured question consists of some information given in the question followed by a number of questions based upon the information given. Usually there are spaces for you to fill in the answers. Bear in mind the amount of space you are given. If you are given three lines the examiner is expecting more than one or two words. Also the number of marks for each part is given, and if two marks, for example, are available usually more than a single word would be required.

On pages 228–242 there is a selection of GCSE structured questions.

Comprehension questions

Comprehension questions appear on GCSE papers and provide a convenient way of introducing the candidate to up-to-date information, especially about the social, economic and environmental aspects of chemistry.

It is most important to read the information thoroughly before attempting to answer the question. Candidates usually score good marks on this type of question. However, there is a temptation to spend too much time on the comprehension questions.

On pages 249–252 there are some sample comprehension questions.

Essay questions

Essay questions are suitable only for candidates attempting to achieve grades A, B or C. Apart from chemical knowledge and understanding, the candidate needs to be able to select, organize and present the information in an acceptable form.

Usually to help the candidate the question is broken down into parts and each part has a separate mark allocation. This should help you to know how much time to spend on each part. Just as you would with an English essay, you should plan your essay and there is nothing wrong with putting your essay plan down on the answer paper and then neatly crossing it out. It does at least show the examiner that there was planning!

Do not just 'waffle'. In chemistry credit is given only for specific points in your answer and so there is no benefit in just writing to produce a long essay. If you do this you are just wasting time.

On pages 246–247 there are some sample essay questions.

Sample questions and answers

Multiple choice questions

For candidates of all abilities. This test should take about three-quarters of an hour.

1 Magnesium (atomic number 12) forms Mg^{2+} ions. The number of electrons in a magnesium ion is

    A   4
    B   6
    C 10
    D 12
    E 14

2 Which one of the following substances dissolves in water to form a solution with a pH greater than 7?

    A Sulphur dioxide
    B Ammonia
    C Chlorine
    D Copper(II) oxide
    E Hydrogen chloride

3 Which one of the following reactions would result in the formation of an element?

    A Burning carbon in excess air
    B Heating copper(II) sulphate crystals
    C Neutralizing an acid with a base
    D Reducing lead(II) oxide with hydrogen
    E Heating lead(II) carbonate

4 Dehydration of methanoic acid (formic acid) HCOOH produces a gas. This gas is

    A carbon monoxide
    B carbon dioxide
    C hydrogen
    D carbon
    E water

5 An indicator is used during a neutralization reaction in order to

    A detect the acid and the alkali
    B show when exactly reacting quantities of acid and alkali are present
    C speed up the rate of reaction between the acid and the alkali
    D measure the amount of heat liberated
    E show whether the reaction is reversible

6 Crystals of sodium carbonate decahydrate (washing soda) are efflorescent. When these crystals are exposed to air the crystals

    A lose mass and remain solid
    B gain mass and remain solid
    C gain mass and become liquid
    D gain mass, change to liquid and evolve bubbles of gas
    E remain unchanged

7 When a piece of copper is added to silver nitrate solution, silver is displaced. Iron reacts slowly with warm, dilute hydrochloric acid to produce hydrogen but silver and copper do not react. The metals in order of reactivity, with the most reactive first, are
    A copper, silver, iron
    B iron, silver, copper
    C iron, copper, silver
    D copper, iron, silver
    E silver, iron, copper

8 Crude oil is separated into fractions with different boiling points by fractional distillation. In which one of the following are the fractions arranged in the correct order of increasing boiling point?
    A Petrol, bitumen, diesel oil, paraffin
    B Bitumen, diesel oil, paraffin, petrol
    C Diesel oil, petrol, bitumen, paraffin
    D Paraffin, diesel oil, bitumen, petrol
    E Petrol, paraffin, diesel oil, bitumen

9 2.38 g of tin, when treated with concentrated nitric acid and heated, produced 3.02 g of anhydrous tin oxide. What is the formula of this oxide? ($A_r(O) = 16$, $A_r(Sn) = 119$)
    A SnO
    B SnO_2
    C Sn_2O
    D Sn_2O_3
    E SnO_3

10 $2NH_3(g) + 3CuO(s) \rightarrow N_2(g) + 3H_2O(g) + 3Cu(s)$
What is the volume of the gaseous product formed when 80 cm^3 of ammonia is passed over heated copper(II) oxide?
(All volumes measured at room temperature and pressure.)
    A   20 cm^3
    B   40 cm^3
    C   80 cm^3
    D 120 cm^3
    E 160 cm^3

Questions 11–15 refer to the following types of chemical reaction

    A Hydrolysis
    B Polymerization
    C Dehydration
    D Neutralization
    E Precipitation

Select the term from the list above which best describes the reaction represented by each of the following equations:

11 $(C_6H_{10}O_5)_n(aq) + nH_2O(l) \rightarrow nC_6H_{12}O_6(aq)$

12 $OH^-(aq) + H^+(aq) \rightarrow H_2O(l)$

13 $C_2H_5OH(g) \rightarrow C_2H_4(g) + H_2O(g)$

14 $MgO(s) + 2HNO_3(aq) \rightarrow Mg(NO_3)_2(aq) + H_2O(l)$

15 $MgSO_4(aq) + Na_2CO_3(aq) \rightarrow MgCO_3(s) + Na_2SO_4(aq)$

16 The diagram represents apparatus which can be used to pass a measured quantity of air, to and fro, over heated copper wire until no further reaction occurs.

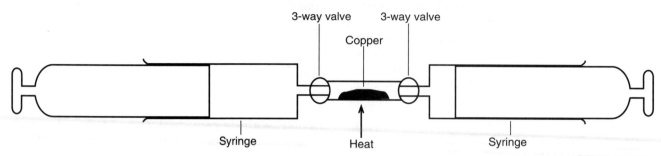

In one experiment it was found that 16 cm³ of gas remained after the apparatus had cooled. How many cubic centimetres of air were there in the apparatus at the beginning of the experiment?

    A   20
    B   40
    C   60
    D   80
    E   100

17 Three liquids were available:
    (i)   a solution of dry hydrogen chloride dissolved in dry methylbenzene (toluene)
    (ii) pure ethanol
    (iii) pure water

Which one of the following would have a pH less than 7?

    A   (i)
    B   (ii)
    C   (i) and (ii) mixed together
    D   (i) and (iii) mixed together
    E   (ii) and (iii) mixed together

18 A metal M forms a hydroxide $M(OH)_3$. The relative formula mass of his hydroxide is 78. What is the relative atomic mass of the metal M? ($A_r(H) = 1$, $A_r(O) = 16$)

    A 27
    B 30
    C 59
    D 61
    E 75

19 A metallic element X forms an ion X^{3+}. What will be the formula of the sulphate of X?

    A XSO_4
    B $X(SO_4)_3$
    C $X_2(SO_4)_3$
    D X_3SO_4
    E $X_3(SO_4)_2$

20 An ion with a single positive charge becomes an atom by
    A losing an electron
    B losing a neutron
    C gaining a proton
    D gaining a neutron
    E gaining an electron

21 If a mixture of fine pollen grains in water is examined closely it will be seen that the pollen grains are always in motion.

This motion is most likely to be due to
   A   the convection currents in the water
   B   the chemical reaction between the pollen and the water
   C   the attraction and repulsion between charged particles
   D   the collisions between pollen grains and water molecules
   E   the diffusion of pollen grains

22 The products of the hydrolysis of starch with hydrochloric acid can be identified using
   A   iodine
   B   sodium carbonate
   C   chromatography
   D   distillation
   E   enzymes

Questions 23–26 refer to the experiment described below

The apparatus shown in the diagram was used to produce a sample of ethene from liquid paraffin.

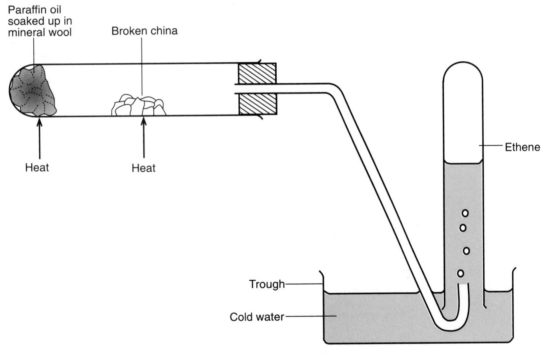

23 What is the reason for using the mineral wool?
   A   To act as a catalyst for the reaction
   B   To prevent heat escaping from the test tube
   C   To prevent water from the trough entering the test tube
   D   To hold the liquid paraffin at the end of the tube
   E   To lower the boiling point of the liquid paraffin

24 The process taking place during this experiment is
   A   cracking
   B   polymerization
   C   combustion
   D   distillation
   E   saponification

25 The liquid found floating on the water at the end of the experiment
   A   is produced by reaction between ethene and water
   B   comes from the broken china
   C   is unreacted liquid paraffin
   D   is produced when ethene comes in contact with air
   E   is produced by reaction between ethene and substances in the water

26 Ethene and paraffin can be distinguished *chemically* by the fact that ethene, but not paraffin,

    A   will burn in air
    B   will decolorize bromine water
    C   is a hydrocarbon
    D   can be obtained from crude oil
    E   is a gas at room temperature

Questions 27–30 refer to the curves A–E
Each curve shows the change of a property with time

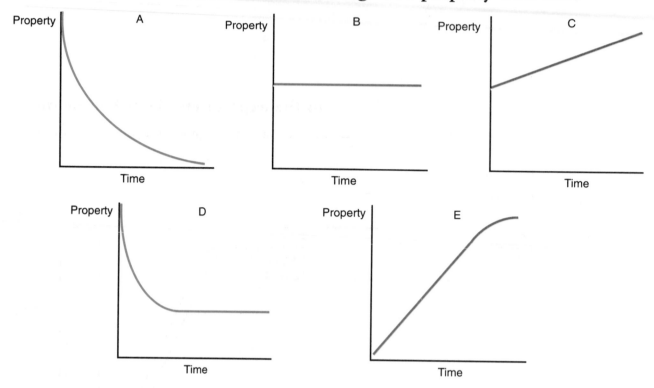

Select the curve which best shows the change of the property in italics with time for each of the following:

27 *The volume of carbon dioxide evolved* during the reaction between calcium carbonate and hydrochloric acid

28 *The mass of a catalyst* during the decomposition of ammonia

29 *The mass of lead(II) oxide* when heated in a stream of hydrogen

30 *The mass of a copper cathode* during the electrolysis of copper(II) sulphate solution with copper electrodes and a constant current

Questions 31–32 refer to the following experiment

Dry air is passed over heated zinc in the apparatus shown in the figure. The gases remaining escape at X.

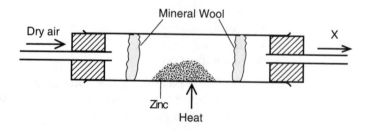

31 The gas leaving the apparatus at X is mainly
    A argon
    B carbon dioxide
    C nitrogen
    D oxygen
    E water vapour

32 The main chemical compound present in the apparatus at the end of the experiment is
    A zinc
    B zinc oxide
    C zinc nitrate
    D zinc nitride
    E zinc hydroxide

33 The table below gives the results of six experiments involving the reaction between zinc and hydrochloric acid. In all experiments 0.2 g of zinc was used together with the same volume of acid.

Experiment number	Concentration of acid	Temperature of acid (°C)	State of division of zinc	Time for the reaction to be completed (s)
1	1 M	25	Foil	190
2	2 M	25	Powder	85
3	2 M	35	Foil	62
4	2 M	50	Powder	15
5	2 M	35	Powder	45
6	3 M	50	Powder	11

Which set of experiments suggests that the speed of a reaction increases with temperature?
    A 1, 3 and 4
    B 2, 3 and 4
    C 2, 3 and 5
    D 2, 4 and 5
    E 2, 5 and 6

34 Which one of the following liquids, when added to a strongly alkaline solution in the correct amount, could produce a solution with a pH of 7?
    A Distilled water
    B Limewater
    C Potassium hydroxide
    D Sulphuric acid
    E Universal Indicator

35 An atom of an element with an atomic number 3 and a mass number 7 contains
    A 3 electrons
    B 3 neutrons
    C 4 electrons
    D 4 protons
    E 7 neutrons

Questions 36–40 refer to the following processes

    A Chromatography
    B Crystallization
    C Distillation
    D Filtration
    E Fractional distillation

Which of the above processes would be most suitable for

36 removing sand from river water?

37 obtaining pure water from sea water? ☐

38 separating a mixture of petrol and diesel oil? ☐

39 investigating the number of colourings added to a fruit drink? ☐

40 obtaining ammonium sulphate from an aqueous solution of ammonium sulphate? ☐

Answers to multiple choice questions

1 C; **2** B; **3** D; **4** A; **5** B; **6** A; **7** C; **8** E; **9** B; **10** B;
11 A; **12** D; **13** C; **14** D; **15** E; **16** A; **17** D; **18** A; **19** C; **20** E;
21 D; **22** C; **23** D; **24** A; **25** C; **26** B; **27** E; **28** B; **29** D; **30** C;
31 C; **32** B; **33** D; **34** D; **35** A; **36** D; **37** C; **38** E; **39** A; **40** B.

Reasoning behind the answers

The answers may not help you to see how to do similar questions in the future. Here briefly is an explanation of how the answers are obtained. This is especially useful where the question tests application of your knowledge to different situations. Where the question is recall, reference is made to the appropriate chapter in the text.

1 A magnesium atom contains 12 electrons and loses two electrons when forming a 2+ ion.

2 See Chapter 7.

3 Reduction is removing oxygen. If oxygen is removed from lead(II) oxide only lead remains.

4 Dehydration is the removal of water. If two hydrogen atoms and one oxygen atom are removed from HCOOH only CO (carbon monoxide) remains.

5 See Chapter 32.

6 Efflorescence is the loss of water to the atmosphere and therefore there would be a loss of mass.

7 Only iron is reactive enough to displace hydrogen from hydrochloric acid. Copper replaces silver and is therefore more reactive than silver.

8 See Chapter 20.

9 2.38 g of tin combine with 0.64 g of oxygen. 0.02 moles of tin atoms combine with 0.04 moles of oxygen atoms.

10 From the equation, 80 cm^3 of NH_3 produces half the volume of nitrogen (40 cm^3). However, candidates often forget that the water has condensed and give an answer of 160 cm^3.

11 Hydrolysis is the splitting up of a compound with water.

12 This is the ionic equation for neutralization.

13 This is removal of water – dehydration.

14 Acid + base, therefore it is neutralization (see Chapter 2).

15 $MgCO_3(s)$ tells you that the solid is precipitated.

16 One fifth of the 'air' removed during the experiment.

17 Water must be present before acid properties are shown.

18 There are three OH^-; mass $3 \times 17 = 51$. Subtract this from 78.

19 The ions are X^{3+} and SO_4^{2-}.

20 Positive ions are formed when atoms lose electrons. Atoms are formed when positive ions gain electrons.

21 Brownian motion.

22 Iodine is used as a test for starch and iodine is a frequent wrong answer here. Starch is split up into sugars by hydrolysis and these can be separated and identified by chromatography.

23 Otherwise the liquid will run along the tube.

24 This is breaking down large molecules in the liquid into smaller molecules in the gas.

25 This liquid is produced by distillation. The liquid paraffin boils. Some of it does not react when passed over the heated china and condenses in contact with the cold water.

26 See Chapter 20. This is frequently not known by candidates.

27 There is no carbon dioxide at the start. The volume increases during the reaction until one or both of the reactants are used up. No further gas is produced.

28 The mass of catalyst remains unchanged.

29 The mass of lead oxide decreases during the reaction until it reaches a minimum.

30 The mass of the cathode increases as copper is deposited and the increase is steady because of the constant current.

31 Oxygen is removed; mainly nitrogen remains.

32 Reaction between zinc and oxygen forms zinc oxide.

33 2, 4 and 5 – all the other conditions apart from temperature are the same – i.e. concentration of acid and state of division. In these three experiments only temperature is different.

34 Sulphuric acid is the only strong acid solution present. When a strong acid and a strong alkali are mixed in the right amounts a neutral solution of pH 7 results.

35 Atomic number 3, mass number 7: 3 protons, 3 electrons and 4 neutrons.

36 This is removing an insoluble solid from a liquid (see Chapter 1).

37 This is separating a solvent from a solution (see Chapter 1).

38 This is separating liquids with different boiling points (see Chapter 1).

39 See Chapter 1.

40 This is obtaining crystals from an aqueous solution.

Short answer questions

Short answer questions are suitable for any level paper. They tend to be used on Central and Basic tier papers. They have the advantage of giving good syllabus coverage. Questions which are starred would be suitable only for Higher level papers.

1 Centrifuging   Decanting   Drying and weighing
  Crystallizing   Dissolving   Evaporating
  Chromatography   Distilling   Filtering

Choose one of these processes to achieve each of the following.

(You may use a process once, more than once or not at all.)

(a) Obtaining pure water from sea water. .... (1)

(b) Removing solid impurities from industrial gases. ....

.... (1)

(c) Removing water from clothes hanging on a clothes line. ....

.... (1)

(d) Removing water from clothes using a spin drier. ....

.... (1)

(e) Separating home-made wine from sediment. .... (1)

(f) Drying a sample of copper(II) oxide completely and checking that it is dry.

.... (1)

(g) Extracting the red colour from a solution obtained from some flower petals.

.... (1)

(h) Discovering whether the red colour extracted in (g) was a single colour or a mixture of colours. .... (1)

MEG 1993

*2 In the spaces provided, write the name of an element that fits the description. The Periodic Table may be helpful.

(a) an element that is liquid at room temperature. .... (1)

(b) an element that has allotropes. .... (1)

(c) an extremely unreactive nonmetal with a relative atomic mass greater than 200.

.... (1)

(d) a metal that has 14 neutrons in one atom of its most common isotope.

.... (1)

(e) an element that forms a compound in which one atom of the element is combined with four atoms of chlorine. .... (1)

(f) a nonmetal that forms oxides of the type X_2O_3 and X_2O_5. .... (1)

(g) an element in group II that is more than reactive than calcium. ....

.... (1)

3 Complete the following table.

Particle	Atomic number	Mass number	Number of		
			protons	neutrons	electrons
carbon atom	6	12			
sodium atom	11			12	
sodium ion Na$^+$					

4 The table shows some information about the samples in a school mineral collection.

Sample	Colour	Streak	Hardness	Acid test	Heaviness
Quartz	colourless	none	hard	no action	light
Feldspar	white	white	hard	no action	light
Pyrites	golden	black	hard	no action	heavy
Calcite	colourless	white	soft	fizzes	light
Gypsum	white	white	soft	no action	light
Haematite	red	red	hard	no action	heavy

A student at the school has started to make a key to identify the samples using the information in the table. Complete the key by adding the information or sample names in the blank spaces.

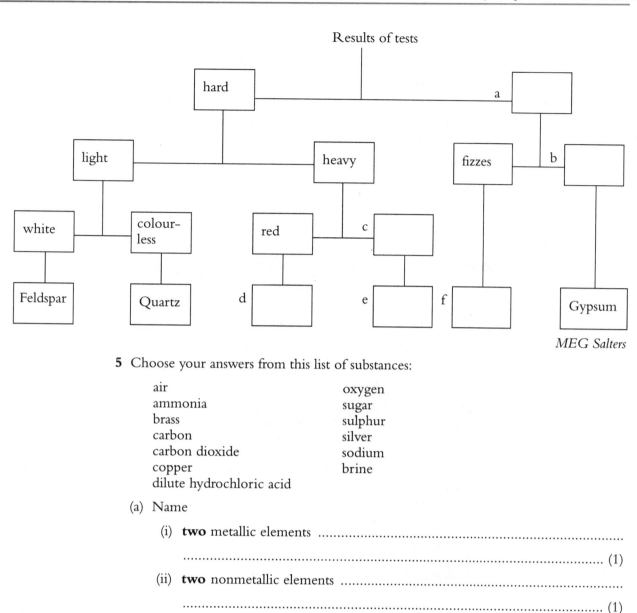

Results of tests

MEG Salters

5 Choose your answers from this list of substances:

air   oxygen
ammonia   sugar
brass   sulphur
carbon   silver
carbon dioxide   sodium
copper   brine
dilute hydrochloric acid

(a) Name

(i) **two** metallic elements ....

.... (1)

(ii) **two** nonmetallic elements ....

.... (1)

(iii) **two** compounds ....

.... (1)

(iv) **two** mixtures ....

.... (1)

(b) State which **one** of the substances is used:

(i) in the manufacture of fertilizers .... (1)

(ii) in the production of sulphuric acid .... (1)

(iii) in photography .... (1)

(iv) to produce chlorine, hydrogen and sodium hydroxide by electrolysis

.... (1)

6 Use the following equations to answer the questions below.

A $C + O_2 \rightarrow CO_2$
B $2Mg + CO_2 \rightarrow 2MgO + C$
C $C + CO_2 \rightarrow 2CO$
D $Fe_2O_3 + 3CO \rightarrow 2Fe + 3CO_2$
E $CaCO_3 \rightarrow CaO + CO_2$
F $2CO + O_2 \rightarrow 2CO_2$

Write the correct letter in the box for:

(i) the reaction in which carbon is oxidized to carbon dioxide ☐

(ii) the reaction in which thermal decomposition occurs ☐

(iii) the reaction in which carbon monoxide reduces a metal oxide ☐

(iv) the reaction in which a metal is oxidized by carbon dioxide ☐

(v) three of the reactions involving solids that take place in the blast furnace

☐ + ☐ + ☐

(7)

MEG

Answers to short answer questions

1 (a) Distilling; (b) filtering; (c) evaporating; (d) centrifuging; (e) decanting; (f) drying and weighing; (g) evaporating; (h) chromatography.

★2 The question asks for names. If you use symbols you will receive credit, e.g. credit for O_2 not for O.

(a) bromine or mercury;
(b) carbon or sulphur (phosphorus, oxygen, arsenic, tin or silicon are also correct but you are unlikely to give these);
(c) radon;
(d) aluminium (not silicon which has 14 neutrons in the atom but is not a metal);
(e) any element in group IV;
(f) any element in group V;
(g) strontium, barium or radium.

3 Carbon atom: 6p, 6n, 6e.
Sodium atom: mass no. 23, 11p, 11e.
Sodium ion (formed when a sodium atom loses an electron): at. no. 11, mass no. 23, 11p, 12n, 10e.

4 a, soft (1); b, no action; c, black/golden; d, haematite; e, pyrites; f, calcite. Six answers. Allow 1 mark for each up to a maximum of 5.

5 (a) (i) Copper, silver, sodium (any 2) (1);
(ii) oxygen, sulphur, carbon (any 2) (1);
(iii) ammonia, carbon dioxide, sugar (any 2) (1);
(iv) dilute hydrochloric acid, brass, air, brine (any 2) (1);
(b) (i) ammonia (1); (ii) sulphur (1); (iii) silver (1); (iv) brine (1).

6 (i) A (1); (ii) E (1); (iii) D (1); (iv) B (1); (v) A (1), D (1), E (1).

Structured questions

In this section questions that are unstarred are suitable for candidates of all abilities. Questions that are starred are intended for candidates aiming at Higher level – grades A★, A and B.

1 The following procedures were used in a set of experiments on the Reactivity Series.

1 Excess magnesium powder was added to 25 cm³ of each solution, all having the same molar concentration.

2   The rise in temperature in each case was recorded.

Molar solution	Rise in temperature (°C)
Copper(II) sulphate	42
Lead(II) nitrate	32
Magnesium sulphate	0
Sodium nitrate	0
Sulphuric acid	38
Zinc sulphate	14

(a)   From the results place the **elements** copper, hydrogen, lead, magnesium and zinc in order of reactivity.

Most reactive ....

....

....

....

Least reactive ....   (2)

(b)   Explain why there is no rise in temperature in two of the experiments.

....

.... (2)

(c)   Suggest the rise in temperature you would expect if excess magnesium powder was added to 25 cm^3 of molar iron(II) sulphate solution.

.... °C   (1)

(d)   Give **TWO** changes, other than a rise in temperature, that are observed when magnesium powder is added to copper(II) sulphate solution.

....

....

....

.... (2)

MEG 1993

2   The alkanes form a homologous series of hydrocarbons.

(a) (i) What is meant by hydrocarbon? ....

.... (2)

(ii) State one chemical characteristic of the alkanes.

.... (1)

(b) The boiling points of some alkanes are given in the table below.

Number of C atoms	2	3	4	5	6	7
Boiling point (°C)	−89	−42	0		69	98

Plot these results on the grid on the following page.

Use the plot to predict the boiling point of pentane, the alkane with five carbon atoms.

Boiling point of pentane = ...°C   (3)

(c) Give the molecular formula of pentane .... (1)

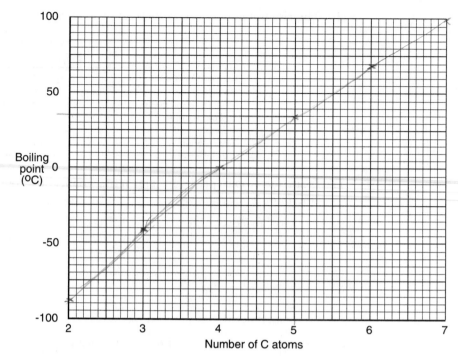

(d) The arrangement of the carbon atoms in the two isomers of butane may be shown in a simplified way as

C — C — C — C   and   C — C — C
                                              |
                                              C

Show in a similar way what you would predict for the arrangement of carbon atoms in the **THREE** isomers of pentane.

(3)

(e) Suggest how you might distinguish by a chemical test between pentane, an alkane, and pentene, an alkene. Name the reagent and state what you would expect to observe.

Reagent ....

Observation with pentane ....

....

Observation with pentene ....

.... (3)

MEG 1993

3 Ethane-1,2-diol has the structural formula shown.

```
        H    H
        |    |
  H —  C  —  C  — H
        |    |
        O    O
        |    |
        H    H
```

When one mole of water is added to one mole of epoxyethane one mole of ethane-1,2-diol is formed as the only product.

(a) (i) Give the molecular formula of ethane-1,2-diol

.... (1)

(ii) Deduce the molecular formula of epoxyethane

.... (1)

(b) The conversion of epoxyethane to ethane-1,2-diol can be carried out in one of two ways.

	Conditions for Process 1	Conditions for Process 2
pH value	7	1–2
Temperature (°C)	200	60
Pressure (atm)	14	1

(i) Suggest a substance that could be added to produce the pH value in Process 2. .... (1)

(ii) List and justify two advantages and one disadvantage of Process 2 compared with Process 1. ....

....

....

....

....

.... (3)

(c) The major use of ethane-1,2-diol is to dissolve in water in the radiator of a car to act as antifreeze. Ethane-1,2-diol freezes at −14 °C and boils at 197 °C.

(i) Name the technique you would use to separate these two components in a mixture from a radiator. .... (1)

(ii) When a sample of the liquid taken from a radiator that contained water and antifreeze was cooled down, crystals first appeared at a temperature of −21 °C. The thermometer was checked and found to be accurate. Explain.

....

.... (1)

MEG 1993

★4 Imagine that you needed to check the concentration of some dilute sulphuric acid. You titrated 25.0 cm³ of the acid with sodium hydroxide solution containing 1.2 mol dm⁻³ NaOH; 35.0 cm³ of the alkali was required for neutralization.

$$2NaOH + H_2SO_4 \rightarrow Na_2SO_4 + 2H_2O$$

(a) (i) With what should you measure out 25.0 cm³ of the acid?

.... (1)

(ii) With what should you measure out 35.0 cm³ of the alkali?

.... (1)

(iii) State clearly, giving a named example, what you would add to the acid in order to know when to stop adding the alkali.

.... (1)

(iv) What would you then observe when 35.0 cm³ of the alkali have been added? .... (1)

(b) (i) How many moles of sodium hydroxide (NaOH) were added in the titration? ....

.... (1)

(ii) With how many moles of sulphuric acid (H_2SO_4) (in the 25.0 cm^3 of solution) would this react? ....
.... (1)

(iii) What is the concentration of the sulphuric acid in mol H_2SO_4 dm^{-3}?
....
.... (1)

(c) If excess magnesium were added to 1.00 dm^3 of the acid what volume of hydrogen, measured at room temperature and pressure, would you expect to be evolved? (1 mole of gas at room temperature and pressure occupies 24 dm^3)

$$Mg(s) + H_2SO_4(aq) \rightarrow MgSO_4(aq) + H_2(g)$$

....
....
.... (3)

ULEAC

⋆5 (a) When zinc burns in oxygen, it gives a white powder, zinc oxide. In an experiment, 2.60 g of zinc gave 3.24 g of zinc oxide. **Show**, using this data, that the formula of the zinc oxide is ZnO. (Relative atomic masses Zn = 65, O = 16)

(4)

(b) When zinc oxide is stirred with water, nothing appears to happen. When dilute hydrochloric acid is added and the mixture is stirred, the powder disappears. Explain why the powder disappears and write an equation for the reaction which occurs. ....
....
....
.... (3)

(c) (i) What kinds of substance **always** contain the ion H$^+$(aq)?
.... (2)

(ii) What kind of reaction is represented by the following reaction?

$$H^+(aq) + OH^-(aq) \rightarrow H_2O(l)$$

.... (1)

ULEAC

6 Small samples of three metallic elements, **P**, **Q** and **R**, were each placed in cold water.

P rushed about the surface, burned with a lilac-pink flame and finally disappeared.
Q sank and showed no change.
R first sank, then started to bubble with ever increasing vigour, sometimes rising to the surface, and finally disappeared leaving a cloudy liquid.

(i) Place **P**, **Q** and **R** in order of activity, **the least active first**.

.... (2)

(ii) Suggest possible identities for **P**, **Q** and **R**.

P might be ....

Q might be ....

R might be .... (3)

(iii) What gas is formed by **R**? .... (1)

(iv) Which of these elements might be suitable for making cold water pipes?

.... (1)

(v) Plan a simple experiment you might do to find if the element you have chosen really is suitable for making water pipes. ....

....

....

.... (2)

(vi) Do you think that your experiment would be a reliable guide? Explain your answer. ....

....

.... (1)

ULEAC

★7 (a) In the manufacture of aluminium (relative atomic mass 27) a molten electrolyte containing aluminium oxide is electrolysed.

$$Al^{3+} + 3e^- \rightarrow Al$$

How much aluminium will be deposited by a current of 20 000 A flowing for one hour?

(Faraday constant = 96 500 coulombs)

(b)

	Relative density	Tensile strength	Electrical conductivity	Hardness	m.p. (°C)
Aluminium	2.70	8.2	38.2	20	660
Steel (iron)	7.86	32.5	10.0	70	1525
Copper	8.92	21.0	59.3	45	1083

Select, and give a reason for your choice, the metal most likely to be used for:

(i) the cable on a passenger lift ....

.... (2)

(ii) unstressed partitions in a passenger aircraft ....

.... (2)

(c) Although copper has a higher electrical conductivity than aluminium, overhead power lines are often made from aluminium. The aluminium cable normally has a core of steel.

Explain why this is so. ....

....

....

.... (4)

ULEAC

★8 One very large use of chlorine in recent years has been the manufacture of CFCs – chlorinated fluorocarbons. CFCs are gases and, after use, they spread out into the atmosphere. Scientists now believe that the chlorine in CFCs may be responsible for destroying ozone in the upper atmosphere.

(a) A chlorine atom contains 17 protons in the nucleus, and 17 electrons. Chlorine is in group VII of the Periodic Table. Draw diagrams of an atom of chlorine, a chloride ion (as found in sodium chloride) and a molecule of chlorine. The diagrams should show the arrangement of electrons in the outer layer.

   (i) a chlorine atom (2)

   (ii) a chloride ion (2)

   (iii) a molecule of chlorine (2)

(b) Which would you expect to be most reactive, a chlorine atom, a chlorine molecule, or a chloride ion in solution? Explain your answer.

....

.... (2)

(c) (i) Complete the equation below to show how a chlorine free radical might be formed from a molecule of dichlorodifluoromethane CCl_2F_2 (a common CFC) in the upper atmosphere.

$$+ \text{ energy } \rightarrow$$ (2)

   (ii) Suggest where the energy needed for this reaction might come from.

   .... (1)

   Ozone is formed naturally in the upper atmosphere.

   $$O_2 + \text{energy} \rightarrow O + O$$

   The oxygen atoms then react with other oxygen molecules to form ozone.

(d) Write an equation to show the reaction between an oxygen atom and an oxygen molecule to form ozone.

(1)

If chlorine free radicals are present in the upper atmosphere, they can destroy ozone:

   reaction I $Cl\cdot + O_3 \rightarrow ClO\cdot + O_2$
   reaction II $ClO\cdot + O \rightarrow Cl\cdot + O_2$

(e) Write a single, simpler, equation which sums up the overall effect of reaction I and reaction II.

(1)

(f) Explain why a single chlorine free radical is able to destroy many molecules of ozone. ....

....

.... (3)

MEG Salters

9   The table gives details of some of the substances present in different types of fatty spread.

Substance present	Spread A	Spread B	Spread C
Water (%)	13.1	5.6	56.0
Saturated fats (%)	61.8	17.4	22.4
Unsaturated fats (%)	25.1	77.0	21.6

(a) Draw sections of molecules which could be part of

   (i) a saturated fat

(1)

   (ii) an unsaturated fat

(2)

To test whether a fat is saturated or unsaturated, a small amount of the fat is mixed with ethanol in a test-tube, then bromine water is added a drop at a time. After each drop is added, the tube is shaken well.

(b) Describe what you would see in the tube

  (i) if the fat is saturated ....

  .... (1)

  (ii) if the fat is unsaturated ....

  .... (2)

(c) What is the purpose of the ethanol in this tube?

.... (1)

(d) The three spreads shown were margarine, slimmers' margarine and butter. Identify the slimmers' margarine from the table, and explain your answer.

....

.... (2)

(e) Spread C is likely to contain a fairly large amount of a certain type of food additive. What is this type of food additive, and why is it necessary?

....

.... (3)

MEG Salters

★10 The diagram shows three electrolysis cells in series.

Cell 1 contains silver electrodes dipping into aqueous silver nitrate solution.
Cell 2 contains copper electrodes dipping into aqueous copper(II) sulphate solution.
Cell 3 contains chromium electrodes dipping into an aqueous chromium salt solution. ($A_r(Ag) = 108$, $A_r(Cu) = 64$, $A_r(Cr) = 52$)

(a) Aqueous copper(II) sulphate solution contains Cu^{2+}, SO_4^{2-}, H^+ and OH^- ions.

Which ions are present in aqueous silver nitrate solution?

.... (1)

(b) One product formed in cell **2** is copper. Write ionic equations for the reactions which take place at the electrodes in cell **2**.

Anode ....

Cathode .... (2)

(c) A current was passed through the circuit. If 0.540 g of silver was deposited at the cathode in cell **1** and 0.130 g of chromium at the cathode in cell **3**:

(i) calculate the mass of copper deposited at the cathode in cell **2**;

(2)

(ii) calculate the charge on the chromium ion in cell **3**.

(3)

MEG Science Sample

★11 (a) Study the information given below, and then answer the questions which follow.

Type of material	Typical properties
Metals	Strong; hard; malleable; high density; conduct heat and electricity well; some react with air, water and acids.
Ceramics	Hard; strong when compressed; weak when stretched; brittle; high melting points; heat resistant; chemically unreactive.
Glasses	Same as ceramics but also transparent.
Plastics	Flexible; easily melted and moulded; wide range of properties depending on specific plastic; some burn when heated in air.
Fibre	Structures are long, strong, hair-like strands; flexible; some burn when heated in air.

Explain which **one** of the above types of material would be best for making each of the following:

(i) An oven door ....
....
.... (2)

(ii) A dustbin ....
....
.... (2)

(b) Explain the difference between a compound and an element. Use the examples of sodium, chlorine and sodium chloride to illustrate your answer.

....
....
....
....
....
....
....
....
.... (6)

SEG

12 The diagram below represents the manufacture of ammonia.

(a) An aqueous solution of ammonia is alkaline.

(i) What colour change would take place if Universal Indicator was added to an aqueous solution of ammonia?

From .... to .... (1)

(ii) What colour changes would you see if nitric acid solution was added slowly to a solution of ammonia containing Universal Indicator?

.... (1)

(b) (i) Write a balanced equation for the formation of ammonia

$$N_2 + H_2 \rightarrow NH_3$$ (1)

(ii) The reaction between nitrogen and hydrogen is **exothermic**. Explain the word **exothermic**. ....

.... (1)

(c) Explain why ammonia is transported as a liquid rather than as a gas.

....

.... (2)

(d) (i) What is done to increase the rate of reaction between nitrogen and hydrogen? ....

.... (2)

(ii) Why are the substances recycled? ....

.... (2)

(e) Ammonia can be converted to nitric acid by first oxidizing the ammonia to nitrogen(II) oxide.

(i) Write a balanced equation for the conversion of ammonia to nitrogen(II) oxide. .... (2)

(ii) Write an ionic equation, including state symbols, for the reaction which occurs between ammonia and nitric acid in aqueous solution.

.... (2)

SEG

★13 In hard water areas limescale is formed on the inside of pipes and boilers.

(a) Use the equation below to explain how limescale is formed.

$$Ca(HCO_3)_2(aq) \rightarrow CaCO_3(s) + H_2O(l) + CO_2(g)$$

....

....

.... (3)

237

(b) Ion exchange resins are used as water softeners. When ready to use, the ions on the resin are sodium ions Na^+.

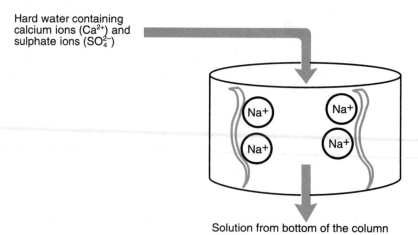

Hard water containing calcium ions (Ca^{2+}) and sulphate ions (SO_4^{2-})

Solution from bottom of the column

(i) What happens to the calcium ions when a solution of calcium sulphate is passed through the column? .... (1)

(ii) What is the name of the solution which comes out from the bottom of the column? .... (1)

(c) Detergents are needed to get things clean when washing with water. The diagrams below show the cleaning process.

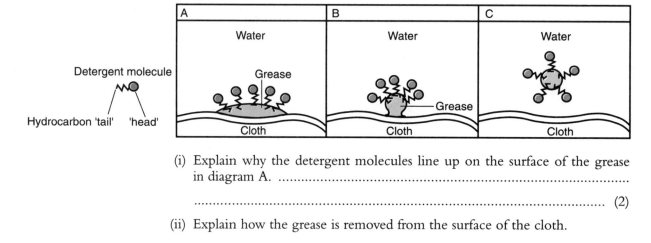

(i) Explain why the detergent molecules line up on the surface of the grease in diagram A. ....

.... (2)

(ii) Explain how the grease is removed from the surface of the cloth.

....

.... (2)

MEG Nuffield

*14 The diagram shows a section through some strata of rocks found in a cliff. The cliff is located many miles from the sea at about 300 m above sea level.

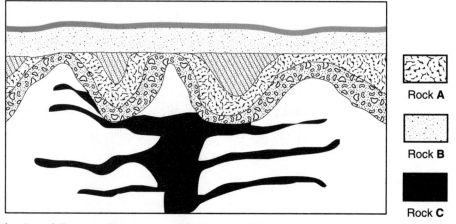

Rock **A**

Rock **B**

Rock **C**

(Rocks **A** and **B** are sedimentary rocks. Rock **C** is igneous.)

(a) How can you account for the shape of the layer of rock **A**?

....

.... (2)

(b) A geologist deduces from the diagram that rock **A** is older than rock **B**. Explain how he reaches this conclusion. ....

....

....

.... (2)

(c) Some igneous rocks contain the radioactive element thorium. Explain what will happen to the thorium atoms over a long period of time.

....

.... (2)

(d) Limestone is deposited in tropical seas. Explain how Britain once had a climate suitable for limestone depositions. ....

....

....

.... (2)

MEG Nuffield

15 The melting points of the first 18 elements in the Periodic Table are shown below.

(i) Name the element with the highest melting point.

.... (1)

(ii) To which group in the Periodic Table does this element belong?

.... (1)

    (iii) Name the two elements with the lowest melting points.

.... (2)

    (iv) Give the electron arrangement of the element with atomic number 11.

.... (1)

    (v) From the graph, work out whether elements 7, 8, 9 and 10 are all solids or all liquids or all gases at room temperature.

.... (1)

MEG 1988

16 Venus is one of the planets in the solar system. The atmosphere of Venus was investigated by the space vehicle 'Pioneer Venus' in 1978.

A comparison with the Earth's atmosphere is shown below.

Substance	Approximate percentage in atmosphere	
	Venus	Earth
Carbon dioxide	96	0.03
Nitrogen	3	78
Water vapour	0.4	traces
Oxygen	0.006	21
Carbon monoxide	0.005	traces
Noble gases	traces	1

(a) Explain whether or not you think it is possible for humans to survive in the atmosphere of Venus. Give your reasons.

.... (1)

(b) Would an iron nail rust faster on Venus or on Earth? Explain your answer.

.... (1)

(c) The apparatus below could be used to measure the amount of carbon dioxide in 50 cm^3 of the Venus atmosphere.

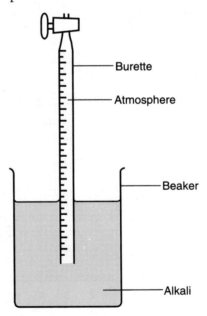

    (i) Name a suitable alkali to place in the beaker.

.... (1)

    (ii) Describe what would happen in the burette when the apparatus was left for several hours? .... (1)

(iii) How would you expect the experimental observations to differ if a sample of the Earth's atmosphere was used in the place of the Venus sample?

....

.... (2)

(iv) What industrial uses are made of calcium carbonate and the products of its decomposition on Earth? ....

....

.... (3)

(v) Name a compound produced by the reaction of the alkali with carbon dioxide. .... (1)

(d) Name **two** noble gases that are present in the Earth's atmosphere.

....

.... (2)

(e) The large amount of carbon dioxide in the atmosphere of Venus has probably been caused by the decomposition of rocks containing carbonates such as calcium carbonate.

(i) What is meant by decomposition?

.... (1)

(ii) Write a balanced equation for the decomposition of calcium carbonate ($CaCO_3$) into calcium oxide and carbon dioxide.

.... (2)

Cambridge International GCSE 1988

⋆17 Germanium (Ge) is an element in group IV which has similar properties and structure to diamond and silicon.

(a) Germanium is obtained by heating germanium(IV) oxide in hydrogen. The main use of the element is in semiconductors and it is needed in a high state of purity. Slight traces of impurities change its electrical properties, e.g. resistance. Germanium is purified by zone refining.

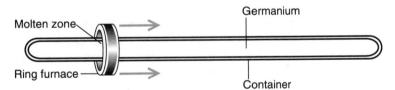

A ring furnace is moved along the rod in the direction shown. The high temperature inside the ring melts the impure germanium. A solution of the impurities in molten germanium is formed.

As the ring surface moves along the rod, the molten zone travels with it to the end of the rod.

The principle of zone refining is that when a dilute solution is cooled only the pure *solvent* crystallizes.

(i) Write an equation for the reduction of germanium(IV) oxide to germanium by hydrogen. ....

.... (1)

(ii) What is the usual laboratory method of showing that a solid is pure?

.... (1)

(iii) Suggest a better method than the one given in part (ii) for testing the purity of germanium. .... (1)

(iv) The furnace has passed along the rod once. Indicate using the letter X on the diagram where the germanium has the highest purity. Use the letter Y to indicate where there is the greatest concentration of impurities. (2)

(v) Suggest how the principle of zone refining could be used to provide pure water from sea water. ....

....

.... (2)

(b) (i) By considering the position of the element in the Periodic Table, predict two physical properties of germanium.

....

.... (1)

(ii) Germanium(IV) oxide is a white crystalline solid which has a high melting point. Describe its structure.

....

.... (2)

(iii) Draw a diagram which shows the arrangement of valency electrons in a compound of germanium and chlorine.

(2)

(iv) A compound of germanium and hydrogen contains 96.05 per cent of germanium. Calculate its **empirical** formula. (A_r(Ge) = 73, A_r(H) = 1)
    If the relative molecular mass of this compound is 152, what is its molecular formula? Draw its structural formula.

(4)

Cambridge International GCSE 1988

Answers to structured questions

1 (a) Magnesium, zinc, lead, hydrogen, copper. (2)
    1 mark if magnesium is first and copper is last.
    (b) Sodium is more reactive than magnesium. (1)
    Magnesium will not displace itself. (1)
    (c) Between 15 and 31. (1)
    (d) Blue colour goes or goes colourless;
        pink/brown/red precipitate;
        fizzes/gas produced;
        magnesium dissolves.   Any 2 points (2)

2 (a) (i) Compound of carbon and hydrogen (1) only. (1)
        The word 'only' is important as it rules out compounds like sugars which are compounds of carbon and hydrogen but have one or more other elements also present.
    (ii) Burn or unreactive or substitution reactions. (1)
    (b) Points correctly plotted. (1)   Smooth curve. (1)
    Boiling point read from your graph (34–38 °C). (1)
    (c) C_5H_{12}. (1)
    (d) C — C — C — C — C   C — C — C — C   C
                                              | |
                                              C   C — C — C
                                                                  |
                                                                  C
                                                                  (1 mark for each)

(e) Bromine (aqueous solution or dissolved in a suitable solvent); (1)
no reaction/no colour change/slow reaction with pentane; (1)
decolorized/goes colourless/loses its colour with pentene. (1)

3 (a) (i) $C_2H_6O_2$. (1)   (ii) C_2H_4O. (1)
   (b) (i) Name strong acid, e.g. sulphuric acid.
        (ii) Advantages – lower temperature and so less energy required;
                   lower pressure and so safer or less expensive.
            Disadvantage – requires acid which is extra cost or dangerous;
                   lower temperature means slower reaction.
   (c) (i) Fractional distillation. (1)
        (ii) Impurities lower the freezing point or a mixture freezes at a lower
             temperature than the pure substances. (1)

*4 (a) (i) Pipette. (1)   (ii) Burette. (1)   (iii) An indicator (named or not). (1)
        (iv) A colour change to match the indicator chosen;
             e.g. phenolphthalein, colourless to pink. (1)
   (b) (i) $35.0/1000 \times 1.2 = 0.042$. (1)
        (ii) 0.5×0.042 (1) $= 0.021$.

N.B. The mark here is given for the chemistry, realizing that the number of moles of sulphuric acid is half the number of moles of sodium hydroxide. This comes from the equation (2 NaOH to 1 H_2SO_4). The mark is not given for the arithmetic. If you had got the wrong answer in (b)(i) but divided the answer from (b)(i) by 2 you would still get the mark. This is called consequential marking and uses the important principle that you should not be penalized twice for the same mistake.

        (iii) $1000/25 \times 0.021 = 0.84$ mol dm^{-3}. (1)

Again, if you had the wrong answer in (b)(ii) but multiplied it by 1000 and divided it by 25, you would still get the mark.

   (c) Moles $H_2 = 0.84$. (1) This should be the same answer as (b)(iii) and if it is you will get credit.

        Volume of hydrogen $= 0.84 \times 24$ (1)
                   $= 20.16$ dm^3. (1)

*5 (a) You are given the formula here and you must show the steps you have to make
        to get it.   Mass of oxygen $= 0.64$ g. (1)
                   Ratio Zn/O $= (2.6/65)/(6.4/16)$ (1) $= 1$. (1)
                   Hence formula is ZnO. (1)
   (b) Zinc chloride is formed (1) which is soluble in water. (1)

        $$ZnO + 2HCl \rightarrow ZnCl_2 + H_2O \quad (1)$$

   (c) (i) Aqueous solutions (1) of acids. (1)
        (ii) Neutralization. (1)

6 (i) **Q, R, P**. (2)
   (ii) **P** – potassium; (1) **Q** – zinc/lead/copper; (1) **R** – calcium/lithium. (1)
   (iii) Hydrogen. (1)
   (iv) **Q**. (1)
   (v) e.g. leave **Q** in water **for a long time** OR heat OR add some acid. (1)
        Look for specified evidence of corrosion. (1)
   (vi) Reference to enormous time of contact required or possible toxicity of **Q**. (1)
        There is only one mark for this part. There is no mark for your yes/no answer without support.

*7 (a) $Q = It = 20\,000$ A $\times 3600$ s (1)
            $= 72\,000\,000$ coulombs

                $3 \times 96\,500$ (1) coulombs $\rightarrow 27$ g Al (1)
                   $72\,000\,000$ coulombs $\rightarrow \dfrac{27 \times 72\,000\,000}{3 \times 96\,500}$ g Al (1)

                   $= 6715$ g (1)

(b) (i) Steel. (1)
      Greater tensile strength. (1)
  (ii) Aluminium. (1)
      Lowest density. (1)
(c) Aluminium has the lowest density therefore more easily supported. (1)
    Poor tensile strength. (1)
    Fails to support weight. (1)
    Needs high tensile strength steel core. (1)

*8 (a) (i)   (ii)   (iii)

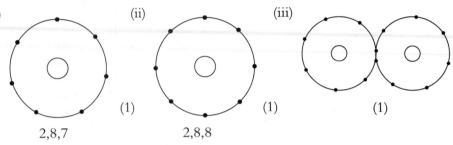

          (1)   (1)   (1)

      2,8,7   2,8,8

N.B. In (a)(iii) an examiner would allow Cl : Cl but not Cl –Cl or Cl_2.

(b) Atom. (1)
Contains unpaired electrons/is a free radical/has not a completed octet. (1)
(c) (i) CCl_2F_2 + energy $\rightarrow$ $CClF_2 \cdot$ + Cl· (1 mark for each product)
  (ii) Sunlight/UV light/solar radiation. (1)
(d) $O + O_2 \rightarrow O_3$ (1)
(e) $O + O_3 \rightarrow 2O_2$ (1)
(f) Cl· acts as a catalyst. (1)
    After attacking ozone it is regenerated in reaction II. (1)
    So able to attack another ozone molecule. (1)
    This type of reaction is called a chain reaction, but you would not be expected
    to know this.

9 (a) (i) Your diagram must show at least two carbon atoms and they must be joined
         by a single bond, i.e. C – C. (1)
    (ii) Double bond shown by a double line, i.e. ==. (1)
         Double bond between two carbon atoms. (1)
  (b) (i) Yellow/brown/red colour of bromine remains. (1)
    (ii) Bromine colour fades/bleached/disappeared. (1)
         Colour still seen if too much bromine added. (1)
  (c) Solvent/to help mix the fat and the bromine solution. (1)
  (d) C. (1)   Less fat. (1)
  (e) Emulsifier. (1)   Water and fat do not mix easily. (1)
    Large amounts of fat and water present in C. (1)

*10 (a) Ag^+, NO_3^-, H^+, OH^-: all required. (1)
  (b) Anode: $Cu \rightarrow Cu^{2+} + 2e^-$ (1)
    Cathode: $Cu^{2+} + 2e^- \rightarrow Cu$ (1)
  (c) (i) 32 g of copper would be deposited for each 108 g of silver. (1)
         Mass deposited = $1/200 \times 32$ = 0.16 g. (1)
    (ii) Number of moles of electrons = 0.005. (1)
         Number of moles of chromium = 0.0025. (1)
         Therefore each chromium ion has a 2+ charge. (1)

*11   (a) (i) Glass. (1) Transparent. (1) OR Metal. (1) Strong. (1)
       (ii) Plastic. (1) Unreactive/low density. (1) OR Metal. (1) Strong/fire proof. (1)
  (b) The atoms which make up the element are all the same. (1)
    A compound contains more than one type of element/atom combined
    together/chemical bonding involved (1)/in fixed proportions. (1)
    In sodium chloride there are sodium and chlorine atoms/ions. (1) In chlorine
    there are only chlorine atoms joined in pairs as chlorine molecules. (1)

12 (a) (i) From orange to blue/purple. (1)
    (ii) Purple/blue to green to red. (1)

(b) (i) $N_2 + 3H_2 \rightarrow 2NH_3$ (1)
    (ii) A reaction in which heat/energy is given out. (1)
(c) Gases take up much more space (1) than the same mass of liquid. (1)
(d) (i) Conditions include high temperature, high pressure, catalyst. All three (2)
                                                            Any two (1)
    (ii) The nitrogen and hydrogen do not react completely. (2)
(e) (i) $4NH_3 + 5O_2 \rightarrow 4NO + 6H_2O$
      Reactants and products correct. (1) Balanced correctly. (1)
    (ii) $H^+(aq) + OH^-(aq) \rightarrow H_2O(l)$
      Reactants and products correct. (1) State symbols correct. (1)

★**13** (a) When water is heated (1) soluble calcium hydrogencarbonate (1) converted/decomposed into insoluble calcium carbonate. (1)
(b) (i) Exchanged for the sodium ions. (1)
    (ii) Sodium sulphate. (1)
(c) (i) Heads are soluble in water/heads ionic. (1)
      Hydrocarbon 'tails' are soluble in grease/oil. (1)
    (ii) Detergent molecules roll grease up into ball. (1)
      Grease–detergent particles washed off cloth by water. (1)

★**14** (a) Horizontal (sedimentary) layers deformed (1) by sideways pressure/pressure near plate margins. (1)
(b) Sedimentary rocks laid down under seas in time sequence. (1)
    Rock A has been eroded, therefore rock B must have been laid down later. (1)
(c) Radioactivity will decrease/decay over time. (1)
    Some indication of nuclear changes. (1)
(d) Where Britain is now was once completely under the sea/no deposits from rivers/clear water. (1)
    Some reference to climatic change. (1)

15 (i) Carbon.
    (ii) Group IV.
    (iii) Hydrogen and helium.
    (iv) 2,8,1.
    (v) They are all gases at room temperature.

16 (a) Impossible: there is virtually no oxygen in the atmosphere of Venus.
(b) On Earth: rusting requires oxygen and water.
(c) (i) Sodium hydroxide or potassium hydroxide.
    (ii) Alkali level would rise until the burette is nearly filled. (Only about 2 cm³ of gas would remain, the carbon dioxide (96 per cent) will have been absorbed by the alkali.)
    (iii) The alkali level in the burette would not change visibly.
    (iv) Carbon dioxide is used as a refrigerant and in fire extinguishers; calcium oxide is used to produce hydrated lime which is used to neutralize acidity in soil.
    (v) Calcium carbonate.
(d) Argon, neon (also, in smaller amounts, helium, krypton and zenon).
(e) (i) The breakdown of a compound into smaller compounds and/or its pure elements.
    (ii) $CaCO_3(s) \rightarrow CaO(s) + CO_2(g)$

★**17** (a) (i) $GeO_2(s) + 2H_2(g) \rightarrow Ge(s) + 2H_2O(g)$
    (ii) A pure substance melts at a definite and sharp melting point.
    (iii) Test the electrical conductivity.
    (iv) X at the left-hand end of the container; Y just to the right of the ring surface.
    (v) Use a rod of frozen water inside a suitable metal container. After repeated movements of the ring furnace from left to right, pure frozen water will collect at the left-hand end.
(b) (i) Solid, high melting point.
    (ii) Giant structure of ions.

(iii)

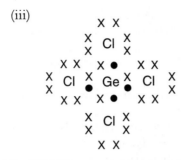

(iv) 96.05% germanium; 3.95% hydrogen (total 100%):

	Ge	H
Percentage	96.05	3.95
Relative atomic mass (RAM)	73	1
Percentage/RAM	1.32	3.95
Divide by 1.32	1	2.99 ($\approx$ 3)

Empirical formula: GeH_3.

The relative molecular mass of GeH_3 would be 76 (73 + 3 × 1); since we are told the relative molecular mass of the hydride is 152 (76 × 2), the **molecular formula** must be Ge_2H_6.

H — Ge — Ge — H

Essay questions

Essay questions are used for candidates aiming at A★, A, B and C grades.

1   (a) "Chemicals can be both used and abused".
        For each of the three substances
            a fertilizer
            the lead compound in petrol
            a pesticide
        describe how it can
            (i) be of benefit,
            (ii) present a problem.

   (b) (i) Outline the production of reasonably pure ethanol from the sugar glucose, $C_6H_{12}O_6$, by fermentation. State the conditions, any other reagents used and how you would obtain reasonably pure ethanol. Give an equation.
       (ii) Ethanol can also be produced by reacting ethene with steam at high pressure using a catalyst. Almost pure ethanol is obtained directly from the process. Write the equation for the reaction and suggest why high pressure is used.
       (iii) A developing country wishes to make ethanol for use as a fuel. Describe some of the factors that would influence the decision as to which process (fermentation or from ethene) would be best to use. (17)

MEG

2   Choose TWO properties of any metal and TWO properties of any fibre (natural or synthetic) and explain how these properties arise from the molecular or crystal structure of each. (10)

ULEAC

3 (a) A farming cooperative was offered ammonium nitrate, NH_4NO_3, at £200 per tonne, and urea, $CO(NH_2)_2$, at £280 per tonne. **Show by calculation** which nitrogenous fertilizer appears to be the 'best buy' in terms of its nitrogen content and price. (5)

(b) Similar calculations on potassium nitrate showed that it was a much more expensive way to buy 'fixed' nitrogen than either ammonium nitrate or urea, but the cooperative purchased a considerable quantity of this salt. Explain TWO advantages offered by potassium nitrate over urea. (2)

(c) 'Bone ash' is mainly calcium phosphate, $Ca_3(PO_4)_2$. This solid is almost completely insoluble in water. If it is treated with concentrated sulphuric acid it forms a mixture called 'superphosphate'.

$$Ca_3(PO_4)_2 + 2H_2SO_4 \rightarrow Ca(H_2PO_4)_2 + 2CaSO_4$$

The calcium sulphate is harmless and the new phosphorus-containing salt dissolves according to the following equation.

$$Ca(H_2PO_4)_2(s) \rightarrow Ca^{2+}(aq) + 2H^+(aq) + 2HPO_4^{2-}(aq)$$

'Bone ash' and 'superphosphate' are both used by farmers as fertilizers. Use the information you have been given to compare their relative merits for this purpose. (3)

ULEAC

4 Carbon dioxide is taken in by plants to form a sugar which may provide food for animals. The animals later convert this sugar back into carbon dioxide to provide them with vital energy.
Rewrite the above passage, using scientific terms to describe the chemical and energy changes: include chemical formulae and equations where you can. Your account should indicate where the energy needed by the animals originated, and how it is stored.

ULEAC

5 (a) Sodium hydroxide is manufactured from brine on a large scale, using electrolytic methods. Describe *one* such method. In your account, you should draw a simple labelled diagram of the cell, state the materials of which the electrodes are made, write ionic equations for the reactions taking place at the electrodes and list any by-products which are obtained.

(b) For *two* of the by-products which are obtained, give two uses of each and say how the materials so obtained have benefited society. (25)

Answers to essay questions

1 (a)

	Benefit	Problem
Fertilizer	increased yield	eutrophication
Lead compounds in petrol	smooth running/ more power	lead poisoning/ brain damage
Pesticide	increase *crop* yield (not just kills pests)	nonselective/gets into food chains

1 mark for each point (6)

(b) (i) Yeast (or zymase). (1) In solution. (1) Temperature 25–40 °C. (1)

$$C_6H_{12}O_6 \rightarrow 2C_2H_5OH + 2CO_2 \text{ (1)}$$

Fractional distillation. (1)

(ii) $C_2H_4 + H_2O \rightarrow C_2H_5OH$ (1)

Speeds up reaction/increases yield. (1)

    (iii) Any four points from the following:
availability of oil/ethene/sugar;
cost/availability of technology for ethene process;
cost/availability of catalyst;
transport costs;
labour costs.

2   For the metal **and** for the fibre:
details of structure (2)
For two properties,
each property (1) explained. (1)
maximum no. of points 12. Count to a maximum of 10.
Example:

Copper: Regular arrangement of cations (1) in a sea of electrons. (1)
Conducts electricity well (1) because electrons are mobile. (1)
High melting point (1) because metallic bonding/forces between cations and electrons is strong. (1)

Nylon: Very long (chain) (1) covalent molecules. (1)
Electrical insulator (1) because no free electrons. (1)
Fairly low melting point (1) because forces between covalent molecules relatively weak. (1)

3   (a) Ammonium nitrate
N costs $200 \times 80/28$ (1) = £571 per tonne (1)
Urea
N costs $280 \times 60/28$ (1) = £600 per tonne (1)
Therefore, ammonium nitrate is the 'best buy'. (1)

    (b) Potassium nitrate is faster acting because nitrate is taken up directly by plant roots. (1)
Potassium nitrate contains potassium which is essential for plant growth. (1)

    (c) Bone ash is less soluble and thus has long-term advantages. (1)
Superphosphate is more soluble and is thus quicker acting. (1)
Bone ash will not be leached from the soil so easily because less soluble. (1)
Bone ash more suitable in acid soils because superphosphate releases H^+. (1)
Bone ash cheaper because superphosphate requires more processing. (1)
(Any three marks)

4   Sample answer:
Carbon dioxide and water (1) are converted by the plant into glucose (1) and oxygen (1) by photosynthesis (1), an endothermic (1) process catalysed (1) by chlorophyll (1). Energy is supplied in the form of light. (1)

$$6CO_2 + 6H_2O \rightarrow C_6H_{12}O_6 + 6O_2$$

Formulae (1) balance (1)

Animals metabolize the glucose in the process of respiration (1), the reverse of photosynthesis (1), which is exothermic. (1)   (Maximum 10 marks)

5   (a) A longer question which emphasizes the trends towards a social angle to chemistry. The two possible methods are given in Chapter 23. The Diaphragm cell method is becoming far more popular, and will be used for our sample answer:

Diagram (2) with additional marks for the following correctly labelled: sodium chloride solution entering cell (1), hydrogen escaping from cell (1), chlorine escaping from cell (1), anode correctly labelled (1), cathode correctly labelled (1), diaphragm correctly labelled (1), solution leaving cell containing sodium chloride and sodium hydroxide (1).

Electrodes made of titanium (anode) (1), steel (cathode) (1).

$$2Cl^- \rightarrow Cl_2 + 2e^- \quad (2)$$

$$2H^+ + 2e^- \rightarrow H_2 \quad (2)$$

By-products: hydrogen (1), chlorine (1), sodium chloride (1)   (Any 2 marks)

(b)

	Uses	Benefit
Hydrogen:	used for making ammonia (1)	ammonia used for artificial fertilizers (1)
	used for hardening oils to make margarine (1) (or a pollution-free fuel)	as a substitute for butter (1)
Chlorine:	used for making PVC (1)	PVC used as a substitute for glass – does not shatter and less dense (1)
	used for water purification (or bleaches) (1)	kills germs and prevents transfer of disease (1)

Comprehension questions

Unstarred questions are for all candidates. Starred questions are for A★, A, B and C candidates.

1   Read the following passage and answer the questions which follow:

Aircraft manufacturers are preparing for one of the biggest technological revolutions in the way they build planes since aluminium replaced canvas-and-wood frames more than 50 years ago. It involves the use of aluminium–lithium, a new alloy that is up to 20 per cent lighter than traditional materials.

So enthusiastic are the manufacturers that British Alcan Aluminium, one of the two companies leading the worldwide charge of the light brigade, believes 'al-li' alloys could replace up to 75 per cent of conventional metals over the next decade.

Lithium, the lightest metallic element, is mined in America, Australia and Africa. Research into its properties when mixed with aluminium has been going on since the 1920s.

The industry really started to get interested in the 1970s after the oil crisis, when soaring prices made fuel saving important. Lighter planes fly further.

Several technological problems have to be overcome. Though lithium is already widely used in batteries and in atomic power generation, it can be tricky stuff to handle. It oxidizes rapidly in air and in its molten state is highly reactive.

In recent years these problems have largely been overcome. Only the financial problem – the high price of lithium alloys – remained. However, oil prices rose so fast in the 1970s that high strength al-li alloys are now cost effective at three times the price of conventional aluminium.

These alloys are not only lighter, they are also stiffer, stronger and more corrosion resistant.

Sunday Times

(a) What is meant by the word '*alloy*'?   (1)

(b) Why is it an advantage to use lighter alloys in aircraft construction?   (1)

(c) What information in the passage suggests that lithium is a reactive metal?   (1)

(d) Give *three* advantages, apart from lightness, of using aluminium–lithium alloys rather than aluminium.   (3)

(e) Give one disadvantage of aluminium–lithium alloys.   (1)

★2 Carefully read the following passage and then answer the questions which follow it.

The map on the next page shows the location of a fertilizer factory and two power stations in the Belfast area.

All the raw materials needed at the power stations and fertilizer factory must be imported, although it is hoped to generate power from locally mined lignite at some time in the future.

The location of the power stations means that the giant cooling towers seen at power stations in England are not needed.

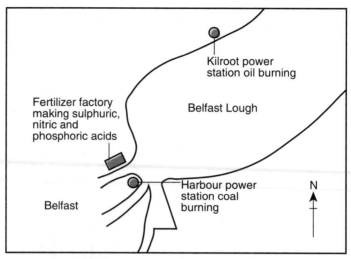

Both sulphuric and nitric acids are manufactured in the fertilizer factory. The sulphuric acid produced at the fertilizer factory is used to make phosphoric acid from phosphate rock. The fertilizer factory markets fertilizers which are mixtures of the ammonium salts of the acids made at the factory. A plume of brown smoke is often seen rising from the nitric acid plant, and this, and other gases from the factory and power stations, contribute to the atmospheric pollution in the area.

(a) List *four* raw materials which must be imported for use either in the power stations, or in the fertilizer factory. (4)

(b) (i) Name the main chemical found in phosphate rock. (1)
(ii) Write a word equation for the reaction between sulphuric acid and phosphate rock. (1)
(iii) Write a word equation for the reaction between ammonia and phosphoric acid. (1)

(c) Write a symbol equation for the reaction between ammonia and sulphuric acid. (2)

(d) Name another chemical made at the factory which is an ingredient of the mixed fertilizers. (1)

(e) (i) Name the brown gas in the smoke given off at the fertilizer factory. (1)
(ii) Name *two* other gases which pollute the atmosphere over these industries and state which process gives off the gas. (4)

(f) Winds in the Belfast area blow mostly from the south west. Does this have any effect on atmospheric pollution over Belfast caused by these industries? (1)

(g) (i) Why are large cooling towers not needed at the power stations? (1)
(ii) How does this affect the environment? (1)

(h) Would burning lignite make much change to atmospheric pollution? Give a reason for your answer. (2)

NICCEA

3   Read the following passage about pollution and answer the questions which follow.

The control of atmospheric pollution is one of the major problems facing our technological society. In the United Kingdom many millions of tonnes of carbon monoxide, sulphur dioxide and oxides of nitrogen are released into the atmosphere each year. Under certain conditions, these gases become trapped near the ground, resulting in an increase in lung cancer, bronchitis and other respiratory diseases.

The carbon monoxide problem can be reduced by improving the design of car engines to allow hydrocarbon fuels to burn more efficiently. Catalytic converters can also be put into the exhaust systems of cars. These help the oxidation of carbon monoxide and also remove oxides of nitrogen which are formed from the gases in the atmosphere. These converters can only work efficiently if unleaded petrol is used.

The main sources of sulphur dioxide pollution are coal-burning power stations and factories producing metals from sulphide ores. As sulphur dioxide is carried in the atmosphere it reacts with moisture to form acid rain. The pH value of acid rain can be as low as 3.5. The effect of acid rain on stone buildings and steel structures is easy to see. The effect it has on forests and lakes takes longer to develop.

The melting of acid snow in Scandinavia releases huge quantities of acidic water into lakes and rivers. This dissolves away essential minerals in the soil and can cause the death of a large number of trees. The high acidity also results in the death of fish and water plants, causing lakes and rivers to become lifeless.

Lime is added to lakes in Sweden, but little can be done to treat acid snow and the water which is running in small streams. The only effective answer is prevention at source. Some of the worst polluters are already fitting expensive equipment to absorb the acidic gases they produce.

(a) (i) What measures have factories taken to minimize contaminated air being trapped at ground level?

    (ii) A coal-fired power station burns 1000 tonnes of coal a day. Calculate the mass of sulphur dioxide released if the coal contains one per cent of sulphur. (Relative atomic masses: O = 16; S = 32.)   (3)

(b) (i) What is meant by the term 'hydrocarbon fuels'?

    (ii) Explain the meaning of the term 'catalytic' used to describe the device for converting carbon monoxide to carbon dioxide.

    (iii) Write an equation for the reaction between carbon monoxide and nitrogen oxide (NO) which takes place in the catalytic converter and results in the formation of two harmless gaseous products.   (5)

(c) Discuss how pollution and its treatment can affect:
(i) tourism; (ii) the cost of running a health service; (iii) the cost of manufactured goods.   (6)

NEAB 1988

★4 Dating the remains of living things by analysis of fluoride ion content

Two calcium phosphate minerals are hydroxyapatite, $Ca_3(PO_4)_2 \cdot Ca(OH)_2$, and fluorapatite, $Ca_3(PO_4)_2 \cdot CaF_2$. Hydroxyapatite forms part of the structure of bones and teeth. Hydroxyapatite is more soluble than fluorapatite in water and acid. Since the fluoride ion and the hydroxide ion are of similar size, one ion can be replaced by the other in the minerals.

If bones and teeth are buried in moist soil for long periods, fluoride ions from the ground water replace hydroxide ions to form the fluorapatite. Thus the concentration of fluoride ion can be used to estimate the age of buried bones and teeth. About 80 years ago Dawson claimed to have found the remains – some skull fragments, part of a jawbone and a tooth – of early man in a Sussex gravel pit. At the time, amid much debate, the remains of this 'Piltdown man' were accepted by the British Museum as over 500 000 years old. However, when modern methods of dating became available the fluoride ion content of the skull fragments was found to be four times that of the jawbone and tooth.

(a) Write down the symbols for
(i) the calcium ion; (ii) the fluoride ion; (iii) the phosphate ion.   (4)

(b) How does the concentration of fluoride ions in buried bones in moist soil change with time?   (1)

(c) Which of the compounds calcium fluoride or calcium hydroxide is more soluble in water? Give a reason for your answer.   (2)

(d) Why do you think that the British Dental Association recommends the addition of fluoride ion to drinking water?   (3)

(e) Would the addition of iodide ions to drinking water have the same effect as the addition of fluoride ions? Give a reason for your answer.   (3)

(f) In dental care it is considered that the use of 'fluoride toothpaste' is less effective than adding fluoride ion to drinking water. Why do you think this is so?   (2)

(g) Why is the 'Piltdown man' now considered to be a fraud? (2)

(h) What further information would be required to date the remains found in the Sussex gravel pit? (3)

NICCEA 1988

Answers to comprehension questions

1 (a) An alloy is a mixture of metals.
   (b) Lighter aircraft fly further on the same amount of fuel.
   (c) It oxidizes rapidly in the air.
   (d) It is stiffer, stronger and more corrosion resistant.
   (e) High price.

★2 (a) Sulphur, phosphate rock, coal (or coke), oil.
   (b) (i) Calcium phosphate.
      (ii) Calcium phosphate + sulphuric acid → phosphoric acid + calcium sulphate.
      (iii) Ammonia + phosphoric acid → ammonium phosphate.
   (c) $2NH_3(g) + H_2SO_4(aq) \rightarrow (NH_4)_2SO_4(aq)$.
   (d) Nitric acid.
   (e) (i) Nitrogen dioxide.
      (ii) Carbon dioxide and sulphur dioxide – burning coal.
   (f) Gases are blown away from Belfast over the Lough.
   (g) (i) Cooling water is discharged into the sea.
      (ii) It may raise the temperature of the water with some effect on the natural life of Belfast Lough.
   (h) The answer should argue possible pollutant effects of burning lignite.

3 (a) (i) Expensive equipment has been installed to absorb acidic gases at source.
      (ii) 1000 tonnes of coal will contain 10 tonnes of sulphur (one per cent). The equation for the reaction is: $S + O_2 \rightarrow SO_2$.
   Using relative atomic masses: 32 tonnes of sulphur will react with 32 (16×2) tonnes of oxygen to produce 64 tonnes of sulphur dioxide; therefore 10 tonnes of sulphur will produce 20 tonnes of sulphur dioxide.
   (b) (i) Compounds of carbon and hydrogen only, which, when burnt in air or oxygen, produce energy.
      (ii) A catalyst is a substance which speeds up a reaction without being used up: in this case, the 'catalytic' device speeds up the conversion of carbon monoxide to carbon dioxide, without itself being used up.
      (iii) $2CO(g) + 2NO(g) \rightarrow 2CO_2(g) + N_2(g)$
   (c) A variety of answers will be correct for this question.
      (i) Pollution will make people less likely to visit an area – not only countryside, buildings can also become unsightly due to the effects of atmospheric pollution.
      (ii) Pollution will make more people ill, especially elderly people and people already suffering from other illnesses. Treating pollution should reduce illness, especially respiratory illnesses, and thereby reduce the costs of running a health service.
      (iii) Treating pollution can be expensive; manufactured goods will cost more when the costs are passed on by the manufacturers.

★4 (a) (i) Ca^{2+} (ii) F^- (iii) PO_4^{3-}
   (b) Fluoride ions from ground water gradually replace hydroxide ions in the hydroxyapatite of bones and teeth. The fluoride concentration in the buried teeth and bones will increase with time.
   (c) Calcium hydroxide is more soluble in water than calcium fluoride; hydroxyapatite is more soluble than fluorapatite.

(d) Teeth are hardened by fluoride when fluorapatite is formed. Fluorapatite is less soluble in acid, the main cause of tooth decay.

(e) No: Fluoride and hydroxide ions exchange because they are similar in size. Iodide ions are considerably larger than fluoride ions so would not exchange with the hydroxide ions in the hydroxyapatite of the teeth.

(f) Treating water with fluoride means everybody has their teeth hardened without having to make a choice. People can choose not to use a fluoride toothpaste. (The removal of choice is the reason that many people object to fluoridation of tap water.)

(g) The fluoride concentrations found in different parts of the 'Piltdown man' skull were different, indicating that the parts are of different ages and therefore could not have come from the same skull.

(h) The fluoride concentrations in the ground water.

Coursework

During your Chemistry course you will be expected to complete **whole investigations**. These investigations involve you scoring marks in three separate strands:

- Strand (i) **Predicting** (Asking questions, predicting what might happen, making hypotheses)
- Strand (ii) **Implementing** (Observing, measuring and manipulating variables)
- Strand (iii) **Concluding** (Interpreting your results and evaluating the scientific evidence)

In each investigation you will score a mark out of 10 for each strand. Your best mark in each strand will be carried forward as your score out of 30. As was explained in the Introduction section, a mark for spelling, punctuation and grammar will be added by your teacher.

Your marks and samples of work from your school or college will be checked (moderated) by an expert from outside your school to make sure that the marking is the same in all schools and colleges.

Table 1 on the next page shows the marks or levels which can be awarded in each strand. The wording at each level is very precise and it is not necessary to understand its exact meaning. It is important to know that you do not have to score 10, 10, 10 in the three strands to be given an A★ grade for Coursework.

Table 2 is perhaps a little easier for you to understand. It explains what is expected of a candidate at levels 7, 8, 9 and 10.

There follows some helpful advice on each strand to help you to get the highest marks.

Strand (i) Predicting

This is a very important strand because if you fail to get this right it may prevent you scoring in other strands.

The first point to make is perhaps a very obvious one. If you are being entered for a Chemistry examination, the subject of your coursework must be chemical. You cannot use a coursework which is about the motion of a pendulum, even though it is marked against the same criteria. You might, however, use an investigation about electrolysis in Chemistry and Physics or one about rates of reaction using enzymes in Chemistry and Biology.

Unlike previous coursework systems, this system requires you to have factual subject knowledge. If you are doing an investigation based on electrolysis, make sure you have studied the subject beforehand. You are not going to use your investigation to 'discover' something that is already in the book. It is important in Chemistry that you study the subject quantitatively if you want to achieve the highest levels. If you are planning an investigation in electrolysis, make sure you know how the quantity of product is related to current, time, etc.

Your investigation must have a **prediction**. Without this it is worthless. Your teacher will probably point you in the right direction, without telling you exactly what to do. He/she will have to make sure that the investigations are manageable and worthwhile. You need to say something like:

I think .... will happen because ....

To help you get a suitable 'because' it may be best to include a section of theory which you consider relevant. You do not have to remember this as you do have access to

Table 1

Pupils should be engaged in activities which encourage the ability to plan and carry out investigations in which they:

	Strand (i) Predicting	Strand (ii) Implementing	Strand (iii) Concluding
Level 1		observe familiar materials and events. (1 mark)	
Level 2	ask questions such as "how . . . ?", "why . . . ?", and "what will happen if . . . ?", suggest ideas and make predictions. (2 marks)	make a series of related observations. (1 mark)	use their observations to support conclusions and compare what they have observed with what they expected. (2 marks)
Level 3	suggest questions, ideas and predictions, based on everyday experience, which can be tested. (1 mark)	observe closely and quantify by measuring using appropriate instruments. (1 mark)	recognise that their conclusions may not be valid unless a fair test has been carried out. distinguish between a description of what they observed and a simple explanation of how and why it happened. (1 mark)
Level 4	ask questions, suggest ideas and make predictions, based on some relevant prior knowledge, in a form which can be investigated. (1 mark)	carry out a fair test in which they select and use appropriate instruments to measure quantities such as volume and temperature. (1 mark)	draw conclusions which link patterns in observations or results to the original question, prediction or idea. (1 mark)
Level 5	formulate hypotheses where the causal link is based on scientific knowledge, understanding or theory. (1 mark)	choose the range of each of the variables involved to produce meaningful results. (1 mark)	evaluate the validity of their conclusions by considering different interpretations of their experimental evidence. (1 mark)
Level 6	use scientific knowledge, understanding or theory to predict relationships between continuous variables. (1 mark)	consider the range of factors involved, identify the key variables and those to be controlled and/or taken account of, and make qualitative or quantitative observations involving fine discrimination. (1 mark)	use their results to draw conclusions, explain the relationship between variables and refer to a model to explain the results. (1 mark)
Level 7	use scientific knowledge, understanding or theory to predict the relative effect of a number of variables. (1 mark)	manipulate or take account of the relative effect of two or more independent variables. (1 mark)	use observations or results to draw conclusions which state the relative effects of the independent variables and explain the limitations of the evidence obtained. (1 mark)
Level 8	use scientific knowledge, understanding or theory to generate quantitative predictions and a strategy for the investigation. (1 mark)	select and use measuring instruments which provide the degreeof accuracy commensurate with the outcome they have predicted. (1 mark)	justify each aspect of the investigation in terms of the contribution to the overall conclusion. (1 mark)
Level 9	use a scientific theory to make quantitative predictions and organise the collection of valid and reliable data. (1 mark)	systematically use a range of investigatory techniques to judge the relative effect of the factors involved. (1 mark)	analyse and interpret the data obtained, in terms of complex functions where appropriate, in a way which demonstrates an appreciation of the uncertainty of evidence and the tentative nature of conclusions. (1 mark)
Level 10	use scientific knowledge and an understanding of laws, theories and models to develop hypotheses which seek to explain the behaviour of objects and events they have studied. (1 mark)	collect data which are sufficiently valid and reliable to enable them to make a critical evaluation of the law, theory or model. (1 mark)	use and analyse the data obtained to evaluate the law, theory or model in terms of the extent to which it can explain the observed behaviour. (1 mark)
	(10 marks)	(10 marks)	(10 marks)
MAXIMUM OVERALL TOTAL = 30 MARKS			

Table 2

The table gives a guide to what is required for Sc1 in each strand at levels 7–10.

	Strand (i)	Strand (ii)	Strand (iii)
Level 7	Identify at least two factors that could affect your investigation. Use scientific knowledge and understanding to explain which one you think will have the greater effect.	You need to vary the factors you have chosen in a way that will enable you to compare their relative effects. For example, if you have predicted that doubling one factor will have more effect than doubling another factor, then your results should allow you to make this comparison.	Draw a conclusion based on your results. Your conclusion should relate clearly to your prediction about the relative effects of two variables. Examine your results for possible sources of uncertainty.
Level 8	The prediction should be quantitative, i.e. relate to measurable physical quantities. You should justify the prediction using your knowledge and understanding of science.	Take care with choosing measuring instruments so that you can take readings with sufficient precision to be able to draw conclusions.	Draw a conclusion that is based on your results and that links together the separate factors you have investigated.
Level 9	In addition to level 8, you need to plan in advance how you are going to organise your investigation and collect reliable data.	In addition to level 8, use more than one technique in your investigation to judge the relative effects of two or more factors. Your second technique could involve using information from book or a computer.	In addition to level 8, use graphs to help you analyse your data to justify or refute your predictions. Suggest an alternative relationship or compare what you have found out with information from other sources.
Level 10	In addition to level 9, use a high-level scientific model or theory to explain your prediction.	In addition to level 9, you need to collect data that is reliable enough to enable you to evaluate your prediction. You should consider wheter you have enough data to support a valid conclusion.	In addition to level 9, link your conclusion to the scientific theory. Make a critical evaluation of the extent to which your prediction is supported by the data you have collected.

books, etc. You now have a suitable prediction which you can use as the basis for planning your investigation.

At this stage we must consider the topic of **variables**. Suppose you are measuring the volume of carbon dioxide produced by reacting different masses of marble with a fixed volume of dilute hydrochloric acid at room temperature. Clearly the mass of marble and the volume of carbon dioxide are related. The more marble you use, the more carbon dioxide you will produce. The mass of marble is an independent variable. This means it can be what you chose it to be. The volume of carbon dioxide is a dependent variable. This is because it depends upon the mass of marble used.

There are other variables in this investigation which you have fixed:

1 The volume of hydrochloric acid

2 The temperature – room temperature

3 The concentration of the acid

4 The form of the marble – is it lumps or grains or fine powder?

When you are planning it is important to identify all of your variables and decide which ones you are going to vary and which ones you are going to keep unchanged. It is very unwise to vary too many variables at the same time. When you start varying a new variable, compare the new results with your previous ones. If you are making predictions about the effects of different variables, try to predict the effect before you start and try to give a scientific reason why. It does not matter if you are wrong.

Ensure that your planning is clearly written out in a form which your teacher and the external moderator can follow. Remember marks can only be given for what is written down. You cannot get marks for thoughts you had but did not write down.

At this stage your teacher may look at your plan and may even make suggestions – especially for your safety!

Strand (ii) Implementing

This strand is probably the most familiar to teachers and students. Here you carry out your plan. As you do this, you will make detailed observations and/or measurements. Hopefully if you are aiming at the highest levels there will be measurements.

Make sure you write down your observations and measurements straight away. Use a suitable table or tables if possible. There are two reasons why you should record your observations and measurements immediately:

1. In case you lose them. This is not as silly as it seems. It does happen.

2. It enables you to see possible errors or gaps in your results and helps you to see patterns that exist in them.

Make sure your observations are detailed. If you are observing the formation of a precipitate, record its colour accurately, for example as dark green rather than just green. Does the precipitate redissolve in excess reagent?

If you are taking measurements, are you taking them to the right degree of accuracy? If you are using a burette, it can be read to the nearest 0.05 cm^3. A measuring cylinder may not be more accurate than the nearest 1 cm^3. Is doing the experiment once sufficient or should you do the experiment a number of times and average the results?

If you are carrying out a titration and you get the following results:

$$25.00 \text{ cm}^3 \quad 25.00 \text{ cm}^3 \quad 25.00 \text{ cm}^3 \quad 26.00 \text{ cm}^3$$

is it right to work out an average of 25.25 cm^3? It is likely that the 26.00 cm^3 value is wrong, and you would be better taking a value of 25.00 cm^3 and ignoring the 'wrong' results.

Again, if you get the following values:

$$24.70 \text{ cm}^3 \quad 24.95 \text{ cm}^3 \quad 24.80 \text{ cm}^3 \quad 24.80 \text{ cm}^3$$

and you average them you get a value of 24.8125 cm^3, but you would be wrong to use this as it suggests a degree of accuracy to four decimal places, which you cannot justify. A value of 24.80 cm^3 would be best.

Do not be afraid to modify or change your plan. You may wish to increase the temperature range in an investigation or take more measurements.

You may be able to introduce a second technique into your investigation. For example, if you were measuring the volume of gas which was produced from marble chips and hydrochloric acid, you might decide to measure the loss of mass as carbon dioxide gas escapes. You could also introduce computer simulations or models to give a new view of your investigation.

Strand (iii) Concluding

Having got all of your experimental information, now is the time to try and make sense of it. Go back and remind yourself of your original prediction. Look objectively at your results. Do they support your prediction? If you have altered two or more variables, what effect does each one have on your experiment? You may find that altering one variable has much more effect than varying the other. If your prediction is not right, try and see why not.

Your results are often best displayed in graphs or charts. Remember to choose your scales carefully to fill most of the piece of graph paper. Label your axes and draw the best graph line. Put an appropriate title on your graph.

Suggest alternative explanations for the results from your experiments. What would you do next if you had more time? How would you alter the investigation if you did it again?

Glossary

Absolute temperature There is a minimum temperature below which it will never be possible to cool anything. This is called **absolute zero** and is −273 °C. This is the starting point for the **Kelvin** or absolute temperature scale: e.g. 0 °C is the same as 273 K on the absolute temperature scale.

Acid A substance that dissolves in water to form a solution with a pH below 7. An acid contains hydrogen which can be replaced by a metal to form a salt. The three mineral acids are sulphuric acid H_2SO_4, hydrochloric acid HCl and nitric acid HNO_3.

Alcohol An alcohol is an organic compound containing an OH group. A common alcohol is ethanol C_2H_5OH.

Alkali A base that dissolves in water to form a solution with a pH above 7. Alkalis are neutralized by acids to form salts. Common alkalis include sodium hydroxide $NaOH$, potassium hydroxide KOH and calcium hydroxide $Ca(OH)_2$.

Alkali metal A metal in group I of the Periodic Table. Common alkali metals include lithium, sodium and potassium.

Alkaline earth metal A metal in group II of the Periodic Table. Common alkaline earth metals include calcium and magnesium.

Alkane A family of hydrocarbons with a general formula C_nH_{2n+2}. The simplest alkane is methane CH_4. This is the main ingredient of natural gas.

Alkene A family of hydrocarbons with a general formula C_nH_{2n}. The simplest alkene is ethene C_2H_4. This is a very important chemical in industry.

Allotropy When an element can exist in two or more forms in the same physical state, it is said to show allotropy. The different forms are called **allotropes**. Diamond and graphite are two solid allotropes of carbon. Different allotropes exist because of different arrangements of atoms.

Alloy A metal made by mixing two or more metals together, e.g. brass is an alloy of copper and zinc.

Amalgam Many metals form alloys when mixed with mercury. These alloys are called amalgams. The mixture used to fill teeth is an amalgam.

Amorphous Without definite or regular shape.

Analysis Finding out the elements present in a substance is called **qualitative analysis. Quantitative analysis** is finding out how much of each element is present.

Anhydride An anhydride (sometimes called an acid anhydride) is an oxide of a nonmetal which dissolves in water to form an acid. Carbon dioxide is an anhydride, dissolving in water to form carbonic acid.

Anhydrous A substance without water. Often used to describe salts which have lost water of crystallization.

Anion A negatively charged ion which moves towards the anode during electrolysis, e.g. Cl^-.

Anode The positively charged electrode in electrolysis.

Aqueous solution A solution made by dissolving a substance in water. The solvent in an aqueous solution is always water.

Atom The smallest part of an element that can exist.

Atomic number The atomic number is the number of protons in the nucleus of an atom. It is equal to the number of electrons in the atom. The elements in the Periodic Table are arranged in order of atomic number.

Base A substance which reacts with an acid to form a salt and water only. Metal oxides are bases. A base which is soluble in water forms an alkaline solution.

Battery A battery is a source of electricity. A carbon–zinc battery is the type of battery used in a torch. The battery in a car is a lead–acid battery which stores electricity. It can be recharged.

Boiling When a liquid turns rapidly to its vapour at a fixed temperature called the

boiling point. The boiling point of a liquid varies with pressure. The lower the pressure the lower the boiling point.

Calorimeter Apparatus used for measuring heat.

Carbohydrates Compounds of carbon, hydrogen and oxygen. The number of hydrogen atoms in each molecule is twice the number of oxygen atoms. These compounds are energy foods, e.g. glucose $C_6H_{12}O_6$.

Catalyst A substance which alters the rate of a chemical reaction but is not used up in the reaction.

Cathode The negatively charged electrode in electrolysis.

Cation Positively charged ion which moves towards the cathode in electrolysis, e.g. H^+.

Chemical change A change which results in the formation of new substances. A chemical reaction is not easily reversed.

Chromatography A way of separating mixtures, especially of coloured substances, by letting them spread across filter paper or through a powder.

Combination The joining together of atoms of different elements to form a compound (see **synthesis**).

Combustion Burning is a combination of a substance with oxygen. Combustion is another word for **burning**.

Compound A substance formed by joining atoms of different elements together. The properties of a compound are different from the elements that make it up. The proportions of the different elements in a particular compound are fixed.

Condensation When a vapour turns to a liquid on cooling. Heat is given out. Condensation is the opposite of evaporation.

Conductor A conductor will allow electricity to pass through it (electrical conductor) or heat to pass through it (heat conductor). Metals are good conductors of heat and electricity. Carbon, in the form of graphite, is a good electrical conductor but a poor heat conductor.

Corrosion Corrosion is the wearing away of the surface of a metal by chemical attack. The rusting of iron is an example of corrosion. Rusting requires the presence of oxygen and water.

Cracking Cracking is the breaking down of long hydrocarbon molecules with heat and/or a catalyst to produce short hydrocarbon molecules. The short molecules are much easier to sell, especially for making plastics.

Crystal A piece of a substance that has a definite regular shape. Crystals of the same substance have the same shape. Slow **crystallization** will produce larger crystals.

Decomposition A chemical reaction that results in the breaking down of substances into simpler ones. This is often brought about by heating, when it is called **thermal decomposition**.

Dehydration A reaction where water (or the elements of water – hydrogen and oxygen) are removed. Dehydration of ethanol produces ethene. The substance which brings about this reaction, e.g. concentrated sulphuric acid, is the **dehydrating agent**.

Density The mass of a particular volume of a substance. It is expressed as kg/m^3 or g/cm^3.

Detergent A detergent is a cleansing agent. There are two main types of detergent – soaps and soapless detergents.

Diatomic An element whose molecules are composed of two atoms is said to be diatomic. The common gases oxygen, hydrogen, nitrogen and chlorine are all diatomic and are written as O_2, H_2, N_2 and Cl_2.

Diffusion The spreading out of a substance to fill all of the available space. Diffusion takes place quickly with gases and liquids.

Discharge An ion may be converted to a neutral atom at an electrode during electrolysis by loss or gain of electrons. This is called discharging of ions.

Dissolving When a substance is added to water it can disappear from view when stirred. This disappearance is called dissolving. The substance is still there and can be recovered by evaporation.

Distillation A way of purifying a liquid or obtaining the solvent from a solution. The liquid is vaporized and the vapour condensed to reform the liquid. The condensed liquid is called the **distillate**.

Ductile Metals are said to be ductile as they can be drawn into thin wires.

Effervescence If a gas is produced during a chemical reaction, bubbles of the gas can be seen to escape from the solution. This 'fizzing' is called effervescence. This word is frequently confused with **efflorescence**, which is in fact the loss of water of crystallization from a hydrated compound.

Electrode The conducting rod or plate which carries electricity in and out of an electrolyte during electrolysis. Graphite and platinum are good unreactive or inert electrodes.

Electrolysis The passing of a direct electric current (d.c.) through an electrolyte dissolved in water or in the molten state, resulting in the splitting up of the electrolyte at the electrodes. Lead bromide, for example, is split up into lead (formed at the negative electrode) and bromine (formed at the positive electrode).

Electrolyte A chemical compound which, in aqueous solution or when molten conducts electricity and is split up by it. Acids, bases, alkalis and salts are all electrolytes.

Element A single pure substance that cannot be split up into anything simpler.

Endothermic reaction A reaction which takes in heat.

Environment The surroundings in which we and other animals and plants live. A person who studies the environment may be called an **environmentalist**.

Enzyme An enzyme is a protein which acts as a biological catalyst. Certain enzymes only work with certain reactions. The action of an enzyme is best under certain temperature and pH conditions. Enzymes are part of biotechnology.

Evaporation The process by which a liquid changes to its vapour. This happens at a temperatures below its boiling point but is fastest when the liquid is boiling.

Excess In a chemical reaction there is a connection between the quantities of substances reacting. In practice one of the reactants is present in larger quantities than is required for the reaction and is said to be in excess.

Exothermic reaction A reaction that gives out heat, e.g. the burning of coal. A reaction which takes in heat is called an **endothermic reaction**.

Extraction The removal of one thing from a group of other things, e.g. separating iron from iron ore.

Fermentation Enzymes in yeast convert glucose into ethanol and carbon dioxide. This process can be used to dispose of waste sugars in industry.

Filtrate The liquid that comes through the filter paper during filtration.

Filtration (or filtering) A method of separating a solid from a liquid. The solid is 'trapped' on the filter paper and the liquid runs through.

Flammable Describes a substance, e.g. petrol, that catches fire easily.

Fractional distillation A method of separating a mixture of different liquids that mix together. The process depends upon the different boiling points of the liquids. The liquid with the lowest boiling point boils off first and is condensed. As the temperature is raised, liquids with higher boiling points distil over.

Freezing When a liquid changes to a solid. It does this at the **freezing point**. A pure substance has a definite freezing point.

Fuel A substance that burns easily to produce heat and light. A **fossil fuel** is present in the earth in only limited amounts and cannot be readily replaced, e.g. coal, petroleum.

Funnel A piece of glass or plastic apparatus used for filtering. A **Buchner funnel** is a particular type of funnel usually made of china. It produces quicker filtration because the filtrate is sucked through the filter paper.

Giant structure This is a crystal structure in which all of the particles are strongly linked together by a network of bonds extending through the crystal, e.g. diamond.

Group Vertical column in the Periodic Table. Elements in the same group have similar chemical properties.

Halogen An element in group VII of the Periodic Table. The word halogen means 'salt producer'. Common halogens are chlorine, bromine and iodine.

Homologous series The name given to a family of organic compounds, e.g. alkanes.

Hydrated Contains water.

Hydrocarbon Compounds made up from the elements hydrogen and carbon only.

Hydrolysis The splitting up of a compound with water.

Igneous Rocks that have cooled and solidified from molten rock material produced deep in the earth. Granite is an example of an igneous rock. In an igneous rock there are interlocking crystals.

Immiscible Two liquids that do not mix are said to be immiscible, e.g. oil and water.

Indicator A chemical that can distinguish between an alkali and an acid by changing colour, e.g. litmus is red in acids and blue in alkalis.

In situ It is sometimes necessary to prepare a chemical as it is required, by mixing other chemicals. Ammonium nitrate, which is inclined to be explosive because of impurities, can be prepared by mixing ammonium chloride and sodium nitrate. The ammonium chloride is said to be prepared *in situ*.

Insoluble Describes a substance that will not dissolve in a particular solvent.

Insulator A substance which does not conduct electricity, e.g. rubber or plastic. Insulators may be called **non-conductors**.

Ion A positively or negatively charged particle formed when an atom or group of atoms lose or gain electrons.

Ion exchange A process in which ions are taken from water and replaced by others. In an ion exchange column used to soften hard water, calcium and magnesium ions are removed from the water and replaced by sodium ions.

Malleable Metals are very malleable as they can be beaten into thin sheets or different shapes.

Melt A solid changes to a liquid at the **melting point**.

Metal An element that is shiny, conducts heat and electricity, can be beaten into thin sheets (**malleable**) or drawn into wires (**ductile**) is probably a metal. Metals usually have high melting points and boiling points and high densities. Metals burn in oxygen to form neutral or alkaline oxides.

Metamorphic Rocks that were originally either igneous or sedimentary rocks and which have been thoroughly altered by heat or pressure within the crust of the Earth, without melting. Marble is an example of a metamorphic rock.

Mineral A naturally occurring substance of which rocks are made.

Mixture A substance made by just mixing other substances together. The substances can easily be separated again.

Molecule The smallest part of an element or compound that can exist on its own. A molecule usually consists of a small number of atoms joined together.

Neutralization A reaction where an acid is cancelled out by a base or alkali.

Non-aqueous solution Solution where the solvent is not water, e.g. iodine dissolved in hexane.

Oxidation This is a reaction where a substance gains oxygen or loses hydrogen.

Oxides are compounds of an element with oxygen. A **basic** oxide is an oxide of a metal. It reacts with an acid to give a salt and water only. Some basic oxides dissolve in water to form **alkalis**. A **neutral** oxide such as carbon monoxide CO does not react with acids or alkalis and has a pH of 7. An **acidic** oxide dissolves in alkalis to form a salt and water only. It has a pH of less than 7. An **amphoteric** oxide can act as either an acidic or a basic oxide depending upon conditions. Examples of amphoteric oxides include zinc oxide ZnO and aluminium oxide Al_2O_3.

Oxidizing agent An oxidizing agent, e.g. concentrated sulphuric acid, oxidizes another substance. It is itself reduced.

Period A horizontal row in the Periodic Table.

pH A measure of the acidity or alkalinity of a solution. The scale is from 0 to 14. Numbers less than 7 represent acids; the smaller the number the stronger the acid. Numbers greater than 7 represent alkalis; the larger the number the stronger the alkali. pH 7 is neutral.

Polar solvent The molecules of some solvents, such as water, contain slight positive and negative charges. A stream of a polar solvent is deflected by a charged rod. A polar solvent dissolves substances containing ionic bonds. Solvents without these charges are called **nonpolar solvents**.

Pollution The presence in the environment of substances which are harmful to living things.

Polymer A long chain molecule built up of a number of smaller units, called **monomers**, joined together by a process called **polymerization**. Polymers are often called plastics, e.g. poly(ethene) is a polymer made up from ethene molecules linked together.

Precipitate An insoluble substance formed in a chemical reaction. This usually causes a cloudiness to appear in the liquid and eventually the solid sinks to the bottom. The precipitate can be removed by filtering or centrifuging. **OR**

Precipitate If a solid which is insoluble in water is produced during a chemical reaction in solution, the particles of solid formed are called a precipitate and the process is called **precipitation**.

Product A substance formed in a chemical reaction.

Properties A description of a substance and how it behaves. **Physical properties** include density and melting point. **Chemical properties** describe chemical changes.

Proportional If a car is driving along at a constant speed the amount of petrol used increases regularly as the distance increases. The amount of petrol used is said to be proportional to the distance travelled.

Pure substance A single substance that contains nothing apart from the substance itself. Pure substances have definite melting and boiling points.

Qualitative A qualitative study is one which depends upon changes in appearance only. A **quantitative** study requires a study of quantities, e.g. mass, volume, etc.

Reactant A chemical substance which takes part in a chemical reaction.

Redox reaction A reaction where both oxidation and reduction take place.

Reduction Reduction is the opposite of oxidation. This is a reaction where oxygen is lost or hydrogen is gained. A **reducing agent**, e.g. carbon monoxide, reduces another substance and is itself oxidized.

Reversible reaction A reversible reaction is a reaction which can go either forwards or backwards depending upon the conditions. A reversible reaction will include the sign $\rightleftharpoons$ in the equation.

Salt A substance which is formed as a product of neutralization reaction. A salt is the product obtained when hydrogen in an acid is replaced by a metal.

Saturated compound A saturated compound is a compound which contains only single bonds, e.g. ethane C_2H_6.

Saturated solution A solution in which no more of the solute will dissolve providing the temperature remains unchanged.

Sedimentary Rocks, e.g. sandstone, that are composed of compacted fragments of older rocks and other minerals which have accumulated on the floor of an ancient sea or lake, etc.

Semi-conductor Some substances, e.g. silicon, have a very slight ability to conduct electricity. They are called semi-conductors and are used to make microchips.

Solubility The number of grams of a solute that will dissolve in 100 g of solvent at a particular temperature.

Solute The substance that dissolves in a solvent to form a solution.

Solvent The liquid in which a solute dissolves.

Spectroscopy The study of the light coming from a substance. Helium was first discovered by examining light from the sun. Helium must be present on the sun.

Sublimation When a solid changes straight from a gas to a solid **or** solid to a gas, missing out the liquid. The solid collected is called the **sublimate**.

Surface tension A measure of the attraction between molecules at the surface of a liquid. Water has a high surface tension.

Suspension A mixture of a liquid and an insoluble substance where the insoluble substance does not sink to the bottom but stays evenly divided throughout the liquid.

Synthesis The formation of a compound from the elements that make it up. This is usually accompanied by a loss of energy.

Titration A method of investigating the volumes of solution that react together.

Transition metal A block of metals between the two parts of the main block in the Periodic Table. Transition metals are usually dense metals that are much less reactive than alkali metals.

Vapour A vapour is a gas that will condense to a liquid on cooling to room temperature.

Viscous A viscous liquid is thick and 'treacle-like'. It is difficult to pour.

Volatile Describes a liquid which is easily turned to a vapour, e.g. petrol.

Water of crystallization A definite amount of water bound up in the crystal, e.g. $CuSO_4 \cdot 5H_2O$.

Index